# CHINA
### Through My Window

# CHINA
## Through My Window
### NAOMI WORONOV

## An East Gate Book
### M. E. Sharpe INC.
**Armonk, New York**
**London, England**

**An East Gate Book**

Available in the United Kingdom and Europe from M. E. Sharpe,
Publishers, 3 Henrietta Street, London WC2E 8LU.


**Library of Congress Cataloging-in-Publication Data**

Woronov, Naomi.
    China through my window.

    ''An East gate book.''
    1. China—Description and travel—1976–
2. Woronov, Naomi—Journeys—China.   I. Title.
DS712.W67   1988    952.05′8        88–4519
ISBN 0-87332-474-9

Printed in the United States of America

China's revolution has now led to some convergence of Chinese and foreign elements in a new Chinese cultural synthesis. But do not jump to the conclusion that *they* are becoming more like *us*. It can also be argued that under the pressure of numbers and uncontrolled social evils, *we* are obliged to become more like *them*. Admittedly the modernization influences on China have come thus far mainly from outside, but in the future that we all face together, the balance may someday shift.

John King Fairbank
*The Great Chinese Revolution: 1800–1985*

# Contents

# Acknowledgments

I want first to thank the writers and old China hands who made invaluable comments on the content and form of various drafts of this book: Lynn Belaief, Eliot Glass, Tom Grunfeld, Virginia Hazzard, Marvine Howe, Helen Rosen, Sheila Klass, and Terry Woronov. I am indebted to Hayes Jacobs, whose sincere encouragement and expert guidance helped me to persist and to hone my craft, and to Sid Passin, whose sensitive, skillful attention to every word and detail helped refine the final draft. But I am most indebted to Kathy Chamberlain, whose writing and editing skills are evident in every chapter. It is she who coached and coaxed me through each stage of the joyous misery of writing and publishing a book.

I am grateful to the David and Sadie Klau Foundation for a grant (I call her Sadie Klaus), and to the City University of New York for a Scholar Incentive Award. Thanks, too, to Ruth Misheloff and Dell Bisdorf, who photocopied and mailed to friends and relations each of my lengthy letters from China which are the basis of this book, to my editor, Douglas Merwin, who has been patient and helpful at every turn, and to my copy editor, Anita O'Brien, who did a fine job on the manuscript.

Finally, to my Chinese friends, colleagues, and students, I express my apologies for the cultural faux pas and inaccuracies of this book, as well as my eternal gratitude: in ways neither they nor I may ever fully appreciate, they have helped make a new woman of me.

# Romanization and Currency

The official pinyin system of romanization is used in this book to render Chinese names, places, and terms.

### Pinyin Alphabet Pronunciation Guide

(Letters in parentheses are equivalents used in traditional Wade-Giles spellings)

| | | | |
|---|---|---|---|
| a (a) | Vowel as in *far* | y | Semi-vowel in syllables |
| c (ts') | Consonant as in *chip* | | beginning with i or u |
| g (k') | Consonant as in *go* | | when not preceded by |
| i (i) | Vowel as in *eat* or as in *sir* | | consonants, as in *yet* |
| o (o) | Vowel as in *law* | q (ch') | Consonant as in *cheek* |
| u (u) | Vowel as in *too* | zh (ch) | Consonant as in *jump* |
| x (hs) | Consonant as in *she* | | |

*Source:* Abridged from Frederick Kaplan, Julian Sobin, Arne de Kaiser, *The China Guidebook*, ninth ed., Teaneck, N.J.: Eurasia Press, 1988, p. 733.

### The Renminbi/U.S. Dollar Exchange Ratio in August 1979

| | | | |
|---|---|---|---|
| ¥ 1 = $ .62.5 | | 100 = | 62.50 |
| 5 = 3.12 | | 500 = | 312.50 |
| 10 = 6.25 | | 550 = | 343.75 |
| 20 = 12.50 | | 1000 = | 625.00 |
| 50 = 31.25 | | | |

(80 *fen* = 50¢)

# CHINA
Through My Window

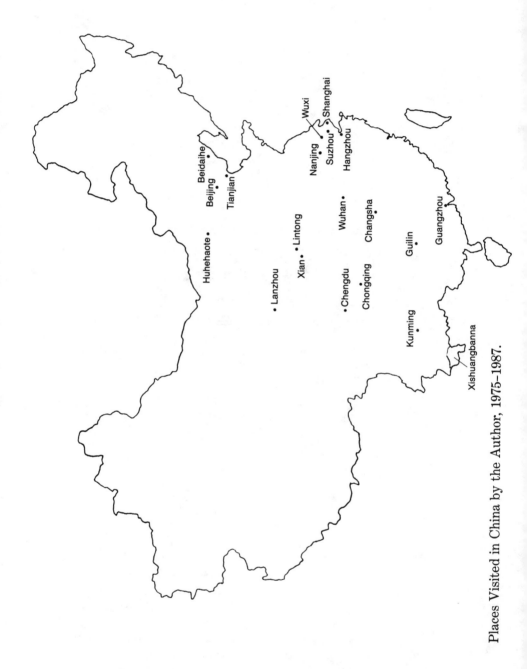

Places Visited in China by the Author, 1975–1987.

# Introduction

A balcony is not a place to take the summer's sun in China. It is not a place to sit and type your lessons or to lean over the railing and study your neighbors' living habits. A balcony is a place to hang laundry. From here your just-washed sheets fall on the muddy ground and your unseemly Western underwear blows into your neighbor's garden because you don't have much experience wielding six-foot bamboo poles. Here you watch your jeans turn into ice legs in the winter while you wonder how the granny next door manages to get her clothes dry enough to put next to her skin.

A few days after I moved into my apartment just outside the gates of Zhejiang University, I set up a little table on my balcony so I could enjoy the spring sunshine, type my lessons, and study my neighbors' daily habits, but I soon discovered that while I was reading my neighbors they were also reading me. And why not? Given the ugly history of foreign intervention in China, perhaps the people didn't want me here at all. I was the first foreign teacher to live in the community in more than thirty years—perhaps I seemed like a Martian to them.

As I stood on my balcony thinking these thoughts, a small fleet of neatly constructed paper airplanes and missiles landed on my table. On them were crayoned, in Chinese and in English, the words "friend" and "comrade."

I was deeply moved by this welcome. In the two years I lived and worked in China, though I often found myself at odds with institutions, I always felt welcome and comfortable among the people. I learned, concretely, what we all abstractly know: people are the same all over the world—and very different. The young people, in particular, helped me articulate the similarities: people want a decent standard of living; some degree of vocational, financial, educational, and health care security; sufficient love and affection; some fun; and, finally, a useful

3

Scene from my Zhe Da apartment window.

and meaningful existence.

But how we define these apparently simple matters depends largely on our history. Before I moved to the university, for example, I visited teachers living in new apartments with running water, Western-style toilets, and bathtubs. But no one took baths. My goodness, I thought, soaking in my nice hot tub at the Hangzhou Hotel, people have been provided with modern bathrooms and they don't even know what a tub is for.

Then I moved into one of those flats. Water pipes were still being laid and the water often went off. If you didn't keep your bathtub filled with water to flush the toilet and wash your vegetables and your face, you had to go off to the local well to pump it and carry it home. There was no hot running water at all. If you wanted a hot bath you'd have to heat a dozen pots of water which would consume an inordinate amount of your monthly coal supply, and if there were four people in the family . . . .

By now you're no doubt asking what made a person like me pick up and go to China, of all places. It began with every cliché in the book: burn-out, midlife crisis, and an intense love affair that promised to go nowhere. My own life seemed empty, decaying; China somehow seemed to represent energy, growth, purpose.

On my fortieth birthday, I received a letter from my pension fund saying that if I continued to teach until the year 2003, I could retire and live happily—if poorly—ever after. Oh, my God! A few quick calculations threw up before me the staggering prospect of grading *another* 80,000 freshman compositions, mostly confined to such subjects as drug abuse, alcohol abuse, child abuse, wife abuse, discrimination, crime, unemployment—the stuff of university-wide freshman English exams topics.

Before the New York City budget crisis of the mid-seventies, teaching gave satisfaction and meaning to my life. We taught nine hours a week of composition, and three of literature. Writing classes were restricted to twenty-two students, and it was possible to teach people to write reasonably well-organized, reasonably correct essays by the end of the semester. Our literature courses bubbled with lively discussion, for our students—working adults and teenagers, black and white, from North Carolina and Brooklyn and nearly any tiny corner of the globe you could put your fingernail on—brought with them a wealth of experiences and ideas.

But in 1976 the city laid off more than a thousand full-time faculty and staff. At our school (one of the eighteen branches of the City University of New York), we lost 120 teachers including 15 of the full-time English staff of 40. Classes grew so swollen that I—who had pursued students by mail, phone, and foot—sighed with relief when someone disappeared from class. The number of literature courses was severely reduced; bitter battles ensued over who was to acquire these precious commodities. I became another one of those people who go to work, do the best they can without killing themselves, and collect their paychecks. I had lost my sense of purpose; I was not a person I admired very much.

And now I was 40, that marker at which one contemplates the past and asks oneself a lot of nasty questions: What have I done with my life? Now that women are so much freer, how can I release the creative capacities I know are hidden down there somewhere? Life is nearly half over: What have I done to be proud of in the first half? What will I speak of with pride forty years from now?

And I was unattached. It seems, though, that sometimes you exude some sense of self that is responded to. That same October I met Nayim. Things developed as these things do, but there were from the start restrictions on our relationship. Nayim had come to the States four years earlier to study English literature, but his heart was in his homeland and he insisted he must return when he completed his doctorate. Furthermore, despite the fact that we share a name—Nayim is the male equivalent of Naomi—he is an Arab and I a Jew; his deeply patriotic and Christian family would suffer as much as my pro-Zionist family should our relationship become known. A touch of the Romeo and Juliet scenario creates stronger bonds, but it makes for a whole lot of heartache as well. Clearly, we said, there is no future for us, so we'll simply enjoy our relationship as long as it lasts and go our separate ways.

My way was to China.

I didn't want to go somewhere to "help the poor natives." I wanted to be in a place in upward motion, to contribute whatever little I could to a nation in progress, to be part of a new history in the making. China, it seemed to me, was as close as you could get to that kind of place at this moment of history. Trying to modernize, to raise the standard of living of the people, to raise the cultural, scientific, and technical level of the nation, China urgently needed English teachers.

In 1975 I led a women's delegation to China under the auspices of the U.S.-China Peoples Friendship Association. I knew from books and from acquaintances who had lived and traveled in China how it had been before 1949, before "Liberation." I was immensely impressed with the changes I found in 1975. At the time, I believed everything I was told: No one was hungry anymore. There were no drugs, no beggars, no prostitutes, no unemployed. Though the standard of living was very low, it was significantly higher than before Liberation. Women held up half the sky, did precisely the same work as men, were paid the same, and shared the housework with their husbands.

But so much had changed in the few years since 1975. That great, confusing upheaval, the Cultural Revolution, was over, and tales of blood began to trickle out of China. What was one to believe? I had walked the streets of Shanghai and other large cities and never seen a sign of dire poverty, never a beggar, never a prostitute—had it all somehow been hidden from my eyes? Had I fallen prey to Cultural Revolution propaganda? What is socialism anyway? How does it work? *Does* it work? What aspects of Chinese life are molded by Chinese culture and character, by centuries of feudalism, by socialism?

So many questions. I wasn't naïve enough to believe I could answer all these questions in a couple of years, but at least, I thought, I could make a start. And China needed English teachers.

Did I, after all, make inroads into all these profound matters? Yes and no. I learned very little about the "isms," about the functioning of the government or the Chinese Communist Party. I understood that

China was moving into a new phase, that this was a transition period, but I hadn't a clue how cataclysmic those changes would be. Today I recognize that the years of my stay in China, 1979–1981, constitute an historic period in its own right, a 7 on any sociopolitical Richter scale. Many Chinese are nostalgic for that period, for the pace and values described in this book. For better and for worse, so much is being pushed aside by the pressure to modernize, to produce, to compete as a growing national power.

I met and talked to a great many people, from Dai peasants in tropical Yunnan near the Laotian border to herdsmen in Inner Mongolia in the North. On long train rides in the hard-berth cars, in homes, and in work places, with my students and other friends as guides and translators, I listened to people speak of their lives and joys and anguish, of their aspirations for themselves, their children, and their nation.

But it was principally through the eyes of China's intellectuals that I came to see China. These are the people with whom I lived and worked, with whom I became friends, with whom I shared the personal and national tragedies of the Cultural Revolution, with whom I spoke late into the night of China's past and future, with whom I lived China's present.

There was a foreign community of six living in the Hangzhou Hotel, but none of us was overly fond of any of the others of us, so I found myself alone with a multitude of experiences, impressions, sensations, delights, and fears, and I began to put them, unedited, into longer and longer letters back home.

Photocopied and distributed to a handful of friends and relatives, these ten- to twenty-page letters on tissue-thin paper passed from hand to hand. By the end of my first year in China, the letters went out to a paid subscription list of nearly a hundred all over the United States. Out of these letters has come this book.

I kept a diary, too, at least for the first year, but it served mainly as analgesic for the long-term, long-distance heartache that beat back and forth between Nayim and myself in a situation where our letters arrived in one another's hands some three to six weeks after we'd written them. These, too, are briefly excerpted in this book.

I learned much about America in those two years, for the conflict and confluence of cultures and the questions Chinese people asked forced me to reflect more deeply on American institutions and people than I had ever done before.

And I certainly discovered a lot about myself in this new setting. I watched myself fight for what I believed was right, and I watched myself be just plain pigheaded and foolish. My value system often became confused and distorted with regard to money, time, energy, resources, friendship, the relation of self to society.

"Is everything in this book true?" the reader may ask. Yes and no. Every event in this book occurred, every person is real, every conversation took place. However, most names, professions, and locations have been altered in an effort to protect people from those petty bureaucrats who remain hostile to Chinese-Western contact (and who may have some influence over the lives of my Chinese friends), and conversations have been reconstructed—who sits at the dinner table writing down what everyone is saying?

This, then, is China through *my* window. It is the story of one American teacher who traipsed halfway around the world to learn a little about China, about America, and about herself.

# 1
# Ducks and Grapes

"Oh, Naomi dear, bring back grapes," said my mother when I called her in 1975 to tell her I was going to China for a month.

"Grapes, Mother? From China? Why would—"

"Naomi, don't be silly," she said, "I mean *jade* grapes."

This, as it turned out, was no mean trick, not because China wasn't dripping with jade grapes, but because in those Cultural Revolution days a tour of China was school after factory after revolutionary opera. As the tour leader, I was daily squeezed between our guides' drive to stuff as much politics as possible into our month-long tour and the tour members' drive to stuff as much Chinese merchandise as possible into their suitcases. One of the tour members snuck off to the local Friendship Shop one day during lunch and rushed back to tell me that the place had great grapes. I went at once. I was missed by our guide, Mr. Lu. I explained at length about the urgent request from aging, ailing mother—which did stop him for a minute—but I was still forced to sit through a lengthy lecture on the seriousness of my leadership responsibilities and the frivolity of shopping.

This was the China I knew, a China thoroughly disdainful of such mundane matters as money. This was the China I envisioned returning to as I called Mother in 1979 to tell her I was going back to China to teach. This time, however, Mother's thoughts had turned from fruits to just deserts:

"What salary are they giving you?" she asked.

"I don't know, Mom."

"You don't know? Well, where are you going to live?"

"I don't know, Mom."

"What is all this 'I don't know' business? What does your contract say?"

"Well I don't exactly have a contract."

"But you must at least have a letter of appointment."

This was getting embarrassing. I had no contract, no letter of appointment. I had nothing but the word of Wang Fusheng at the Chinese Mission to the United Nations that I had a job at Zhejiang University in Hangzhou.

"How do you know they'll even have a job for you when you get there?" asked Mother, picturing me, no doubt, stranded in some Pearl Buck rice paddy.

"They wouldn't give me a plane ticket to China if there were no job for me," I answered, glad that I could at last say something reasonable.

Of course I had no plane ticket in hand, but what bothered me was not my ticket or wages or work conditions; I trusted the Chinese implicitly and was awash with idealistic notions about living under Chinese conditions, regardless of discomfort, and on a Chinese salary. What bothered me was that I had no idea what I was going to teach to whom, so I had little notion how to prepare.

On March 1 I wrote a letter to Zhejiang University asking if I'd be teaching language or literature courses, how many classes I'd have with how many students in each, who my students would be (undergraduates, graduates, English teachers?), and what was their level of proficiency in spoken and written English. I also wanted to know what sort of duplicating equipment (if any) was available, what teaching materials (if any) they had, what restrictions (if any) there were on what I could bring into the country, and whether or not I could bring an electric typewriter—so much for living under *any* conditions.

March went by. So did April. I was beginning to think that Mother was right, that Zhejiang University was a complete fiction, when I received this memorandum in my mailbox at school:

**Borough of Manhattan Community College**

TO: All Faculty
DATE: May 14, 1979
FROM: President Smith
RE: Chinese Delegation Visit, May 18, 1979

A group of eight Chinese professors from Zhejiang University (formerly spelled Chekiang) in Hangzhou (formerly spelled Hangchow) will visit the College from 9:30 to noon on May 18. BMCC will be the first institution on their tour of American colleges and universities, and the only community college on their agenda. By a most surprising coincidence, Prof. Naomi Woronov will be teaching next year at Zhejiang University, and will meet with the group on May 18.

By another "surprising coincidence," this was the first I had heard of this visit. A few days later I met with eight jolly gentlemen in modest, ill-fitting Western suits. They smiled uncomfortably, sometimes even giggled, for this was their first day in the United States, and even those with Ph.D.s from American universities had rarely spoken English in the last thirty years.

Vice-President Liu Dan looked like somebody's sweet old grand-father. He had a full head of white hair, wore rimless glasses on his round, gently wrinkled face, and was soft-spoken despite his near deaf-ness. I later learned he was fitted in the States for a hearing-aid; he had lost his hearing during an interrogation session in the mid-sixties when students boxed his ears and assigned him to the post of school garden-er—an idea borrowed, no doubt, from the fate of China's last emperor, Pu-yi, who was made a gardener in Beijing in the 1950s and later wrote a two-volume autobiography called *From Emperor to Citizen*.

In the fifteen minutes I spent with them, they talked about the Hangzhou weather and the beauty of West Lake. They gave my trip some size and shape, but none of them could tell me anything about what I was expected to teach to whom.

Nor was it much help when a letter finally did arrive from the Foreign Language Teaching Group of Zhejiang University saying that I'd be teaching a little bit of everything to everyone, that they had virtually no teaching materials and no restrictions on the material I could bring with me, that I could bring an electric typewriter, and that I must excuse their delay in writing to me "as a number of things haven't been decided yet."

Fortunately, long before the arrival of the letter or the appearance of the Zhejiang Eight, I had begun collecting books. I had called several publishers in New York City (many of whom had recently been on a publishers' tour of China and were well aware of the dearth of teaching materials). Books poured into my office. Many of the publishers, I think, genuinely wanted to contribute needed materials, while others surely dreamed of hordes of English-hungry Chinese rushing to buy their books. Their dreams were not unfounded. I quickly discovered that hordes of English-hungry students *were* rushing to buy their books—in pirated editions.

I also dunned my colleagues for texts and lighter reading from their own libraries (mysteries, science fiction, short stories, novels), urging them to cull literature as modern yet as modest as possible, for I did not wish to be the purveyor of illicit material to what I knew to be a pristine society. Now quick: how many modern novels can you name with little or no prurient interest?

When I hinted to my colleagues in the fall of 1978 that I was going to teach in China, the reaction was pure fifties: "Red China? Communist

China? Aren't you afraid of being jailed and tortured?" On January 1, 1979, however, relations between the United States and China were normalized, and the Land of the Yellow Peril was transformed into the scene of a grand adventure movie.

So my colleagues piled their books on top of the publishers', I pulled out more than half of my own library, and Nayim returned from excursions to the Barnes and Noble Annex with armloads of English-as-a-Second-Language texts, books on cross-cultural understanding, and the most demure literature he could find. He even donated his two-volume *Oxford English Dictionary* (the one with the magnifying glass in a drawer on top).

In all, I collected nineteen very large cartons of books. O.K. Now what? How do I get nineteen very large cartons of books to China?

Tourist agencies and trade companies proved useless. I called the U.S.-China Peoples Friendship Association for help. They helped. They had a tour of twenty-two people going to Beijing on a Swissair night flight. Each person could take one box as part of his or her luggage.

I rented a truck for $50 and drove with a friend to the airport, but he could only help in the morning, so I sat in the Swissair terminal from 11 a.m. to 7 p.m. guarding my treasure.

At long last the tour members began to arrive—all twelve of them. But I had nineteen boxes of books. I explained my dilemma to Swissair. They totaled up the cost (in hundreds of dollars) of sending the other seven cartons. I said I couldn't pay. They said they couldn't send the books.

"Are you ready to open a check-in counter library?" I asked.

"Huh?" the man said.

"I mean I have no way of getting these boxes back home," I said, and went on and on about how badly they were needed in China. I thought of Mother: how embarrassed I had always been watching her wheedle and cajole strangers into giving her something she wanted.

"No way, lady," said the Swissair supervisor. I followed the poor man from office to office and counter to counter, joking, crying, laughing, pestering the hell out of him. It was minutes before the flight.

"Lady," he said, "put the damn boxes on the conveyor belt and get the hell out of here, will you?"

I did. All nineteen cartons arrived in Beijing, where they were collected by my future employer (the Chinese Academy of Sciences) and shipped down to Hangzhou to await me like old friends when I arrived at the end of August.

I needed not only demure reading matter for China, but decorous attire as well. I hoped to make myself as inconspicuous as a foreigner can be, remembering that in 1975 it had taken only seconds to gather a crowd of several hundred people—friendly, but nonetheless disconcerting. I took a few loose shirts, sweaters, and jackets to wear over loose jeans, and planned to fill in with Chinese clothes.

But there was another, more perplexing problem. At the time I applied for a job in China, Nayim and I had had a date or two; there had been no reason to write anything but "single" on my application. Now, however, we were living together, and the question of marital status was a dilemma: the Chinese government would invite my husband—but not my lover—to China after I had been there one year. I began to fantasize about our travels together, picturing us sipping tea on a train headed for the Xinjiang Autonomous Region in the northwest, heatedly discussing Third World politics and cultures. The Chinese consider it a moral (rather than religious) sin to live together without benefit of bureaucrat, but they find nothing strange about one partner going off for years without the other.

On the other hand, claiming nuptial bonds meant having nothing to do with other men in China. Hadn't Nayim made it perfectly clear that in a few years he was going home? It would be stupid of me to close off the possibility of meeting other men. Now I saw myself exploring revolutionary Yan'an with some recent divorcé who had run off to China, as I had, or with some fascinating Chinese widower with a tragic story about losing his wife during the Cultural Revolution.

I agonized over this a long time and tried to discuss it with Nayim and with friends familiar with China. Sure enough, someone came up with a solution: I could straddle the contradiction by referring to him as my *ai ren*, meaning "loved one," the term many Chinese now use to refer to their husbands or wives to undercut the sexist connotations of the old words *tai tai* (for wife) or *nan ren* ("male person" for husband). It was understood that one did not have (or at least admit to) an *airen* to whom one wasn't married, but it seemed to give a Westerner a way out if needed. "Oh, I didn't mean I was actually *married* . . . ."

August 12, 1979. JFK. I'll take Air France to Paris, spend a week, then get CAAC (China's airline) to Beijing. Terrible scene. Nayim is silent, miserable. I'm sure I've made an awful mistake. I can still call it off, simply not get on the plane, turn around, and go home with him. Minutes to departure. I must leave. I leave. It's done. I manage to get as far as the security check point with my heavy camera bag, my "portable" electric typewriter, my briefcase loaded with books, a bag filled with a week's worth of summer clothes for Paris, and another bag with things that just wouldn't fit in any other bag.

"Excuse me, Madam" says a polite guard. "It will be necessary to unpack your belongings."

"You're kidding," I manage through my tears.

"I'm sorry, Madam," he says, "it's for your own safety." I have never before or since had to unpack my belongings at an airport. But unpack I do, and then attempt to stuff everything back into some corner of some piece of luggage and can't, and end up dragging things along onto the plane like a bag lady, looking even more lunatic, no doubt, because I'm smiling at the picture I must present to the flight attendant who awaits me at the top of the metal stairs.

It's a winter-cold August in Paris. I've checked everything but a few summer clothes at the airport. I never do figure out how to light the gas burner in the basement apartment borrowed from a friend of a friend. I call people I know in Paris, but everyone is out of town for August, so I spend most of the week huddled under the blankets, feeling dark, dreary, damp, and cold, writing long, gushy, painful letters to Nayim, and ripping them up. Whatever made me do such a dumb thing? What if he meets another woman this very week, this very day, some young, lovely, interesting woman? I gorge on bread and cheese and chocolates and oranges.

By the time a week in Paris has shivered by, I'm more than ready to get back to the airport and leave for China where I will surely be well cared for. Had not some Chinese person jumped each time someone sneezed during our 1975 tour? Everything will be fine once I put myself in the hands of the Chinese.

In New York, Air France had paid no heed to the number, weight, size, or shape of my bags. As Air France is CAAC's agent in Paris, I anticipate no problems. I lug all my stuff from the checkroom to the check-in counter where they ticket each bag, dump it on the conveyor belt, and send me to the cashier's window. Four hundred francs or about $40 is what I understand I must pay. Well, that's reasonable enough for all that tonnage.

But it turns out to be 4,000 francs, or $400.

"I don't have that amount of money," I say simply to the cashier.

"Oh, that's all right," she says, "you can put it on your credit card."

"I can put it on my credit card, all right," I say, "but I have no way to pay the bill. I'm going to China where I'll be paid in Chinese dollars which are useless anywhere else in the world."

We finally get to the French equivalent of "Well, lady, I just work here," and someone goes off to find the Chinese person in charge of CAAC.

"Oh, good," I think, "now we'll get this settled." I explain where I'm going and why, that I had not been charged in New York and had no reason to expect I would be in Paris, and that it doesn't matter as I don't have the money anyway.

"Madam," he says, in excellent French, "if you cannot pay the bill you cannot get on the airplane."

I'm dumbfounded, suddenly a little scared, and more than a little irked.

"Good," I say, the French pouring out of me from some unknown source, "give me back my bags and I will present them to you as a gift as all my clothes put together are not worth $400."

"That cannot be done," he replies calmly, "because the luggage has already been loaded on the airplane."

"Swell. You send my baggage on to Beijing and *you* explain to the authorities there why their English teacher is still sitting in Orly airport."

"The Chinese government reimburses Western employees for excess baggage costs," he assures me. I cannot dispute this, but it's a moot point as they cannot pay me back what I cannot issue forth.

"What *can* you pay?" he finally asks.

"I can pay the 400 francs I originally understood the bill to be," I say.

So that's what I pay. But the incident isn't comforting for someone going off to the other side of the world without a contract, without a letter of appointment, without a hint of what's to come.

On the plane I read a delightful Roger Simon detective story called *Peking Duck*. It's all about foreigners and Chinese entangled in a messy conspiracy to purloin a jade duck from the Summer Palace.

"Good grief," I say to myself, noting that I am now in much better humor, "jade grapes, jade ducks. What next?"

# 2
# Snakes and Dragons

"He's a snake," says Suzy Fast, slumped down in a papa bear chair with grey slipcovers. The Chinese must have had in mind the anatomy of Russians—not themselves—when they cluttered every room from the Great Hall of the People to Paul and Suzy Fast's suite in the Hangzhou Hotel with these oversized chairs. Resting her elbows on aged-grey doilies, Suzy slowly spoons carefully leveled teaspoons of peanut butter out of the jar and between her lips. She's lovely. She looks so cool and classy in her simple cotton skirt and blouse, her long legs trim down to the polished toenails, her soft red hair, with just the right amount of natural curl, both sensuous and neat.

Paul sits opposite her in a straight-backed desk chair. He, too, is crisp and clean in his light blue bermuda shorts and open-necked shirt, but his straight black hair makes him look more in place in China than Suzy does. As I've been in Hangzhou barely a week, they are my voices of experience. Paul sits relaxed, drinking a beer, neither confirming nor contradicting his wife's description of Lao Fan, the man who will be my coteacher, guide, translator, and daily companion for the next two years. All "foreign experts" have *wai ban* or "handlers," intermediaries between us and the layers of powers that be.

"How long have you guys been here?" I ask.

"We've been at Zhe Da for eight months," Paul answers.

I know what Zhe Da means: When I arrived in China I stayed at the Friendship Hotel in Beijing, a large complex stuffed with "foreign experts" like me who refer to their universities as Bei Da (Beijing University) or Wu Da (Wuhan University). "I'll be at Zhe Da" I responded to inquiries, feeling very sophisticated. *Xue*, I learned, means "school": a *daxue* is a "big school" or university, an elementary school is a *xiaoxue* or "small school," and a high school is a *zhongxue*, literally, "middle school." China is Zhongguo or "Middle Kingdom."

"Just watch out for him. The man is a snake," Suzy repeats between spoonings.

"What makes you say that?" I ask, feeling confused and unsure of my judgments, for I had liked Lao Fan the moment I met him at the train station the night I arrived in Hangzhou.

"Oh, he's very sweet, very polite," says Suzy, licking like a cat at the precious peanut butter. When she learned of my arrival in China, Suzy sent a request for "gold paste" through the foreign expert grapevine at the Friendship Hotel, and I schlepped three jars down here for her. Eyeing their little stash of cans, boxes, and bottles of Western food and scotch (along with Chinese beer and brandy), I wonder what I should have stocked for myself.

Suzy mimics Lao Fan: "'Would you please prepare a lecture every week. Would you please record these rather short science texts—oh, yes, and, sorry, but we must have them this afternoon. Oh, and we're giving an exam tomorrow. Would you please check it right now. And please be ready at 7 a.m. tomorrow morning when vice-president blah blah will visit you in your room. And would you please repeat yesterday's lecture at the Branch Campus on Thursday at three. Oh, and would you just be sure to give me copies of the lessons you prepare for every one of your twenty-three hours a week in the classroom.'"

I laugh my way through to the last line. This, however, is serious business: Twenty-three hours a week in the classroom?

"Not any more," says Paul. "But the first semester here we were very compliant—said we'd do whatever was needed—so they actually scheduled twenty-three classroom hours for each of us."

"Many thanks for the warning," I say, noting that some people are coming to my room this afternoon to discuss my teaching program.

"We have sixteen hours this semester," says Paul, "and that's O.K. Also, now that you're here, we can each do a lecture every *three* weeks. That's a relief."

"Some relief!" Suzy comments.

"It's not a big deal," Paul says. "You can just tell them something about America, or show slides if you have them."

"I took a lot of slides in New York City just before I left. Someone warned me about this 'lecture' business."

"Don't soft peddle it," says Suzy. "It's not so simple. There isn't a God damn thing in this place. There are no books. And you have to fight for every God damn piece of paper. I'm sick and tired of the bunch of them," she concludes, screwing the lid back on the half-eaten jar of peanut butter. "All very polite, all nicey-nicey. And *they* teach six hours a week. 'But English is your native language,' says Lao Fan when you confront him. Bullshit. It's just bullshit. I'm exhausted and fed up with the bunch of them. That lying snake will work you to death if you let him."

Paul laughs lightly at Suzy's fury. "And wait 'til you get a load of the Dragon Lady!" he adds.

The Chinese-style roof and the delicate architectural balance of the Hangzhou Hotel create its exterior elegance, but the interior decor announces loudly that the hotel was built in the fifties for Russian guests. I go two flights up the great marble staircase from Paul and Suzy's second floor suite to my own on the fourth floor. It's enormous. New Yorkers would kick and claw for an apartment the size of my bathroom where, were I the primping kind, I could sit on a little stool before the three-way mirrored vanity, or where, as I *am* the soaking kind, I can luxuriate in a big tub of hot water and fiddle with the French telephone shower.

My rooms are filled with massive, functional, blond furniture. Only one decorative piece, a long, tall, elegantly carved, highly polished table against the wall, says "China." But imagine eighteen-foot ceilings and French doors leading onto a balcony overlooking West Lake, glorious West Lake with tall pines in front, and in the distance jagged mountain peaks that shift in shape and hue with every change of weather. My little guide to Zhejiang University—dated by its pre-pinyin spelling of "Chekiang"—embodies the locals' love of West Lake: "Its surface sparkling in the sun and far hills glinting through veils of mists, the West Lake is one of the most famous scenic resorts in the world—a picture of hill beyond hill, lake within lake." Oh, how lucky I am!

The Snake and the Dragon Lady seat themselves in my share of the nation's papa bear chairs, though mine are covered in balding red velvet rather than neat grey cotton. Next to me on the frayed red velvet couch sits a fragile-looking, sweet-faced woman named Li Xumei. Her feet in black, laced shoes and white socks barely touch the off-white carpet. (The carpet has bamboo trees delicately carved into it, but it's so old and worn that I won't notice them until months later when I search on my hands and knees for some lost item.)

With grudging respect, Suzy calls Li Xumei "our Commie," for she is the party branch secretary of the Zhejiang University Foreign Language Teaching Group—our "unit." Short, straight, black hair parted in the middle and tucked behind her ears, the smooth skin on her high forehead and cheekbones obscured by large, round, plastic-framed glasses that dominate her face, Li looks like a stereotypic schoolteacher in her late thirties. In fact she's fifty. (I soon discover that it's impossible for me to make even wild guesses about Chinese age.) Once the amenities are over, she's a lively and forceful woman. I feel that I

West Lake in winter from my Hangzhou Hotel window.

have an ally in the room.

Madam Lo, the "Dragon Lady," is head of the Foreign Affairs Of-fice—*ergo* in charge of the foreign experts, Paul and Suzy and me. And she does have an air of authority. While others deal with the little formalities of greeting the foreigner, she impatiently awaits the serious business of the day. Clearly, she has more important things to do. Like Li Xumei, Madam Lo wears a white blouse over black pants, but her plump body makes her look uncomfortable even in loose clothes, and she fans herself a good deal with an unornamented palm fan. Her hacked off hair is parted near the center and dragged off to the sides; she habitually pushes wisps off her face with an air that blames the greying hairs for purposely annoying her. She is the only person I will meet in two years in China who is addressed as "Madam."

Zhang Chefu, our driver, pulls a straight-backed chair into our circle and quietly seats his five-year-old granddaughter, Zhang Wei, on his knee. I will soon get used to the presence of children on all occasions, business and pleasure, and begin to think how much familiarity they have with adults and with the everyday affairs of the adult world by the time they reach adolescence.

Lao Fan is tall by Chinese standards, about 5′ 11″. He has a thin, sallow face, a long, straight, un-Chinese nose, and a becoming Western hairstyle parted on the left and combed back off his forehead. Though nearing fifty, he moves with the grace and ease of a loose-limbed basketball player—or a snake, depending on your point of view.

First comes the chit-chat. "Are your rooms satisfactory?" asks Li. This is a rhetorical question, and I try to express my embarrassment at living in such luxury. Of course they don't believe me; they're certain that life in the Hangzhou Hotel pales in comparison with my palace and servants in America.

"Do you need anything?" Lao Fan asks. Another rhetorical question. They know perfectly well that I don't have to lift a finger. I do no shopping, no cooking, no cleaning. I don't even have to do my own laundry if I'm too lazy. I can give it to the *fuyuyuan* (the hotel attendants we call the "fu") and get back a neat little pile of freshly pressed jeans, blouses, underwear, and socks. In fact, my living conditions here are close to ideal, but no cigar because it's so noisy: the tourists are loud and gay until all hours of the morning, and as far as I can tell, the only traffic rule is that all vehicles blast their horns at all cyclists, who, in response, jangle none-too-dainty bike bells.

I offer tea. Every room in every hotel in China, from the ritziest to the shabbiest, has a thermos of boiled water, lidded cups, and a canister of tea, the quality of tea varying in direct correlation to the quality of hotel.

"Oh, no, no," says Li with a slight wave of the hand. "No, no, please don't be bothered," says Lao Fan. Madam Lo moves her hand through the air in a guillotine gesture that makes me feel guilty for offering.

At last we get to the business at hand. What would they like me to teach? There's no consensus.

"Forgive me," begins Li, "my English is very poor." I already recognize this phrase as a formality requiring minimal response. In fact, Li's English isn't bad at all, though her perpetual confusion of "he" and "she" leads to much misinformation and comedy. The written characters for "he" and "she" differ in Chinese, but the spoken "ta" is the same, so most Chinese have a terrible time with "he" and "she" and "his" and "her."

"As you know," Li says, "we have embarked on the road to the Four Modernizations in industry, agriculture, science, and defense. We are trying to make China a strong, modern, socialist nation by the year 2000. As one of China's key universities of science and technology, Zhe Da has a significant role to play in achieving the Four Modernizations, and we take our responsibility very seriously. For our nation, this is a transition period of the utmost importance. To achieve the Four Modernizations, all of us—teachers and students alike—must become proficient in English."

Despite the clusters of clichés, Li's speech is so sincere that it makes me feel just a little bit more important in the world than I did a minute ago.

"Our science professors need to improve their English to study foreign methods and texts, and many of them will soon go abroad as visiting scholars. The English teachers already have several hours with Mr. and Mrs. Fast, but they would also like to learn from you. Our postgraduates will need to pass English tests soon in order to qualify to go abroad. Lao Fan will teach another intensive English class for scientists from all over China who will soon go abroad, and he needs your help with that group, which has not yet been selected. Our freshman teachers have asked that you serve as their adviser . . . ."

"*Deng yi xia, deng yi xia,*" I say, amusing Li with one of the first Chinese phrases I've learned. "Wait a minute. Wait a minute. I'm only one person. We have to establish priorities."

As Li and Lo begin to chatter in Chinese, Lao Fan slides his leg over and lightly steps on my sandal-clad foot. I look up in surprise.

"The tea," he whispers.

"But you all said you didn't want tea," I whisper back.

"Never mind," he answers, smiling. "Just get it."

I bring the tea canister, five lidded cups, and the thermos to the table. But I'm not sure what to do. I know I'm supposed to pinch some tea into the cups, but how much? Seeing my hesitation, Lao Fan moves in and takes over. I get a plate of cookies and hand one to Zhang Wei, who looks at her grandfather. He nods. She smiles a big smile and takes the cookie. Everybody drinks tea, eats cookies, and discusses the heat and the humidity. From time to time, Lao Fan refills the cups with boiling water without adding new tea. Aha, so that's how consistent strength is maintained. I'm learning. I'm also learning about "yes" and "no." It's insulting for a guest to ask for anything from the host or hostess upon whom it is incumbent to think of all needs and offer first. But whatever is offered, the guest must flatly and repeatedly refuse until the food or drink is set before him. It's understood that "no" means "of course." For me this creates a serious dilemma: there's no way *really* to say no, no way to indicate that you really and truly don't want something. In the months ahead I will often feel like the force-fed ducks I saw on a commune outside Beijing.

"You had better tell us what you wish to teach," says Madam Lo in a distinctly British accent and idiom, and a tone of voice that makes every word a reprimand. I note that she's the first person I've encountered to omit the opening gambit of denigrating her English.

We talk back and forth for an hour or more and arrive at a smorgasboard schedule: I will have two hours on Friday afternoons with the teachers, four hours once a week with the postgraduates, two hours a week with a group of freshmen who know no English (illustrating for teachers who will sit in on the class how to teach English *in* English to people who know no English), and eight hours a week with the scientists, sharing the class with Lao Fan, who will give them another ten hours a week. Our first task will be to make up the exam given at scientific institutes throughout China to determine who the lucky ones will be.

We agree on maximum class size—twenty-four—on one lecture every three weeks, and on miscellaneous recording and correcting tasks. It sounds like a whole lot of work, but I'm full of enthusiasm, raring to unpack my books and prepare for classes. I've taught English for eighteen years, but I've never taught English as a Second Language (ESL). I have much to learn. Furthermore, it's September and I'm a teacher. Like ground hogs and grizzly bears, teachers have internal clocks—we're eager to get back to work in the fall.

Not yet. First I must endure two weeks of exhausting fun and relaxation. All this seems strange. Before I left the States, the university urged me to come to Hanzghou "early in September" to avoid the heat. Fine. My plan was to arrive in Beijing in mid-August, travel a bit, and visit with people who had been working here for some time, but Zhe Da dispatched an English teacher to meet me at the airport on my arrival. She booked rooms at the Friendship Hotel, handed me a three-hundred yuan advance on my salary, and put two weeks of whirlwind sightseeing in the capital on a Zhe Da expense account. As her daughter and niece were in Beijing at the time, the four of us went everywhere together and had a grand old time, compliments of Zhejiang University. I was finally getting to my own travel plans when the urgent call came to be in Hangzhou by August 28.

I expected to be set to work at once, but I've done nothing for nearly two weeks, and here are two more weeks of "vacation." With our driver Zhang Chefu at our beck and call, Lao Fan takes me on the rounds of Hangzhou's scenic spots. Maybe there's method in all this sightseeing madness: Make the "foreign guest" so sick of scenic sites she'll gladly devote herself to her work for a long time to come.

But it's impossible to tire of Hangzhou. Even the heat, sometimes 100° in the shade—and we're rarely in the shade—cannot weaken the impact of West Lake, the surrounding hills, the magnificent gardens and bamboo forests, the temples and pagodas. Marco Polo was right. Some seven hundred years before my arrival, he was dazzled by the city and its inhabitants. Leaving Suju (Suzhou), "The City of the Earth," whose people are "a mean-spirited race and solely occupied with trade and manufacture," Marco Polo travelled south to the "noble and magnificent" city of Kinsai (Hangzhou), "The City of Heaven":

This name it merits from its preeminence, among all others in the world, in point of grandeur and beauty, as well as from its many charms, which might lead an inhabitant to imagine himself in paradise.

Of the people Marco Polo says:

By nature the inhabitants of Kinsai are peaceful, and by the example of their former kings, who were themselves unwarlike, they have become accustomed to tranquility. . . . They are not quarrelsome and they conduct their business affairs with perfect candor and honesty. They are friendly toward each other, and persons who live on the same street, both men and women, are like part of one family.

Sounds promising. If Marco Polo is as accurate about the people as he is about the scenery, I'm in for a grand adventure.

At the West Lake boat dock, Lao Fan and I climb into a boat with a dozen other sightseers. Paradise notwithstanding, I am always at least temporarily *the* scenic sight. Was Marco Polo as exotic at the end of the thirteenth century as I am at the end of the twentieth?

A sturdy woman pushes the boat off shore with a long pole. On the Island of Little Oceans we slowly turn our heads to view fields of rose and red and yolk-centered, white-petaled lilies and lotus flowers on large green leaves swallow up the shoreline; willows weep in the light breeze; gently arched bridges and small boats dot the landscape; lush hills lie like perfect paintings in the background.

"Would you like to know how West Lake came to be?" asks Lao Fan.

"Came to be? I thought West Lake was natural," I respond.

"What is 'natural'?" he asks enigmatically.

"Well, how *did* West Lake come to be?" I ask.

"I thought you'd never ask," he says. I'm surprised and amused by this man's cache of English idioms.

"Once upon a time . . . ," says Lao Fan, and we both laugh, he because he's fooled me, I because he's mastered even the rhythms of the English language:

Once upon a time there lived in a cave east of the Milky Way a wondrous white dragon, while in a forest west of the Milky Way a majestic gold phoenix dwelled. Strolling together one day, the phoenix and the dragon came upon a stone whose brilliance astonished and transfixed them. Together they worked on it, day and night, year in and year out, until they fashioned it into a smooth, round, shining pearl. But the Queen Mother of the West was covetous, and during a battle over the bright pearl it rolled out of the heavens and down to earth. Thus came into being Hangzhou's magnificent West Lake.

We tour the lake, and climb the hills, and visit the zoo, and line up to have our pictures taken before the stone tiger at Tiger Spring. After much fussing about where to stand and where to put the hands and how to hold the head, a man gets under the black cloth above the big box mounted on a tripod and squeezes the rubber ball.

"Would you like to have a rest?" asks Lao Fan.

"Oh, no, I'm fine," I answer.

"Are you sure you wouldn't like a rest?" he urges.

"Oh, no. I feel great. Where do we go next?"

"It's time for a rest," Lao Fan says sternly.

"Oh." We look each other in the eye and laugh again. "Why didn't you say so in the first place?" I say to myself, as yet unable to understand that it's impolite for Chinese to say directly what they mean. Learning to interpret the signals is as important—and as difficult—as learning the language.

At Tiger Spring we engage in the favorite Chinese pastime of feeding goldfish flashing their shining skins of yellow, orange, and red. Along with Dragon Well tea and bowls of warm, sweet lotus root soup, each table is supplied with a glass of Tiger Spring water with which visitors test their dexterity in floating coins. I can't do it. Zhang Chefu can— much to the delight of his granddaughter.

As we sip tea and chat, I think of Suzy Fast's characterization of Lao Fan. "A snake," she'd said. "Watch out for him—the man is a snake." I feel comfortable with him, entirely at ease. It's true that I don't understand Chinese ways, but he seems to accept my ignorance and has taken it upon himself to train me. Am I being taken in, set up for something?

"A penny for your thoughts," says Lao Fan.

"I was thinking about my *airen*," I lie. It's an easy lie; Nayim is never far from my thoughts in these leisure weeks when I so wish he were here to share all this with me.

"Your husband? Your curriculum vitae says that you're single."

"I was when I sent in the vitae," I lie again, "but we married soon thereafter."

Lao Fan seems very pleased. "We must arrange to bring your husband here to be with you," he says, and I realize that the whole silly business has been settled in a word; for better or for worse, Nayim is now my husband.

"Where did you learn to speak English so well?" I ask.

"Oh, my English is very poor," he says, and we both laugh because he knows how silly that sounds to me.

"I studied English on and off during my school years before Liber-ation, and then it became my major when I was recruited for the Ministry of Commerce in Beijing in the fifties."

"How long have you been at Zhe Da?"

"I was transferred down here in '77, after the fall of the Gang of Four." I'm to hear this phrase again and again. On October 6, 1976, the so-called Gang of Four (including Mao's wife Jiang Qing) were arrested. The date has become an historic marker like "before Liberation" in China or "after World War II" in the West. Little by little over the next two years the significance of this date will unfold for me.

"Were your wife and son with you in Beijing?"

"No. Ming and Fan Ming were here in Hangzhou," he says casually. "It wasn't so bad. I got to spend a few months a year at home because Hangzhou is on my way back to Beijing from the Canton Trade Fair."

"Oh, you worked as an interpreter at the Trade Fair?"

"Yes, for several years."

"So you've had a lot of dealings with foreigners and all our weird-ness."

"Sure," he says, already picking up my Americanisms.

"So that's how come you're not offended by my endless blunders?" I want Lao Fan to know that I know and appreciate his patience and training. If, as Suzy says, this man has some deep ulterior motive for being so friendly and helpful, I guess I'll find out in time. If he wants me to work hard, well, what's wrong with that? I'll work as hard as I can; I'll draw my own lines. In the meantime, I like him.

And I adore Zhang Chefu. He has a gentle strength that makes me feel oddly secure. Though I barely know him and though we share no common language, I know I would trust this man with my life. Every-body calls him Zhang Chefu, so I thought it was his name, but it turns out that *chefu* means "master," a term of utmost respect for an older person highly skilled in his or her craft or trade. As his son and daugh-ter-in-law have been assigned to work in different cities, Zhang Chefu is raising his granddaughter. It's a delight to bask in the sunshine he showers upon her, a warmth she radiates back into the world. What a secure, happy adult she'll surely be.

Zhang Chefu has his own store of Hangzhou fairy tales. En route to the silk embroidery factory, he relates in dramatic detail how Hangzhou acquired "the secret of the gods." Lao Fan translates:

> Once there was a little girl named Lei Lei who loved her father dearly, but she ran away one bitter winter day from her cruel stepmother. The child walked and wept until a great white bird, taking pity on her, led her

into a valley spring-rich in flowers and foliage. Here she was taught to pick the tenderest leaves of the mulberry tree by day, to feed them to the snowy white worms at night, and then to reel the fine threads into cloth for the colorful cloud-weaving maidens.

The days flew by pleasantly, but Lei Lei missed her father. One day, with a basket of worms and mulberry seeds still on her arm, she ran home through the woods to find that her stepmother was dead and her father a greybeard, for she had in fact been gone a score of years or more. Lei Lei rushed to her father, spilling the contents of her basket upon the ground. The very next day full-grown mulberry trees stood in the fields. When the eggs hatched she taught the villagers to weave and dye the silk. And thus it is that the people of Hangzhou came to share this sensuous secret of the gods.

Bolts of heavy silk—the sort used for tablecloths, cushion covers, or cheongsam (those very sexy dresses for very skinny oriental women outside of China)—roll off the silk factory machines, miles of turquoise and fuchsia and gold with intricate designs in contrasting colors, scenes of daily life in ancient courtyards, elaborate gardens replete with flora and fauna.

The eye is dazzled. The ear is tormented. I can't wait to move on to the "computer room" where a few dozen women sit before large peg-boards in the manner of telephone operators at switchboard consoles. Male supervisors walk behind their chairs. By hand, each woman punches a cluster of tiny holes in a computer card she then hangs on a particular set of pins on the board. Thousands of hand-punched cards tell the machines precisely where to sew threads of which color. For China, this is very modern, but I think I'd rather spend my days hand-embroidering tablecloths than punching tiny holes in rectangular cards.

Teacups in hand, we settle into those enormous grey-clad chairs. Ms. Gao, the silk company's "meet and greet" person, tells me that porcelain, lacquer, and silk are three of China's great gifts to the world. Silk was invented some 3,500 years ago, and Hangzhou has for centuries been the silk center of the world.

Each spring, persnickety silkworms, which, like me, thrive only in a tranquil environment, are hand-fed mulberry leaves until they spin their cocoons. Mulberry trees, continually pruned to five or six feet, will live more than fifty years. In the fall the cocoons are dried to kill insects, then trucked or shipped on the Grand Canal to Hangzhou where workers sort the larva cases, boil them to loosen the filament, then attach an end to a spool that unwinds the strands. About a ton of cocoons yields about 250 pounds of raw silk.

I express my awe at the process and product but want to know if there isn't a problem at the factory with hearing impairment.

"Oh, yes," answers Ms. Gao. "Recently we began hiring deaf workers [giggle], and we do take precautions: our workers wear earplugs, they rotate jobs every four hours and every six months of the year. Still . . . ." Such candor. No one would have admitted the existence of a noise problem in 1975.

"Why do you have so many women workers and so many men supervisors?" I ask.

"Women are by nature better suited to handling small, repetitive tasks," answers Ms. Gao matter-of-factly. "They are by nature more patient than men."

"Yes," I comment, "like Comrade Jiang Qing."

Nodding heads pop up. Did they hear correctly? Lao Fan gives me a dirty look—and neglects to translate.

Silk. Li Xumei looks at me sweating profusely in my summer cottons. "You must buy some silk," she urges.

Silk? The word reeks of Saks Fifth Avenue, of pre-Liberation Chinese ladies in slinky cheongsams slit up to the thigh, of imperialists lording it over the natives. And silk in all this heat? Absurd.

I'm wrong on all counts. Li puts my hand on her own black slacks and white blouse made of Hangzhou silk, cheaper and easier to come by than cotton which requires coupons. Li and I shop together, she insisting on bright patterns for me, I on subdued solids. "But you are a foreigner," she says. "You may wear whatever you like." Clearly an envied prerogative, but I will not make myself any more magnetic to the Chinese eye than I already am.

Lao Fan accompanies me to the tailor. Once you've stumbled up the crumbling stairway to the factory above a downtown clothing shop, it's so like New York, where men do the fitting and cutting, women bend over clattering machines. The tailors take measurements, discuss design with me. All this must be very embarrassing (and boring) to Lao Fan, but it is, as he notes whenever I raise the point, his "duty." Feh!

On the way back from the tailor, Zhang Chefu stops the car at a point known as "Lingering Snow on Intersecting Bridge." He launches into a long tale I cannot follow about a small white snake that lived under the bridge and managed, after hundreds of years of concentration and meditation, to turn herself into a beautiful woman called Lady White. Lady White married a mortal and became an apothecary, supplying the populace with marvelous cures in times of grave epidemics. There are other bountiful snake-people in the story, as well as bad monks who try to expose and capture them, but everybody finally lives happily ever after.

Funny about snakes: though they are for the Chinese, as for us, symbols of evil and deceit, they may also be Mary Poppins types in fairy tales. I think of the snake in Saint Exupéry's *The Little Prince*, the snake who at once poisoned and liberated the child. Dragons, too, have a double identity in China: though fiery and fearsome, they can be benign creatures that have come to symbolize the absolute but benevolent power of the emperor.

Following, no doubt, the ancient principle of yin and yang as much as the Marxist-Leninist doctrine of the unity of opposites, Chairman Mao said that one always divides into two. But he added that ultimately the essence of things becomes clear. O.K. We'll see about these snakes and dragons.

# 3
# Ninth Moon: Bits and Pieces

The Chinese have a saying: It is best to be born in Suzhou, live in Hangzhou, eat in Guangzhou, and die in Liuzhou. Suzhou produces the handsomest people; Hangzhou is paradise on earth; Guangzhou (Canton) has the best food; Liuzhou has the best wood for coffins. Since I was born a while ago and have no plans to die soon, it's not a bad bargain to end up living in paradise.

But I would prefer Canton cooking—or Shanghai, or Beijing, or Sichuan, or Hunan. Here at the Hangzhou Hotel, meals are mediocre, unspicy to my taste, and expensive even for us foreign experts—Paul and Suzy and me, and George who teaches at Hang Da down the road a piece. We pay 4 or 5 yuan a day—50-60 percent of tourist prices. For food, hotels, even planes and trains, there's a national four-tier price scale covering Chinese, overseas Chinese, foreign experts, and tourists.

But in the Chinese bureaucratic tradition, if you aren't in some category, you're in trouble. Take Jack and Kyoko. Jack is here on a research fellowship with his Japanese-American wife, Kyoko, and their three-month-old baby, Jeremy. Kyoko is eager to teach Japanese or English at Hang Da (which urgently needs her expertise), but there are no precedents for hiring the spouses of researchers, so she spends her days washing diapers. (She once turned over a few days' worth of Jeremy's diapers to the fu who returned them in a few hours, snowy white and neatly ironed, with a bill for 12 yuan). They were assigned a suite of rooms like mine, then charged full tourist rates—over 40 yuan per day—as well as double our rates for meals. Jack must hire a cab every day to get to and from his institute which apparently has no cars, unlike our school which has a whole fleet of cars, trucks, and buses.

Jack is furious: Whatever dinner conversation is not devoted to excoriating Chinese inefficiency and bureaucracy or to foreigner-gossip (who's sleeping with whom and who has come down with what form of hepatitis) is given over to bitching about prices.

September 9 is the anniversary of Mao's death. I ask Li Xumei why virtually no notice is taken of the occasion. Her answer is a lengthy discourse on the profound love of the Chinese people for Premier Zhou Enlai who always practiced what he preached in his national and international as well as his domestic duties. She tells me, for example, that Zhou's wife was barren, yet he spurned her offer for him to take another wife in order to produce heirs.

Mao's own marital record reminds me of the litany I learned in school about the wives of Henry VIII: divorced, beheaded, died, divorced, beheaded, survived. When Mao was fifteen (1908), his parents arranged his marriage to a woman named Luo whom he soon divorced. He fell in love with and married (1920) Yang Kaihui, who was beheaded by the Kuomintang in 1930—two years after Mao's marriage to He Zizhan, a revolutionary comrade-in-arms and veteran of the Long March. Mao and He Zizhan had five children in seven years. Busy philandering with young actresses in his cave at Yan'an, Mao divorced He Zizhan and then married a young actress named Lan Ping (née Shumeng, later Li Yunhe, pen name Li Jin). She renamed herself Jiang Qing, something like Pure Green Waters. For each this was a fourth (and final) marriage.

Li agrees that New China would not exist without Mao, that his theoretical contributions were earth-shaking. But it was Zhou who lived the exemplary life, who understood both theoretically and practically the nature of and need for China's intelligentsia. It was Premier Zhou, Li reminds me as though I had a personal stake in the matter, who protected foreigners during the Cultural Revolution.

"I guess models are very important to Communists," I offer. "I remember the slogans 'In Agriculture, Learn from Dazhai' and 'In Industry, Learn from Daqing.' Every place we visited in 1975 had model workers and model students and model tea pickers and—"

"That's hardly an invention of communism," Li laughs. "It is a tenet of ancient Chinese philosophy that people are inherently good, but that there are many difficulties in life that can lead them astray. We need models at every level. Thus, if our leaders conduct themselves morally and ethically, we will become better people in a better society. We say 'The ruler is the wind, the people are the grass.'"

"Is that why you and your family are last in line for a new apartment?" I ask.

"Oh, we are not rulers," she says. "But you are right. Cadres must set good examples for the people—even if it hurts a little sometimes."

I want to hug her, but instead take her hand, sensing for a moment an odd feeling of closeness and security. The gesture surprises me; it would never have occurred to me at home to take a woman's hand.

If you're planning to visit Hangzhou late in the ninth moon (September), in the time of the autumnal equinox, you too will have an opportunity to witness the Great Tidal Bore of the Qiantang River. George and Jack get me all excited about it, reading descriptions at the dinner table from their vast store of guidebooks. Who could resist the "deafening roar" of the Tidal Bore, and the "white streak on the horizon" that gradually mounts to a water wall 12 to 20 feet high?

It's one of Hangzhou's many 100° days. All of us foreigners and some twenty of our colleagues from Zhe Da and Hang Da jam into a school bus and lumber off down miserable roads that grow so dusty we have to close the windows and keep handkerchiefs over our mouths. The best place to witness this event is at Haining, some forty-three bumpy, dusty miles from Hangzhou, a good three hours' trip each way—surely a small price to pay to witness such a phenomenon, and fun because our Chinese comrades are lively and playful and full of stories.

All I can see as we drag our aching bones into the noon-day glare is a sea of black umbrellas. Under them, thousands of people are glued together by the sweat of their bodies. We push and shove our way through the crowds (poor Suzy is terrified by this great mass of sweaty flesh), but for once we're only secondary spectacles as all eyes are focused on the river.

We find a spot that gives us some headroom above the crowd. We wait. And wait. I'm utterly miserable. I may pass out. But surely it's worth it all for what's to come, this spectacle of a lifetime. A sudden hush, a little ripple of "ahs."

"What happened?" I yell over to George, who is standing about five bodies away from me.

"Didn't you see it?" George shouts back.

"See what?" I ask.

"The Tidal Bore," he answers, irked.

"You mean that tiny pencil line of white across the river?"

"Sure," he says. "Didn't you see it?"

"Yeah," I say, "I saw it."

"Well, it isn't the same height every year," he says.

Reversing course, we drive for hours in the dusty heat back to beautiful West Lake with its shady weeping willows. George says it'll be better next year. I'm skeptical.

I'm still awaiting a bike coupon. The Friendship Store (where I don't need a coupon) has only men's bikes, and I don't think I can handle that. In the meantime, Zhang Chefu is always at my disposal. The problem is

Anything for a glimpse of the Great Tidal Bore.

this: He picks me up in the morning, deposits me at the classroom door, and is waiting there when I finish class to take me back to the hotel. I am hardly becoming conversant with any Chinese in this situation. The Hangzhou Hotel has guards at the gate, so my students and colleagues feel none too comfortable even with a signed and sealed letter from the Foreign Affairs Office giving them access to the American queen.

I'm very busy. Because I simply can't write separate letters to everybody (except, of course, to Nayim), I've begun to send back "Dear Everybody" letters for circulation to family and friends. Schoolwork seems to multiply. Paul and Suzy and I are going to Mogan Mountain this weekend. Having been here nine months, they're itchy to get out and go places; I'm still at the stage of being astonished when I look up from my typewriter to find the trees and the lake and the mountains right there outside my window. But I'd hardly say no to visiting some scenic spot.

From the diary—*September 23*
*Letter from Martha with dreadful picture of Nayim at a picnic. Her letter dated September 6, and though sent to Hang Da instead of Zhe Da, arrived this afternoon—yet not one letter from N. Know I'll get a bunch all at once, but it's been almost six weeks. . . .*

*September 24*
*Called N today. Landlord's trying to evict him as my name's on lease.*
*Sent lots of letters—doesn't know why I haven't gotten them.*
   *Celebrated Moon Festival this week. Lao Yue, the old man in the*
*moon, is busily engaged in tying together young couples with invisible*
*red silk thread. Incredible night skies, full moon on West Lake. Feel*
*very lonely. Little moon cakes made of lotus and melon seeds or red*
*beans with duck egg yolks set in the center—slice the cake to find a*
*moon inside. Writing Moon, Spoon, June letters to N, urging him to*
*come here in spring.*

*September 27*
*Lao Fan, dripping wet, with whole batch of letters! Knowing how ur-*
*gently I've been awaiting them, he biked here in the pouring rain to*
*bring them to me. Letters, photos, exquisite story he translated. Spirits*
*changed.*

*September 29*
*Two letters full of pain and loneliness. Last night univ. gave me wel-*
*coming banquet (with due apologies for long delay in doing so). V.P. Liu*
*Dan said they're building on-campus housing for foreign experts with*
*heat, hot water, and air conditioning, and "perhaps it will be done by*
*April so we can warmly welcome your husband to our country." Get-*
*ting to hate being cloistered here in the "Imperial Palace" (no dogs or*
*Chinese allowed), but have no landlord, no Con Ed, no Ma Bell—*
*nothing to worry about except being a good teacher. Suzy expends her*
*every free hour bitching. Perhaps, as she says, my attitude will change*
*over the months as small things mount up. We'll see.*

Mogan Mountain: Pathways and stairways wind in and out and up
and down through dense bamboo forests. At one turn a waterfall,
at another a tiny tea house, at a third a small pagoda beckons
you to rest and take in the view. We come across a group of children
from the Young Communist League on an outing, a group of Shanghai
workers here for a series of meetings, and several sets of honey-
mooners.

   There are some six hundred lovely stone houses, hotels, and villas
scattered about the mountain, some with swimming pools and tennis
courts. We pass Chiang Kai-shek's 1930s vacation home. Before
the Cultural Revolution our university owned a house here where
teachers happily came to escape the summer heat of Hangzhou (one
of China's "four furnaces"). Of course, vacations for intellectuals
were not exactly "in" from '66 to '76; the university was forced to give

up its house which it's now trying to reclaim.

We're the only guests in a luxurious hotel, where the rooms are sheer romance and comfort. At *xushi* time (after lunch is always nap time in China), I crawl into a good, hard bed under a warm comforter covered in embroidered silk and smelling as though it just came out of a cedar chest.

Oh, yes, and the meals: turtle, wild duck (we thought it was pigeon— who knows?), and dog! Digging into some unusual sweet meat cooked in an egg batter, we keep asking what it is and people keep telling us it's dog and we keep telling them to quit kidding us and then we figure out that they aren't and Suzy puts her hand over her mouth and runs from the table and everybody laughs. Since I didn't know what I was eating it didn't much bother me. Now snakes and cats, on the other hand . . . .

Coming to and going from Moganshan, we take different roads. Nowhere can you find an inch of uncultivated flatland or hill—typical in China, even in the cities. Here there's mostly rice (bright green and tall as this year's second crop nears harvest), apple and peach orchards, purplish-red mulberry trees, taro, corn, sweet potatoes, hemp, and a heap of other stuff no one can name in English.

Every burden is borne by muscle down here; the veins of humans harnessed to two-wheeled carts bulge under the weight of bamboo handles. I'm amused at the men who watch women hauling huge wheelbarrows of rocks, yet argue the weakness of the sex. In the North mules and horses do much of this work, but down here one sees only a few sheep, a stray dog, and some water buffalo pulling plows through the field. There's a reason: China has so little arable land that the fertile fields of the South cannot be wasted on grazing. Milk coupons are given to people with young children, and cheese is nonexistent down here— southerners say it tastes like spoiled bean curd.

The inhabited part of China is only about half as large as the inhabited part of the United States, but here some two thousand people exist on each square mile of cultivated land. I begin to understand why everyone says population is China's number one problem, and that the one-child family, however odious in personal terms, is crucial to survival, no less improved living conditions.

October 1. A splendid autumn day primed with gold stars on brilliant red flags, red banners with immense yellow or black characters, and big red balloon lanterns hemmed with breeze-blown gold fringe. At noon, a banquet with local and provincial big-wigs, a ten-course meal with endless supplies of rice wine and *mao tai* and too many toasts. All very pleasant. All very boring. Attempts at conversation are met with fresh supplies of fish heads with staring eyes, gangrenous "hundred year old" eggs, and rubber sea slugs—along with a host of fabulous dishes like Hangzhou's famous Beggar's Chicken and West Lake Vinegar Fish. There are toasts. And more toasts. *Gan bei*, I am told again and again, and "dry glass" is to be taken literally. I get half-stewed, stagger back to the hotel, and fall fast asleep.

In the evening we drive into town along the lake shore, all lit up like Christmas. Near the Hall of the People, we sail right into it—a well-organized demonstration perhaps five-thousand-strong. The demonstrators carry picket signs and hunger strike declarations. We can hear chants, speeches, and ritualized wailing of the sort heard at funerals. Madam Lo assures us that the hunger strike is phony, "a bit of drama" she says in her clipped English.

The demonstrators peer into passing cars, apparently searching for provincial officials. I find it rather disconcerting to be the party *inside* the car; I've never been in this situation before, and I don't like it one bit. It's all I can do to keep myself from raising a fist in solidarity as I go by. "Why didn't you?" you might ask. "Because I'm not in America, and don't yet know right from wrong," I would answer.

A few things are clear, though worming even a little information out of our companions is difficult. The demonstrators are "educated youth" (middle school graduates) sent out to work on state farms early in the Cultural Revolution. They are now in their mid-thirties, many married and with children. They have lived on state farms lo these many years, and are sick and tired of the living conditions and the pay (about 30 yuan a month). They want to resettle with their families in Hangzhou—*and* they want jobs. My understanding is that if you've been in the countryside more than eight years, you're permitted to "repatriate" to Hangzhou (or wherever in Zhejiang province you come from), but I'm not clear what that means in terms of jobs or housing or how many people fit into that category. My impression is that officials listen politely, then tell people to go back where they came from and try to be patient because it just can't be done right now—clearly an unsatisfactory response as the demonstrations have been going on for at least a week (generally in the form of sit-ins) and have escalated into hunger strikes.

We join the hand-picked audience in the auditorium for the evening's films, all four hours of them. First comes a documentary on old (sick) and new (healthy) China. The pre-'49 footage is riveting: scenes of mass starvation, opium dens, rickshaw drivers, coolie laborers, women and children workers. The "today" section would have you believe that China has virtually achieved the Four Modernizations. The second film is a dramatic, well-acted depiction of the life of He Long, the Kuomintang general who wakes up one day (or is awakened by the masses) to ask what he is fighting for and why he is fighting the Communists instead of the Japanese. He goes over, becomes a Communist general, and plays a major military role in the liberation of China. Early in the Cultural Revolution he is imprisoned. He dies like a dog, denied both food and medical care. Zhou Enlai tries but fails to help him (Mao is never mentioned as far as I can tell). The film certainly has a good line on women, who play a significant role in the party and the army. But three and a half hours? Poor Lao Fan. Excellent as he is—and he is—he has to quit translating after a couple of hours.

When we come out of the theater the "youths" block the front exits (though consciously leaving others unblocked). Madam Lo and the university higher-ups seem slightly panicky. They bundle us into the car, saying it's late and we're tired. (I have learned better than to say "Oh no, I'm not tired.") Direct questions are met with stiff, frightened responses: "They are disorderly." "They didn't have to come here this evening and spoil October 1st." "This is not the way to settle problems." Hangzhou officials don't deny the legitimacy of the demonstrators' demands, but they feel the youths should do as they're told because that's all that's possible. There is a long tradition in China of experiencing almost any disorder as anarchy, and of course the Cultural Revolution tragedies, so short a time after the anti-Japanese and civil wars, exacerbate this reaction.

The demonstration is not disorderly in any sense that we old sixties activists know and love: police direct traffic, People's Liberation Army soldiers walk around, and no one tries (at least in any obvious way while we're around) to stop or affect the course of the demonstration.

At midnight, on the marble staircase of the Hangzhou Hotel ascending to our respective suites, we talk. Suzy is very frightened; she has never been near a demonstration and is certain that this one portends nothing less than imminent civil war. Jack runs down another of his long lectures on the failure of the socialist system to meet the needs of the people (while demonstrations in America epitomize the excellence of our democratic system). I, who know no more about the situation than any of the rest, find myself defending the authorities (as I often do at the dinner table because blind anti-this and pro-that attitudes always irk me into equally extreme responses). George (the only one among us fluent in Chinese) is determined to go back tomorrow to investigate. Paul smiles at all of us.

What I really think is this: If I'd been stuck out in the boonies feeding the pigs for several years and saw several more years of the same before me, I'd certainly be out there trying to force the municipal authorities to take some kind of action. A letter from a friend in Shanghai says that last February hundreds of thousands of "sent-down" youths home for the New Year joined hundreds of thousands more who were living illegally in Shanghai in a demonstration demanding city jobs, and that similar events have been going on in Beijing and other cities. (Two years hence the official Chinese press will maintain that all "sent-down" youths have been reurbanized. It's hard to imagine this would have been done had the "disorder" of the demonstrations not occurred.)

*October 6*
*Feel like those big, overstuffed chairs—four banquets this week— China's thirtieth birthday. Fabulous food. Fabulous weather. Walk a lot and make new discoveries daily, but jealous when the Fasts go off on their bikes—patience, patience!*

*Lovely letter from N. Told Lao Fan that N wants a visa for spring. No problem. Office asked that he bring an SCM 2200 typewriter like mine. They'll reimburse us in renminbi we can use to travel. Is that something to think about!*

*October 9*
*Wish I had lovely, legible handwriting like Victorian letter writers to answer N's letters so full of pain and tenderness.*

*October 10*
*Today got N's translation of "The Chicken of Jacob's Mother"—de-lightful Middle Eastern story—and blow up of photo I took of him near Cloisters. Large as life. And: "I will do everything I can to be with you in China."*

# 4
# The Heretic

They come in droves, the teachers Wang and Li and Zhong and Yi. They point fingers at twisted, tedious, passive constructions in tired old science texts, asking endless questions about gerunds and participles, about nominatives and imperatives. They come, with time- and weather-worn Chinese-English dictionaries drawn up by what I envision as musty Mandarins in long gowns, greybeards whom Dickens himself would have found quaint. They turn the pages carefully, lest they flake off in their hands, for this is the gospel, all they have to hold of the English language—except for companion turn-of-the-century British grammars. They're terribly distressed to learn that not one of us foreign experts will help them out of their fix: they are for the most part teachers of Russian now teaching "scientific" English *in Chinese* to students whose English is generally far better than their own, "the arcane rules of grammar," as Paul Fast put it, "being the hobby and sole solace of so many of them."

In the first minutes of my first day in the large office I share with Paul and Suzy, the first person at the door is Teacher Zhang. Paul and Suzy laugh—clearly they've seen Teacher Zhang before. Hands stuck high into the too-short sleeves of his Mao jacket, Zhang bows himself into my office with profuse apologies—a black-haired Uriah Heep.

"You too *negga* busy, Professor, yes?" he says.

"No, no. Please come in."

"I very *negga* bother you," he says.

"Not at all," I say, already beginning to feel bothered, especially by the Chinese hesitation word *negga*—something like our "ya know" or "uh"—but painfully close to the English "niggah."

"What can I do for you?"

"Please, Professor. Tomorrow I give *negga* English class. You explain me *negga* sentence." He carefully removes his hands from his sleeves as though they were breakable and takes several books out of his black plastic shoulder bag. He places in my hands a tattered tome (which I quickly convey to my desk lest I be responsible for its demise) and opens it to a page whose text is obscured by underlinings, ink smudges, stars, and arrows, and whose marginalia in English and Chinese constitute a virtual lexicon of grammatical terminology.

He points an ink-stained finger at a sentence that reads: "It has been determined during extensive experimentation in the combustive stages of the nitrates' noncompatible periods that the diffusion of the gasses through the oxygenized substances may cause explosions at temperatures of 62 C or higher."

"Right." I drawl.

"Oh, then know science," he says in awe.

"I know nothing at all about science, Mr.—I'm sorry, I don't know your name."

"Zhang Beihua," he says, and writes some characters on his hand with his fingers as though I could read them.

"I know nothing about science, Mr. Zhang, but perhaps I can help you untangle the sentence. What is your question?"

"Can say *negga* subject 'it' of sentence first member of construct of which *negga* 'diffusion' second and while adjective 'combustive' modifies *negga* second, 'it' is definitive because of position as first member of *negga* construct phrase."

I turn to the window to regain control, and constrain myself from blurting out "D'ya wanna run that by me again?"

"Correct?" he asks in response to my silence.

"I haven't the faintest idea," I answer.

Ah, now he understands. I am being humble. I cannot admit to being a brilliant grammarian able to solve instantly what was for him so complex a riddle.

"Please, Professor, not to be modest," he urges, but I'm sure he's secretly pleased by my modesty—so Chinese a response.

"Mr. Zhang, I cannot tell you about the grammatical structure of this sentence, and furthermore, I don't care." He takes a step backward and replaces his hands in his sleeves. "Can you tell me what the sentence *means*?" I ask.

"Oh, no," he says simply, as though this were an absurd question.

"And if I were able to answer your grammar questions—which I truly am not—would you then know what the sentence means?"

"Oh, no," he answers.

"Then what good is it to ask about its grammatical structure?"

"Tomorrow . . . teach *negga* passage English class. Must know to parse *negga* sentence. Students will—"

"Will what?"

"Must give lesson," he says finally, and bows himself out of the room with profuse apologies for bothering me. He is offended; I feel rotten. I have been neither helpful nor kind—a heretic in the order of grammarians, another foreign devil in China.

Li Xumei, our "Commie," takes me to visit the local elementary school where I sit in on the class of a Ms. Bin. Ms. Bin, it turns out, will be one of my students in the teachers' class that begins this week—who knows by what back door she snuck in, as she isn't a Zhe Da teacher.

Unlike most of the others, she is young and has been trained as an English (not a Russian) teacher. She has a fine collection of large white boards with bright cut-outs of apples and pandas and flowers in sets of threes and fours and fives, and others of children and parents and grandparents in worker, peasant, and soldier attire.

In perfectly articulated English Ms. Bin inquires of her students: "How many people are there in your family?" Fifty hands strain toward her, fingers fluttering. A little person rises and responds: "There are five people in my family: my mother, my father, my grandmother, my sister, and myself."

"Are your parents workers, peasants, or soldiers?" asks Bin, and another youngster answers in excellent English: "My mother is a cadre and my father is a worker, but my two elder brothers are soldiers in the People's Liberation Army."

I compliment Bin on her class and on her English, and then ask her a few simple questions about her own training—none of which she can answer. She has mastered everything in the fifth-grade English text, but is unable either to understand or speak beyond that level.

I meet with Dean Miao, one of the delegation that visited Manhattan Community College last spring. I'm fond of this man; I hardly know him and know nothing of his history, but he has a combination of warmth, seriousness about education, and concern about people that's very winning.

Dean Miao sums up the teachers' plight for me: Most had studied Russian, had come to love the language and literature, had come to feel comfortable and secure as Russian teachers. In the early sixties, after a series of political squabbles, the Russians walked out of China, taking with them not only the funding and equipment for innumerable projects, but the plans as well. Most Russian teachers were soon forced to abandon their field for English. It was like—it *was* starting all over again, and they felt both resentful and inadequate to the task.

In 1966 the Cultural Revolution began, and again the teachers were forced to change course. The study of foreign languages was verboten, the university was closed for three years, and teachers were terrified to teach even when it reopened—what could be more bourgeois than having and passing on knowledge.

For years the teachers sat around doing nothing—literally nothing. Most of their possessions, including books, were confiscated. (To avoid trouble Lao Fan sold his entire library *by the pound*.) No one was permitted to listen to Voice of America or even recordings of something as innocuous as *English 900*. The Russian cum English teachers took up knitting and sewing; several women told me that their husbands became highly skilled at cooking and child-rearing. (It wasn't until later that I began to hear the gory stories about this period.)

In 1976 the Gang of Four fell and the teachers were asked to walk into classrooms and teach English. They didn't know much English, were sure they were now too old to learn it, and, after lolling about for most of ten years, deeply resented being asked to work so hard trying to stay half a step ahead of their students. Dean Miao empathizes, but says it's urgent for a key scientific university like Zhe Da quickly and substantially to raise the level of its English teaching.

Then there's the question of class size. Though teachers have only two three-hour classes per week, they often have ninety or more students in a class. What kind of teaching is that even if you're highly motivated? But this is being rectified; next semester classes will be cut to thirty or forty.

"And finally," Dean Miao says, "so many of them are too old to learn." That again! I haven't been in China a month and I'm already deathly tired of hearing about people in their forties who are "too old to learn."

"I'm too old to learn English," lovely, gentle, forty-one-year-old Pao Nainai said to me last week.

"Oh," I responded, trying to look dejected. "That's too bad. That means there's no chance I'll ever learn Chinese."

"Why?" she asked.

"I'm the same age you are," I answered. "If you're too old to learn English, I'm too old to learn Chinese."

"Oh, but *you're* very smart," she said.

I told her about people in our country who return to school in their fifties and sixties, acquire degrees, and begin new careers or professions. I told her about women with grown children who become scholars, teachers, business executives—anything they choose. I think she thought this was a Chinese-style (i.e., polite) fib.

"Of course," I said, "it's not as easy as it was when you were twenty, but . . . ."

Had I known about him then, I would also have told her about the jazz musician Willie Ruff of the Mitchell-Ruff Duo. In a book called *Willie and Dwike*, William Zinsser describes how "Jazz came to China for the first time on the afternoon of June 2, 1981, when the American bassist and French-horn player Willie Ruff introduced himself and his partner, the pianist Dwike Mitchell, to several hundred students who were crowded into a large room at the Shanghai Conservatory of Music." Ruff did his introductions—and the entire lecture—in Chinese, which he had begun to study in 1979 in preparation for that historic event.

But then Pao would have argued that *he* was very smart, and would have smiled politely, unconvinced, just as Dean Miao agrees politely, unconvinced. (In two years in China I myself learn just enough Chinese to get around; I guess Willie Ruff *is* very smart.)

Friday afternoon. Lunch, *xushi* (nap), and then my very first class. It's hot, so hot that I haven't the strength to be nervous, so hot that the women come in what we call Chinese pajamas, the men in cotton shorts and undershirts. Squashed into old-fashioned double desks nailed to the floor, two dozen grown men and women expend their waning energy fanning their faces in slow, mechanical movements, making some small effort to be attentive to this American woman on a platform before them, the sweat dripping from her scalp into her eyes, nose, and mouth, blouse clinging to her chest and back, pants damp in the crotch and at the backs of the legs. There is already disappointment in the air: for months the teachers have anticipated a woman named "Woronov"— surely, with a name like that, she would speak Russian and they could share with her their old love, and show her their real skills and knowledge.

Having introduced myself and my teaching methods, I ask each of them to do likewise. This creates a palpable, collective tensing of muscles. I call on Pao Nainai. She rises like a schoolgirl, and belches loudly. I turn to write something—anything—on the blackboard, to distract myself from the image of Holden Caulfield in church. It will take me weeks to get used to this perfectly natural custom of belching.

I have schlepped to China twenty-five copies of Studs Terkel's *Working* on the silly assumption that Chinese "people" (undifferentiated) will be interested in what American workers have to say about their jobs and lives, and that this will be an ideal vehicle for teaching idiomatic American English.

For the four teachers whose English skills are already good, the book proves interesting and exciting; for the other twenty-two, it's disastrous. We spend three two-hour sessions getting through about a third of Terkel's steelworker interview. The only English practice anyone gets is to ask the meaning of some word or phrase.

One painful period is devoted to the scene in which steelworker Mike

Lefevre refers to a college kid who's trying to tell him his job as "a nineteen-year-old effete snob." (Spiro who?) Try explaining to the filial Chinese Lefevre's response when Terkel asks him why, then, he wants his own son to go to college: "Yes. I want my kid to look at me and say, 'Dad, you're a nice guy, but you're a fuckin' dummy.' Hell, yes, I want my kid to tell me that he's not gonna be like me . . . ." Hell, no, this is not the text for this class.

A little self-criticism seems in order. I tell the teachers that I'm sorry I didn't make greater efforts to understand the nature and needs of the class before assigning texts. Months later I recognize the importance of this admission of error, for it helps reduce the foreign expert to size, to make me human, and, most important, to exemplify the American concept that it's O.K. to try, to make a mistake, and then to try again—a concept entirely antithetical to the Chinese, for whom a mistake means loss of face.

The result of this deep-rooted face concept is paralysis; because they're terrified of speaking English in public, they (a) won't practice aloud and so can't improve, and (b) teach English in Chinese. Walking the halls of the university, you would never guess there were English classes in progress unless you glimpsed the blackboards or heard the Fasts' or my tape-recorded voice droning on about I-beams and cement mixtures.

After my self-criticism, I offer the teachers several suggestions as to how to proceed. They are teachers, after all, and should surely participate in determining their curriculum, but I dread that no one will say anything and I'll end up debating with myself. All's well. The teachers actively discuss the alternatives I present, and choose to spend half of each class on study skills for ESL students (note-taking, rapid reading, skimming, etc.), and half on simplified reading selections from a text by one of my colleagues, Linda Markstein.

We begin with rapid reading. Another disaster. The teachers insist on taking every word, one at a time, defining it and grammatically categorizing it. I open my Chinese dictionary at random, and ask someone to write on the board the four characters for *xuan bin duo zhu* ("the guest takes precedence over the host" or "a minor takes precedence over a major issue"). "If you do not read the four characters as one phrase," I note, "you cannot comprehend the meaning. The same is true in English." No use.

This becomes an important issue with the graduate students and scientists who are training to go abroad. Until they've checked every word in their "bibles" (as I've come to call their dictionaries), they're unwilling to so much as hazard a guess as to meaning. "In your scientific work it may be essential to understand every word," I note, "though I doubt it. But in ordinary conversation you can't say 'Excuse me a minute. I have to go look up some words in a dictionary.'" They find this amusing, but it makes no dent in their habits.

In the streets of Hangzhou I find the key. "You all know how much Chinese I know." Several people try to hide smiles. "And I know even less *Hangzhouhua* [the local dialect]. Now when I'm walking around Hangzhou and I get hungry, I find a food stall and ask to buy, say, some *youtiao*. Since the vendor is selling *youtiao*," I point out, "he has no trouble following my Chinese. Now, however, he says to me, 'Blah, blah, blah, blah, blah *piao*.' Now I don't understand 'blah, blah, blah, blah, blah' at all, but I know that, in this context, *piao* has to mean 'coupon,' so I hand him my coupon and he's very impressed with my ability to comprehend Chinese." Again there is some "you're smarter than we are" comment, but the concept of contextual interpretation begins to seem possible.

What *does* work in the teachers' class are the simplified essays and stories in Linda Markstein's reader. I begin to understand that I must treat the teachers like any other group of students, assigning and checking homework, and going around the room calling on people to do vocabulary, synonym, grammar, and comprehension exercises.

We discuss O. Henry's "The Last Leaf" in which an elderly artist does a great kindness for a young girl at the cost of his own life. The teachers love the story, appreciate its sentiments, and *giggle* through the death scene.

The general Chinese response to morbid or unhappy situations, I discover, is to giggle. If someone describes how her sister was killed in a car accident, her listeners giggle. If you talk about disease, divorce, death, or violence, the response is laughter—not raucous belly laughter, of course, but laughter nonetheless. This drives Suzy Fast up the wall; she takes it to mean that the Chinese are grossly insensitive, and she will never forgive the people who giggle when she announces she's going home for a while because her father is very ill.

A surprising discussion emerges out of Margaret Mead's essay on the "generation gap." I had anticipated great difficulty with this concept, knowing that filial piety has been the strongest moral force in China since time immemorial, actually predating Confucius, who simply canonized its principles.

But on a Friday evening when a small group of teachers comes to visit me in my rooms (I've arranged these social evenings in hopes of breaking down teachers' reticence to speak), the conversation returns to the topic. China has its own generation gap, Mr. Ma explains. Parents remember the old society and know that whatever setbacks have been suffered over the past ten or even twenty years, the new society is a far,

far cry from the old. The younger generation, however, doesn't remember, looks to the goods flaunted by tourists, and is impatient with the pace of China's development.

Pong Ling adds that many youths are also cynical because so much of what they believed and acted upon during the Cultural Revolution turned out to be so wrong. They are now unwilling to accept a "be patient" attitude from their elders. Lao Li points out that this has two aspects. Young people no longer simply accept what they're told at face value; they want to examine ideas and policies, and to take things into their own hands and change them. On the other hand, not looking at the past and not considering what is objectively possible for the nation at any given period can lead to great danger.

What can be done about this generation gap? Well, the parents try to teach their children about the bitter past, to encourage them to think, but at the same time to discipline them. Mostly they rely on the government, the party, and the Communist Youth League to utilize young people's great enthusiasm for change, but keep it in bounds.

"Do *you* obey your parents without question?" I ask this group of middle-aged men and women, themselves parents. They seem flustered by the question.

"Certainly," says Pong Ling. "How could we be disrespectful to our parents?"

"But suppose your parents are clearly wrong," I argue. "Suppose, for example, you have a girl and they want you to have more children until you have a boy."

"Then we would discuss the matter with them and try to help them understand why that is wrong," says Lao Li.

"And if they persist?"

"In this case," says Pong Ling, "it is easy to save face. You tell them the doctor says you can have no more children." Everyone laughs.

"Question no simple," says Mr. Ma. "We Chinese very like order. Have always rely on government to educate, keep social order. During Gang of Four, two governments, two ideas. Great confusion. Great chaos. Children no listen teachers, parents. Do many thing too terrible. Here," he says, holding a hand palm up, "lose center in government or family, lose order; but here," turning up the other palm, "if follow authority no see, no think, also terrible."

Helping each other with details, vocabulary, and grammar, correcting (correctly and incorrectly) the "he's" and "she's" of it all, the teachers relate to me an ancient tale from the "Twenty-four Examples of Filial Piety":

A poor man has a sick old mother who needs food and medicine he can't afford. The man discusses the problem with his wife, and they decide that the only thing to do is to get rid of their young son. They have only one mother, they reason, but can always have another child. As the man sinks his spade in the earth to dig a hole to bury their son in, he strikes gold. The gods, it seems, are so moved by this example of filial piety, they wish to reward the couple. The old mother gets her food and medicine, the couple and their child live happy lives.

I tell them about Abraham and Isaac. "But the moral is different," I note. "In the Bible God rewards Abraham for his reverence to God, not mother."

In the scientists' class, rapid-fire substitution drills begin at 7:30. Emphasizing rhythms and stress patterns, I say something like "The map is on the wall. Picture." The first student says "The picture is on the wall." I say "maps." The next students says "The maps are on the wall." We continue around the room, substituting singular or plural subjects or alternative objects. Probably because it resembles the rote learning they so cherish, the students enjoy these drills that help to engrave sentence patterns deep into the psyche, so deep that incorrect patterns begin to sound wrong, while correct ones leap to mind.

The key to these drills is pacing. We're doing very well until we get to Xiao Tu, who, as usual, is daydreaming about his fiancée. The youngest and only unmarried person in the group, he is teased unmercifully by his classmates.

We are up to "The books are on the table. Book," when we reach Mr. Jin in the back of the room. Everyone (including me) draws a breath. Mr. Jin struggles, struggles. From all over the room come stage whispers: "Book," says one student, "The book," says another. "Boo-kah," says Mr. Jin, and I exhale, "Yes, good," and move on. Several of the students have gone out of their way to assure me that Mr. Jin is a fine person and a fine scientist. He simply has no aptitude for English. Liang Tai tells me his problem isn't just with English; he's painfully unsocial (as distinct from antisocial) and rarely speaks even to his classmates unless spoken to.

"Boo-kah," on the other hand, is a common problem. Consonant endings are about as painful for my students as Chinese tones are for me. I've thought long and hard about how to grapple with this problem, tried, failed, and tried again, but I think I finally stumbled on a method that at least helps: When, for example, someone says, "I ridah my bikah to workah," that's precisely what I write on the board. I can always count on two or three students pointing out my spelling errors. "I just wrote what you said," I say, and then we practice that sentence for a while.

I've been giving lectures and writing practice dialogues on such subjects as greetings and introductions. These lead me to recognize the need for a session on names. The Han Chinese have only 438 surnames (408 of which are monosyllabic), but endless varieties of given names, for any three (sometimes two) characters can be combined to form a name meaningful to the family. Though we poor Westerners choose from a rather flimsy list of given names, we do have fat phone books full of surnames which, for Chinese-speakers, are tongue-terrible.

We work on some standard given names, male and female, and the stress patterns of some common English, Spanish, and German surnames. I request that each of the scientists choose one form of romanization for his or her name: if, for example, Xu sometimes uses Hsu or Shu (forms often taken by earlier generation Chinese-Americans), neither the U.S. government to whom he's applying for a visa nor the institutions to whom he writes will able to locate his alphabetically filed correspondence. So you can choose to be Chen or Tian or Qian, but you must make a decision and stick to it.

People here often choose new names on special occasions or at turning points of their lives—names they consider better suited to their mature selves or to new historical conditions. Thus, for example, on the eve of Liberation, Li Love Buddha might have become Li Serve the Masses. Along with the drastic limitation of surnames, this custom of periodically assuming new names has resulted in innumerable cases of mistaken identity ranging from comic to tragic.

All this leads me to think about my own name. Whenever I give lectures, neat black lettering on bright red or lavender posters highlights my name in English and Chinese. Lao Fan tells me they sound it out—something like "Fu-na-fu-fa." Intolerable. So I decide to have a Name Naomi Contest.

The name must be appropriate to me (though not necessarily sound like my name), easy for me to pronounce (no mean feat right there), and relatively easy for me to write (another major test of ingenuity). It must be submitted in both pinyin (the romanization system now standard in China) and *Hanzi* (Chinese characters) with a complete explanation of its meaning. Here are some of the submissions:

Ma Lan—Ma is a standard surname, and *ma lan* is a kind of beautiful flower. A folktale says that there was a beautiful and diligent girl named Ma Lan who married a hunter and helped him defeat evil and bring great happiness to the people.

Hai Ming—Hai is a surname meaning "sea" or "ocean." It is a symbol of greatness and infinite wisdom. *Ming* means bright, clear, aboveboard, honest. America and China are divided by the Pacific, but owing to many people's outstanding efforts—including your own—our peoples have come to understand each other and establish friendship.

Ai Min—*Ai* means "love" and *min* means "the people." "Love the People" is a revolutionary name.

Ai Mei—*Ai* means "love" and *mei* is a kind of flower—wintersweet or plum blossom. Chairman Mao and Premier Zhou loved *mei* very much when they were alive. Wintersweet is considered a symbol of a spirit that stands firm and unyielding, yet is modest and prudent. Chairman Mao wrote a poem, "Ode to the Plum Blossom," to praise the noble character of *mei*.

There were many more wonderful entries, but I am now Nan Huamei. "The explanation," says Mr. Liu, "is as follows: Nan is a Chinese surname meaning "south," Hua signifies "China," and Mei means both "America" and "beautiful." The whole meaning expresses directly to us how an American professor came to work with us in South China with a good wish to help the Four Modernizations. If we pronounce Nan Huamei in Shanghai dialect, it sounds just the same as your name, Naomi. It's also easy to write."

Mr. Liu won a silk-covered photo album for his efforts. (Later someone let it out that he was disappointed, having hoped for a book in English from my library.)

I love my new name. Lao Fan has created a signature for me, and I practice a lot. Best of all I love being called Nan Laoshi, Teacher Nan.

# 5
# Tenth Moon: Bits and Pieces

When was the last time you had a birthday party at eight o'clock. On Sunday morning. In your own apartment. It's another glorious tenth moon (October) day, and my room is all cheery with plates of cookies, trays of lidded tea cups, and rows of flowered, pandaed, and scenic-spotted thermoses of boiling water. I was listening to jazz, but at eight sharp I turn to the Voice of America news in "Special English"—that loud, slow speech often mouthed at the blind by the thoughtless. But it's a good English teacher; people listen devotedly, soaking up the propaganda right along with the English lessons.

I feel rather nervous waiting for my visitors, who will certainly arrive in a big bunch, not a few at a time so I could actually greet everyone.

And they come. First the students, about forty of them, the postgraduates with whom I have worked for several weeks now, and the scientists who arrived only recently. They're so sweet, so genuinely friendly, they make me feel that coming here this morning is something they really wanted to do, not something required by duty. They bring all sorts of birthday gifts, gifts surely too expensive for their incomes: a sandalwood fan, a lacquer cup, a package of stationery with delicately printed scenes of Hangzhou, a scroll depicting "Spring in the Garden," a hand-painted silk parasol, a beautiful bamboo vase.

The students, who range in age from thirty to fifty, are spread in a semicircle on the floor while I sit on a little stool holding court and feeling silly. How do you celebrate your birthday in China? We eat noodles. Why? Silly question. Noodles represent long life, and what else should you worry about on your birthday? No parties, no presents—just noodles. Why so many presents for me? You're a foreigner.

We turn to more serious topics. During the Cultural Revolution, some of the graduate students had been undergraduates at Zhe Da.

When one faction of Red Guards decided that the magnificent Buddhas at the Lin Ying Temple were symbols of reaction that must be destroyed, these students organized their schoolmates to protect the temple. I'm proud of them, glad to hear of those who took a stand against absurdity. Though many are very shy, especially in English, I'm enjoying the great exuberance in the room, but I'm told that the teachers waiting at the gate can't come in until the students leave. The students leave.

The teachers come, about thirty of them, bearing a round, gooey cake that says "Happy Birthday" in English. We have tea and cake and break up into groups, more like a party than the "holding court" sort of arrangement I had with the students. The teachers have brought me fine Hangzhou silk for a blouse, and their best calligrapher has written birthday greetings on a silk picture of cranes (another long-life symbol). George comes up to take pictures, and is immediately engaged in conversation in his fluent Chinese. I'm jealous.

Finally, sometime after eleven, the teachers sweep out and Lao Fan and his wife Ming arrive with another cake, this one decorated with the character for long life.

At three o'clock several teachers who were unable to come earlier appear unannounced, and when they finally leave and I can take a breather, George comes up with Great Wall vodka and a book of short stories. We go down to pick up Suzy and Paul. They've set up tall candles in their darkened living room, provided a magnum of Chinese champagne, and given me a very useful gift—clips to keep my pants from getting caught in the spokes of my (nonexistent) bicycle. After a gay and giggly dinner comes cake number three.

Alone at last on my balcony overlooking the lake, I open my cards and letters from home, which help to make this one of the nicest (as well as the longest) birthdays I can remember.

I do tire of "Jingle Bells." It is whistled and hummed by taxi drivers and hotel attendants, sung by passing children, and played every night in the park across the street on sundry instruments I can and cannot identify. Western ditties are everywhere. How bizarre it was the night I arrived in Hangzhou to drift to sleep in this huge, Russian-style hotel in the People's Republic of China serenaded by a harmonica rendering of "Yankee Doodle." But there's a reason: "Yankee Doodle" is the theme song of the Voice of America, which virtually everyone listens to in either English or Chinese.

The mystery of the missing letters has been solved. I came back from school one day to find a telegram lying on the front desk of the hotel. It was addressed to a Mr. Alfred Whitestone, Hangzhou Hotel, Round-the-Lake Road, Hangzhou. Had anyone attempted to find

Mr. Whitestone? No, no. No one reads English, so they hadn't bothered about it.

Can the hotel registration office ascertain Mr. Whitestone's room number? No, no. No one knows who is in which room as room assignments are made by tour group leaders. And would the gentleman kindly provide the names or room numbers of any tour group leaders currently in residence? Silly question.

At dinner time, I go from table to table until I find the grateful Mr. Whitestone. Discussing this over dinner, George and I ask one another why mail addressed to us at our universities arrives within three weeks of posting, while mail addressed to our Round-the-Lake residence rarely reaches its destination. We make a bee-line for the front desk. Scattered in the top drawer are perhaps three dozen letters for all of us, dating all the way back to August. George writes out our names and room numbers in English and Chinese and tapes it up next to the desk. Now we get our mail.

Paul and Suzy Fast have a hot plate (illegal, of course), so they shop in the nearby market and cook most of their meals in their rooms. George normally eats with Jack and Kyoko, and as I am none too fond of macho Jack's attitude toward me or his wife, I normally prefer to eat alone. Sometimes I take a letter to the dining room with me. With my awkward but comprehensible new vocabulary, I order supper and settle into my letter, but soon I have a strange feeling there's a presence at my back. Wrong. There are four presences in white blouses and jackets reading over both of my shoulders. I'm stunned. I pull the pages to my breast and stare at them. They stare back. Confusion all around. One of the young men positions my hand so the letter can be read, points to a very long word, and asks simply: "What means?" "Dissertation" I answer, carefully dividing the word into four syllables. "What means?" he repeats. "A dissertation is a book a student must write to get the highest degree at the university. It is called a doctorate or Ph.D." This explanation seems satisfactory. Two of them walk away, a third brings me silverware and dishes, the fourth continues to stand at my shoulder reciting familiar words.

I begin to understand that letters are not private domain. Really, nothing is. I have come into my room to find mops and brooms and buckets at ease while a young man or woman is "reading" a book that was on my desk or even in a drawer. No harm is meant. Nothing is ever taken. Jack argues that people are spying on us. That may be so, but the kids reading our books and letters hardly know enough English to spy on anybody. As the fu become more familiar, they become more playful; the dining room cashiers often riffle through my pocketbook and hide my wallet or glasses.

Unable to formulate a comprehensible question about the concept of privacy, I look around for an explanation. One thing I notice is that the physical environment of the Chinese family differs from ours. Our goal is privacy; we want to have enough rooms so each member of the family may enjoy his or her own "space"—this is *my* room, my desk, etc. But in a Chinese family, all the space within the family compound walls or any modern apartment seems to be shared by all the family members.

I'm beginning to accept what amounts—in my culture—to a gross invasion of privacy, but I continue to be disturbed by my inability to get the fu to keep my room locked. None of them could possibly get away with my typewriter or camera equipment, but all sorts of people from all over the world pass my open door each day. Ah, well, no point in worrying about it.

*October 21*
*What shall I say? Do? N says he made a big mistake letting me go—I should come home and marry him! I call. He repeats his proposal on the phone and I hear in his voice the expectation that I will get on the next plane and come home. Stare, stare at his picture under the desk glass. What now? I guess Mother was right: look out when things are going well—your whole world's probably about to crumble at your feet.*

*October 22*
*Gloomy morning. Heavy clouds over the mountains. How appropriate! I know how N feels. I nearly went mad that year I was on sabbatical— no job to create a sense of regularity, of balance. But I lived through it and so will he. Besides, if I ran home it might work for a while, but then every time there was a problem between us I'd be screaming about how he made me come home from China to marry him.*

*Oh, love, I know how miserable you are. But I'm happy here, energized, more productive than I've ever been in my life and that is joyous to me. Would you really ask me to come back now so we can be miserable together?*

It's 7:30 a.m. and I've already biked around the lake, had breakfast, and am here at my typewriter looking out over the sun-tipped treetops and the mountains beyond.

The lake is magnificent at sunrise, with dark silhouettes of figures performing tai chi movements, fishing, or sitting and chatting in the morning stillness. An occasional kayak slips through the water. Joggers say "gooda morning" to me as I go by, and tourists are besieged by young people eager to practice English.

I've been longing to join the Fasts on their bike rides around West

Lake, but have, alas, received no bike coupon. So when the Friendship Shop got in the Shanghai Phoenix—purported to be the best brand in China—I decided that if I could learn to ride a bike when I was well over thirty (which I did), I could certainly now learn to ride a man's bike.

Lao Fan and I spend an hour choosing the bike (85 yuan), then I get in the car while he steers his bike with one hand and pushes mine with the other. At the police station we fill out several sets of papers, and I'm presented with a little red plastic book—my very own bicycle license which I am admonished to keep on my person. The police engrave my license number between the handlebars, attach my license plate to the rear fender, and wish me well. Little do they know! We set off for home—sort of. Lao Fan is appalled at my clumsiness and lack of skill, and genuinely worried about my survival. I get a little steadier as we get out of town and head toward West Lake into the sunset.

Still, there's no denying that I am a spectacle: man, woman, or child, so reticent to show almost any other emotion, is easily brought to tears at the sight of the foreigner trying to mount her steed. (In North China, I'm told, a bicycle is called a "foreigner horse.") I can't push off and then throw my leg over the bar—I just don't have that kind of balance. So I have to stand the bike up, throw my leg over the back rack and the bar, then try to push off. If this is not sufficiently comical, add packages to the back rack and you have a scene no doubt described over the dinner table in half the households in Hangzhou.

West Lake at sunset is a thousand picture postcards perfectly framed by weeping willows and dotted with gently arched bridges and beds of four-foot chrysanthemums. The Su Causeway, which divides the inner and outer sections of the lake, is named after the eleventh-century poet-official-landscape artist Su Dongpo (Su Tung-p'o, 1036–1101). An honest official and a wise man, Su is still much loved in Hangzhou. One story has it that on his first day in office he painted scenery on the moldy spots of a local merchant's fans, thereby saving the merchant's business and settling a neighborly quarrel over an unpaid loan.

Su Dongpo wrote a poem about West Lake, comparing it to the ancient beauty Xi Zhi:

Water shimmering—sunny day is best.
Mountains hazy—marvelous even in rain.
Compare West Lake to the beautiful Xi Zhi. She looks
Just as becoming without make-up or richly adorned.

Behind the Hangzhou and Xi Ling hotels are pathways leading up into the mountains. Here George and Kyoko and I stumble upon several ancient temples, some the very ones where Su Dongpo must have passed peaceful hours chatting with monks. In his day Hangzhou is said to have had 360 temples in the city and suburbs. New stone stairways made of centuries-old gravestones with gracefully etched Chinese characters are hauled into place by workers much as the originals must have been.

Some of the old temples now serve as housing complexes. Each family has one or two small, square, dark, cement rooms, but the courtyards (where people spend most of their waking and, in summer, sleeping hours) are full of blooming trees and oddly shaped archways enhanced by delicately carved figures and scenes. The courtyards face West Lake, and behind them the mountains flow upward like traditional Chinese paintings. In this setting we come upon the Quaker Oats Man.

Suddenly we hear a loud bang and much giggling. And there he is, in a cloud of smoke, the Quaker Oats Man. He and his wife travel from one neighborhood to another with their portable apparatus: a small coal oven with a bellows to intensify the heat, and a cannon with a handle to rotate it over the fire.

Beside their contraption sit several baskets containing small bowls of rice, corn, or beans. The old man tilts back his straw hat, wipes his forehead with the back of his sleeve, adds coal to the fire, and cleans out the cannon with a brush. He pours the contents of one bowl into it, adds a little yeast, sometimes a little sugar, sometimes salt. He closes the top and works the bellows with one hand while rotating the cannon with the other.

On the end of the cannon handle is a big thermometer that tells us the moment has arrived. The children hop from one foot to another and giggle again. The old man inserts the cannon into a large wire bag and BOOM, off it goes, producing precisely enough cereal to fill the basket that held the bowl that held the rice.

As smoke clears the people press us to share their goodies. The rice is especially delicious, just like boxed puffed rice, only fresh and warm. The old woman starts the process again. When we try to leave, promising to return soon with our own bowls of corn to be popped, the people rush into their homes and bring us their own provisions. Merry, chattering children follow us down the winding pathways.

Forever and a day, when I sit down to some ordinary, everyday supermarket breakfast cereal, I'll remember my Quaker Oats Man.

# 6
## Visits

A. This person has stepped directly in front of your bicycle, knocked you off into the street, and injured your leg. The accident is clearly *his fault, not yours.*

B. This person has just run directly into you with his bicycle, ripped your pants, and scraped your leg. The accident is clearly *his fault, not yours.*

This morning we try role playing. The notion is so abhorrent to the class that I agreed to supply the situation and assign parts yesterday so people could prepare. Mr. Xu and Mr. Wang stand on the teacher's platform, and in barely audible tones recite a stiff, dull dialogue rendered comical by Mr. Xu's Chinglish, which bears a marked resemblance to that of Hal the Computer, a sort of monotonal march of separated syllables.

Enough of this prepared stuff. I ask two other students to improvise. They can't. They won't. They must go home and prepare first. I point out that in America they will not be able to say "Wait a minute, please. I'll be right back. I have to go home and prepare to converse with you." This is all very amusing, but no one volunteers to stand up and improvise.

I pick on Liang Tai because, as class monitor, he must set a good example, and on our lovelorn classmate, Xiao Tu, a natural comic. Raising voices and gesticulating broadly, they give a very convincing performance which ends with the two of them marching off to the police station in search of a mediator. Other students are emboldened to create English sentences for the incident and to shake their fists at each other. No matter how gentle or how heated the argument, however, it is always resolved by recourse to the traffic police. (No one would venture a guess as to how the police *would* resolve the matter were they in fact asked to do so.)

I try more role-playing situations, choosing topics that will help me explore aspects of my students' daily lives. This time I ask for compositions on "Who does the housework in your family?" Ms. Hua writes:

My husband and I both scientist. Since the character of our work require that we spend spare time to study English and to read and write article and book, so, no matter who, husband or wife, both dislike to do housework. But has to be done. The only way to share. I cook and do the washing and the sewing. My husband does shopping, wash the big sheets, and does some thing which need strong force.

Every student, husband or wife, gives me the same reasonable division of labor line. As easy as that? I don't believe it. The next day I hand Ms. Hua, a nuclear physicist, form B; form A I give to Mr. Li, a biochemist.

A. You have just returned home after a hard day's work to find that the shopping hasn't been done, the food hasn't been cooked, the baby is crying, and the laundry is piling up. Your wife simply refuses to do her share of the housework.

B. You have just returned home from a hard day in the laboratory to find that the shopping hasn't been done, the food hasn't been prepared, the baby's diapers are wet, and the laundry is piling up. Your husband simply will not do his share of the housework.

They whisper conspiratorially for a few minutes, square off, and begin their spontaneous discussion:

"I very busy on laboratory arrive home no dinner," Mr. Li accuses.

"Think I do nothing for hour, no?" answers Ms. Hua. "I split atom, chop vegetable, run computer, pick child day center."

"You too excuse," says Li firmly. "You know I too busy also study English and write article."

"Ho, ho," says Hua, "many good talk, no homework finish."

By this time the entire class is in stitches. It's perfectly clear that all those lovely visions of the peaceful, reasonable division of household labor will have to wait until socialism is transformed into communism, and even the Great Helmsman who was in such a hurry suggested that that would take at least a couple of hundred years. What makes *me* laugh is that, language notwithstanding, the same dialogue is being acted out this very moment in Albany, Atlanta, Altoona.

As comical as all this may be in a classroom exercise, however, the question of who does what chores in a Chinese household is no laughing matter. After all, there are almost no refrigerators or freezers, washers or dryers, Woolite or wash'n'wear. There's no hot running water. In

China, I soon learn, even half the housework is painfully time and energy consuming.

As Yao is preparing an English course she will teach next semester to Tibetan students at the Minorities Institute in Xian, her husband Wu does almost all of the housework. I asked him if I could follow him around for a day to see what that means. He said he leaves the house at 6:30 sharp each day, so I must be prompt. He assumed that I was joking and is surprised to find me at his doorstep at 6:15 on Sunday morning.

Yao and Wu both teach at the university. They have three grown children, all of whom are as yet unmarried and, therefore, living with them. As no single unit of housing was built at the university between 1966 and 1976—it was too bourgeois to think of such material comforts as decent housing—Yao and Wu and their three children have always shared two rooms. When the Fasts and I had dinner with them recently, I was astonished to witness the genuine warmth and friendship developed and sustained among them under such conditions. Surely five Americans in two tiny rooms would tear each other to pieces.

At 6:30 Sunday morning Wu and I set out for the market as he does seven days a week. Bamboo baskets slipped over our arms (I want to look "authentic"), we crush into the crowds buying fresh vegetables and eggs from the peasants, then stand in line at the state market for a small slab of pork and a hunk of pig stomach. On special occasions Wu might buy a chicken or a duck, but it must be killed, bled, cleaned, and plucked before cooking.

In the town of Hangzhou is a new, white-tiled building resembling a small supermarket, but out here at the university rice and flour come from one shop, vinegar, wine, and pickled vegetables from another, vegetable oil, peanuts, coal, noodles, dofu, or dried shrimp from still others.

On the way home we buy some *youtiao* (literally, "oil stick"), something like a deep-fried cruller. Chewing on the crisp *youtiao*, Wu lights the coal burner that sits outside on the balcony so the soot will not blacken their living quarters. He boils enough kettles of water to fill enough large thermoses to meet the family's washing and drinking needs for the day. Now: cook the rice porridge, wash the dishes, fold the quilts, dust and sweep the floor. Take the laundry, a bar of soap, and a thermos of hot water down five flights, scrub the clothes and sheets on a stone slab, rinse out the soap, go back up five flights and hang it all out to dry on six-foot bamboo poles without dropping anything in the mud below or, in winter, developing frostbite.

Wu's neighbor insists that I come over to see her new Chinese-made washing machine—the first on the block. I "oo" and "ah" over her machine, and amuse her family with the story of Mrs. Wang, who told me as we traveled in August from Beijing to Hangzhou that she would never have a washing machine because it tears up your clothes. "How do you wash clothes now?" I had asked her. "Oh," she answered, "I beat them against the rocks."

Washing machines are wonderful, of course, but given the severe shortage and high cost of electricity in China, why not establish public laundries instead of encouraging people to purchase individual washing machines? Furthermore, there's no hot water and no successful cold water detergent, and the machines are incredibly inefficient. You stuff in the clothes, attach a line to the sink or bathtub faucet, fill the tub, turn on the machine which then "agitates" the clothes, empty the dirty, soapy water, fill the machine again, let it push the clothes about again, then fill it yet again in a valiant effort to rinse the soap out. When you remove the clothes from the machine you wring them out and hang them up, and then, as wash'n'wear fabrics are scarce and expensive, iron everything.

Lunch: peel and scrub the vegetables—carefully, as they are fertilized in "night soil" (animal and human excrement)—chop each ingredient, relight the coal burner, make the rice, and set it aside in a padded pot blanket to keep it warm. Cook the dishes (one at a time as there is only one burner). Wash the plates and chopsticks, pots and pans. Then repeat the whole business again at dinner time.

Yao points out that these are just the daily chores. She also makes and mends clothing for the whole family, salts, pickles, and dries various vegetables in season—the list goes on and on. Oy! or "Ai Ya!" as the Chinese say. No wonder the teachers bitch so much about housework.

Soaking in sudsy hot water back in my suite at the Hangzhou Hotel, I muse on my marvelous Sunday excursion and make up my mind to get out of this place. I'm convinced I can only make real friends and learn about the real China *out there*; in here I'm "protected" by officious guards who demand official letters signed and stamped with official seals of high officials. Whenever I talk about moving to the campus they tell me about this forthcoming "foreigner residence"—the foundation has yet to be poured.

Meantime, however, I make arrangements for a series of Sunday excursions. This week I will visit some scenic sites with two of the scientists from our intensive class, and I leave instructions with the hotel guards to let them in. Liang Guixiang and Liang Xianggui walk to the hotel to pick me up. The two women—we call them Da (big) Liang and Xiao (little) Liang—are stopped by the guards and permitted neither to come up nor even to phone me. They walk all the way back to the university and hunt around until they find someone from the Foreign

Affairs Office—it's Sunday, remember—to write and sign and seal a document giving them permission to visit me.

When they arrive (trying hard to mask their fury at this treatment), they find me coughing and wheezing. They insist on taking me to see a doctor. I promise to go quietly if we stop on the way, as planned, at the Tomb and Temple of General Yue Fei.

I've passed the imposing red walls of this monument every day since my arrival in Hangzhou, but I have never been inside. Now the women's excitement is infectious. As we approach the tall iron gates, they fill me in on the history of General Yue Fei (1103–1142), repeatedly referring to something that sounds like "the scum." I can't figure out what they're talking about.

In the main hall is an immense, magnificently painted statue of this Southern Song dynasty hero and martyr. He wears a long, lavender robe embroidered with gold dragons at each knee and across his breast, red slippers with turned up toes, a red belt with mother-of-pearl insets, and a gold and blue hat with a bright red ball atop. His lips, too, are crimson, his eyebrows and heavy mustache and odd little goatee shining black. He's wonderful!

In the twelfth century the Jürched Tartars invaded North China, established the Jin dynasty, and conquered the northern capital of Haifeng. Yue Fei organized a strong and disciplined army ("like Zhu De's Red Army," says Xiao Liang with pride) and soundly defeated the Jin. As Yue Fei was preparing to pounce again and blow them off the face of China, the Southern Song emperor, Gaozong, egged on by his prime minister Qin Gui, got cold feet and signed a humiliating peace treaty with the Jin. Qin Gui lured Yue Fei back to Hangzhou (capital of the Southern Song dynasty) and had him imprisoned and murdered.

Early in the thirteenth century Yue Fei's remains were entombed in a temple on this site, and he came to stand as a symbol of opposition to foreign aggression and appeasement. Two inscriptions are carved in stone above his statue: the first, meaning "Always be loyal to the motherland," was scratched into Yue Fei's shoulders with a needle by his mother. The other reads "Recover our lost territories," a clear reference today to Taiwan and Hong Kong. In the main hall, gay cartoon murals depict such scenes as Yue Fei's mother inscribing her son's spinal column. In courtyards beyond are stone stele (memorial tablets) to Yue Fei, one said to be in Yue Fei's own calligraphy.

And in another courtyard we find them, "the scum." Here are two intricately carved black iron statues on their knees, heads bowed, looking very miserable indeed. And what pleasure visiting peasant women take in spitting on "the scum," Minister Qin and his wife, and knocking them about the head and breasts with their walking sticks.

The temple and tomb were wrecked by Red Guards during the Cultural Revolution; it cost 400,000 yuan to restore the place which was reopened this October 1. It is money well spent, agree the Liangs. It seems odd to me, given the hate-foreigners bent of the Cultural Revolution, that the Red Guards would have struck out at this particular temple, for Yue Fei stood against foreign invasion. I'm being too logical: "Red Guards didn't stop to think beyond the word 'old,'" Da Liang says, "old ideas, old cadres, old temples, old anything." I tell them about the slogan current in America during that same period of history: "Never trust anyone over thirty." They're surprised and amused.

Outside Yue Fei's Temple we walk by little piles of orange peels tossed on the ground or overflowing small baskets. I've seen these in town and around the university and had concluded that it was a form of slobbishness. But here are soldiers loading the orange peels into an army truck. They collect the piles of peels deposited at designated sites, then take them to pharmacists who convert them into vitamins and medicines.

After our morning sojourn and delicious noodles in steaming broth, the two Liangs drag sniffling me off to the hospital where they do a very commendable job as interpreters. Foreign Friend goes to the important people's hospital: neat, lovely grounds, antiseptic halls and rooms, no waiting. Dr. Ma has a warm, quiet smile. Beside him stands his student, Xiao Zhou, an angelic-looking young woman, hair hidden but for wisps, face framed by a snowy white cap. She seems to be holding her breath as though she too could hear while the old gentleman listens intently to the pulses (three, mind you) in each of my wrists, then scrutinizes every detail of my tongue. I ask how he can distinguish the markings of my geographic tongue from signs of illness. He smiles and replies that next week he will eat long noodles for his seventieth birthday.

As he writes out a prescription for me, he explains each detail to Xiao Zhou; neither Liang has the English vocabulary for all the items involved, but at the hospital pharmacy we're given an armload of roots, barks, twigs, leaves, grasses, and seeds. If there are insects nestled in the bramble, I'd rather not know. All of this is taken to the university infirmary, which grinds and cooks it and provides me with little bags of medicine. Dissolved in boiling water, this foul-tasting brown concoction taken three times a day seems like punishment for getting sick.

I've also had endless delegations of fruit- and advice-bearing visitors. A group of teachers arrives. I get the fu down the hall to bring tea things. We sip and chat for an hour, discussing such matters as what I will have for lunch. I say, "Oh, chicken soup, I guess," showing off my common sense. "Oh, no," says Teacher Pao in genuine distress, "that's the worst thing to eat when you're sick." They leave, admonishing me

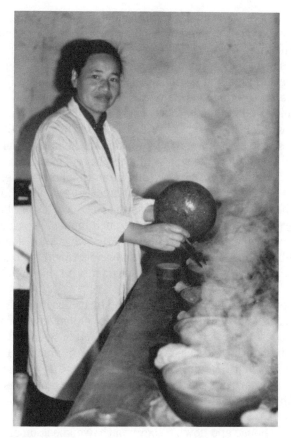

Cooking up cures at the university clinic.

to get lots of rest. Ten minutes later the next group comes and we run through the same scene. Lao Fan and Ming arrive with a dish of *muer*, literally, "wood ears," a type of fungus considered especially healthful. When they've left and I think I'm safe because it's lunchtime, here comes Zhang Beihua with a load of oranges, apologies, and grammar questions. Actually, it's been fun because I'm not *so* sick—just a good healthy cold.

I must be better by Sunday because I have another wonderful excursion planned. As I'm as eager to talk to the local peasants as my students are to practice English, we agreed to meet—outside the hotel—to visit with people in the brigades adjacent to the university. Hoar-frost tips the greening winter wheat crop sown hardly a day after the rice is gathered and the straw cut and piled for use as kitchen fuel. Shooing geese, chickens, and ducks from underfoot, we slosh down a muddy lane and find a woman scrubbing sheets on a large, flat stone laid across bricks in front of the house. We apologize for interrupting her, and she apologizes for the state of her house as she leads us through a sagging doorway into a small, dingy room.

After seating all six of us on rickety bamboo chairs and mini-stools that wobble on the dirt floor, she unscrews the bare bulb that hangs from the ceiling and plugs in the TV set—a good set purchased cheaply by her son who works in a local TV factory. In fact, she is not a peasant but a worker, and as there are four workers in the family (her husband, herself, and two of her five children), they have a great deal of money. (They don't even pay rent as they all live in this house inherited from her family.) A fading picture of Zhou Enlai sits askew above an old wooden table that leans against a soot blackened, crumbling wall. I can't understand why, if they have so much money, they don't spend some of it repairing this dismal abode. Mr. Wang later suggests that they're probably on a waiting list for a new apartment from one of their work units, so they don't want to waste money on this hopeless dwelling.

As I suspiciously eye three or four dead birds drooped in a basket at my left ear, a tall boy with a peaked army hat pulled down over his eyes comes in and slumps against the doorway. He's been out of middle school for six months and has as yet no work assignment. He certainly doesn't work too hard moving out of the doorframe as we leave. I ask if he helps his mother with the laundry and other household tasks, as she, after all, works in a factory six days a week. His silly smile is answer enough.

Behind the house and down a soggy path, we knock on an open door and introduce ourselves to a tiny old woman with bound feet. She is delighted with our visit, insists on serving us tea, then hobbles over to a sideboard where we admire an array of photographs of her children. "My two boys have joined the People's Liberation Army," she says proudly. "My elder daughter is a worker at Zhe Da and my younger daughter is a student there." It is with some difficulty that we get her to settle on a little stool and respond to our questions.

In minutes she's pouring out tales of her life, "speaking bitterness," as the Chinese put it. I would weep with her, for her past is painful indeed, but the more she talks the more she weeps, and the more she weeps the more her nose runs, and the more her nose runs the oftener she blows it, peasant fashion—two fingers and thumb to nose and whacko, in a wide arc onto the cement floor.

As we stroll back to my hotel, I tell my students how much this morning's encounter means to me because of its spontaneity, because it wasn't arranged by China Travel Service or the Zhe Da Foreign Affairs

Department. On Monday morning I find this composition on my desk:

**A Visit**

This morning, Prof. Woronov and we five students visited a peasant family. A granny about sixty-five years old welcomed us, and showed us her clean and tidy house with a kitchen, a pantry, a sitting room and three bedrooms. At our request, she told us her story.

"I was born in Shanghai," she said, "in a poor worker's family. I am the eldest of five children. When I was fourteen, I had to work in a cotton mill and be of help to my family. The child-laborer's life was unspeakably bitter. Three years later, when I finally got over the apprenticeship and could support myself, war broke out. On August 13, 1937, the Japanese aggressor troops occupied Shanghai, trampled on the city and butchered the common people. We ran away in terror. We came to Hangzhou and stayed in a refugee camp near the Qiantang River. There was almost no food. The whole family could only get two little bowls of congee each day. At night, people crowded the camp. We lay down on the wet ground. Lice and bugs were everywhere.

"When circumstances got a little better, we tried to go back to Shanghai, but we had only eight yuan in our pockets. We took jobs here and there, but they didn't last any length of time. We couldn't do anything to help ourselves, so my father sold my two sisters as child-brides. They were nine and eleven years old then. I have never found them till now."

The granny choked with sobs, and tears flowed from her eyes.

"At that time I was nineteen," she said, "and father married me to a poor peasant in this village. My husband had four brothers. He is the oldest, but he hadn't even a house, only a thatched shed.

"It was Liberation that brought an end to those years of suffering. After Liberation our life has gotten better and better. With the help of the government we built this new house."

We asked the granny how she had been affected by the Cultural Revolution. "It meant nothing to us," she said. "If the workers did not work, they still received their guaranteed wage; if we peasants did not work, we did not eat.

"We owe everything to the Communist Party and Chairman Mao." Then, with a smile, the granny said: "I am over sixty. People often advise me, 'You've got old. You'd better stay home instead of working in the fields.' But I still work in the fields every day. I am in good health. And above all, I like to work. The Communist Party and Chairman Mao and Chairman Hua have given me a new life, a happy life. It's a pleasure for me to take part in physical labor."

Class discussion of this essay generates much debate and more writing. In his firm, quiet manner, Mr. Liu points out that while peasants around here are doing very well, those in mountainous regions of the Northwest may live in poverty, earning as little as 20 fen a day to supplement their government grain rations.

A few days later I find on my desk this unsolicited essay from Mr. Liu describing the life of some of China's poorest peasants. (I have made only minor corrections.)

### A Mountain Village

Several classmates and I accompanied Prof. Woronov to visit a peasant family last Sunday. This is quite a rich family and I believe that so are almost all peasant families on the outskirts of Hangzhou, one of the wealthiest areas in China. But elsewhere things are different. I can tell you about it from my own experience.

As a member of a socialist-education work team, I lived in 1965 in a small village in Shaanxi province. The living conditions there were so hard that people who live in the city just can't imagine them. There were no highways, no shops, no cinemas or theatres, no electricity or gas, and even no coal.

Because the village is located in the spur of the huge Qingling Mountain Range, sunshine is very precious, and in addition to the height above sea level, the climate is bitterly cold, so only potatoes and cabbage can be grown—no rice or wheat. All the things that were there were great nature, beautiful and splendid nature: endless mountains, thick woods and bushes, singing brooklets, narrow and steep paths leading to remote places, and wonderful wild animals. In addition, there were terrible, roaring floods in summer, and in winter hundred-foot ice cascades hanging down from the tops of the cliffs.

But there were almost no people. In fact, I could hardly say I lived in a village. In a 13-kilometer-long valley between two enormous mountains, only forty-one persons lived in thirteen households, most in isolated houses a few kilometers apart from each other. I lived in their "center city" where five households nestled together. Before Liberation, most people were refugees who escaped from their native places on the plains to evade the cruel exploitation by landlords. But what awaited them there was another kind of exploitation: in order to survive, they had to do seasonal labor for the mountain lords, cutting down trees and carrying loads of goods like cattle. Most were bachelors because they couldn't support anyone except themselves. It was only after Liberation they were able to marry, and by then most of them were near forty. This is why there were only three people in the average household.

After Liberation great changes took place as the government organized the people to struggle to raise their living standards. Actually, I believe that great nature is fair; it is not partial to people who live in some places while neglecting others who live elsewhere. In such a high and cold mountain area some places are covered with thick forests of bamboo, some so thick that brooms and baskets can be made of them, while others are covered with bushes of which spade stocks and other tools can be made. Thus they earned money to get along. For example, a strong man could make twenty-five spade stocks in a day, but it took him a day to carry them to the people's commune store and another day to return.

Although food and clothing were sufficient, life was very rough. Houses were not tidy for there were no bricks or lime. They built their houses only with stone and soil, and without closets. They owned no clocks or bicycles, for what use could they serve? But you might see ten or more quilts piled up on a bed even though there were only three members in the family.

On the whole, their lives were much happier than before, but their work is still hard. When I watched them carrying 60-kilogram loads of stocks 40 kilometers in a day, I always fancied that it would be wonderful if there were a highway leading to the people's commune, and the commune's truck could come to the front doors of their homes to buy their products. I dreamed that they would set up a small electricity station and small mills to make their products. Of course, we have a long way to go to do all this, but I am sure that, as the four modernizations are developed in our country, such a day will at last come about.

I am still moved by the beauty and sincerity of this piece. It seems to me that the generation educated in the New China of the fifties absorbed a concern for the working people and the nation as a whole that had never before been seen, and certainly doesn't dominate the thinking of the younger generation today. Does it sound foolish to say that I have never before known so many genuinely *good* people? As absurd and counterproductive as it certainly was to send nearly the whole of the nation's intellectuals into rural areas for years on end, there is clearly merit in the idea that many learned about and came to care about how the other 85 percent lived.

# 7
# "Love and Strength for the Next Decade"

Hello from South China—at least they tell me it's south. I'm sitting here at my desk in long-johns, jeans, sweater, wool shirt, and a bright blue down vest I bought here in Hangzhou. The hotel is rumored to have heat—well, maybe when it gets to be winter.

Actually, despite the New York-style cold, I find several layers of clothing adequate, but I'm glad I didn't get sent to Jilin, which is north of North Korea. "I've seen those movies," I told Wang Fusheng in New York when he told me I was given a job in Jilin, "I know how cold it is up there." "Oh, big mistake, big mistake," he replied. "We're sending you south to Hangzhou." Little did I know that "south" means south of the Yangzi, and that heat is provided only north of the Yangzi.

The classrooms are the hardest to take. Despite wool cap, thermal socks, and fuzzy boots, halfway through our four-hour morning sessions the cement floor sends chill-a-grams up through my bones. How odd I must look pacing up and down in front of the students, bundled in layers of padded clothing, double-mittened fingers fumbling to make legible marks on the blackboard. Someone found a big old heater and dragged it up to the fifth-floor classroom Lao Fan and I use regularly for our scientists' class, but there's no outlet for it, so we're waiting for the electricians to rewire.

Paul Fast, a clever fellow indeed, posted a small sign near the hotel's second-floor service room (from whence comes all the warm beer you might wish to buy). His sign said that some American teachers live in the hotel and would much appreciate any reading matter tourists did not wish to lug home. Magazines, newspapers, and books (ranging from *Shogun* to *The Playboy Joke Book* #2) have been anonymously deposited beneath the sign, along with most of a bottle of VSOP cognac; two

66

large packages of spearmint gum; a set of Ohio road maps; an unopened
bottle of Johnny Walker Red; a pamphlet on the Tampa, Florida, Holiday Inn; six coloring books of Washington, D.C.; a jar of instant coffee;
several packages of pop tarts (with a three-year shelf-life); a mostly
used tube of toothpaste; a Sears "Fall Value" catalogue; a jar of Skippy
peanut butter (smooth); a half-full can of Rite-Gard; a bag of Planter's
peanuts; ten packages each of Instant Hot Chocolate and Lipton's Cup-
a-Soup; and sundry postcards of Wall Street, the Statue of Liberty, the
University of Virginia campus, Mount St. Helens, the Lincoln Memorial, and the Watergate apartment complex.

*November 9*
*Friday night. Exhausted. What a fool I am. Wrote frenzied letters in*
*response to N's, and now he writes calmly about his work, his love, his*
*China visa forms.*

*November 15*
*Sitting here in bright blue down vest snapped to neck—look like I just*
*came back from football practice. Think up wild schemes to meet N in*
*Tokyo or Hong Kong during intercession. Oh for a few hours together.*
*Phone calls insane—invariably fall silent as soon as I hear his voice.*

*November 18*
*Sun down. Dark and cold. Two more anguished letters. Well, well. So it*
*"shook my very existence" when I wrote that you are not my whole life.*
*Where is the man who insisted he did not want a traditional woman for*
*whom marriage and children were the be-all and end-all? Now we are*
*"two migrating birds" who need to settle down. Ah, love, I will settle*
*down with you—if only you will wait for me.*

It's a splendid fall day. We've had a week of crisp, sparkling November weather. The tall evergreens that frame my window now contrast
with thinning trees, exposing astonishing new scenes of the lake and
mountains every few days. It's a perfect day to ride my bike around the
lake or out into the countryside, but I, alas, am sick again with an awful
sore throat and swollen glands and must settle for my picture post card
views while I consume my sundry medicines. These consist of throat
lozenges, little bags of herbal medicine mixed in boiling water and
drunk three times a day, and (just in case, I guess, or because Chinese
medicines, though effective, are slow), tetracyline hydrochloride cap-
sules made in Shanghai.

Visitors: Zhang Chefu has brought me *Pan Da Hai*, a cold remedy
that works, I'm certain, by virtue of its aesthetic power. It looks like a

hazel nut, but dropped into a cup of tea it opens like a flower, exuding a sweet scent as its feathery petals open in slow motion, then slowly sink to the bottom.

Lao Fan settles into the red velvet armchair while Li Xumei nests in a corner of the couch. The Dragon Lady sits near her, making me feel horrendously self-conscious in my floor-length, neck-high, long-sleeved black velour bathrobe with pink bands at bottom, wrists, and collarbone. I can't imagine what they think about such attire, but I'm sick and don't care. Much.

They've come about my contract. Yes, now, after all these months they want me to sign a two-year contract. I agree to do so on one condition: that they move me out of the Imperial Palace and into an apartment at the university.

"You are certainly not serious," says Madam Lo seriously.

"I certainly am serious," I answer. Does she think I've been joking about this all these months?

She informs me, in case I'd forgotten, that I am an American and would, ipso facto, be unable to tolerate the conditions under which Chinese people live. I, in turn, inform her that I've visited several Chinese homes (as if she didn't know) and do not find the living conditions so terrible. Furthermore, if she's concerned about my living conditions, I'd be happy to have an electric heater in the apartment, and if she really wants to go nuts, she can send someone to Shanghai to buy an electric water heater. Yes, they exist. I've seen them. Whatever the cost, it has to be infinitely less than the tab on this fancy suite. The university could build a whole language lab, I suggest, for what it costs to keep Paul and Suzy and me in this hotel.

Madam Lo expresses her appreciation for my concern for their finances and goes on to explain why I must stay where I am until the new foreign guest house is completed. I look over at Lao Fan, who has his head buried and his eyes averted—it's crucial that neither of us laugh. Li Xumei is genuinely distressed. I feel badly about causing her more headaches, for I know that everyone turns to her with every problem: marriage and divorce, child-rearing and parent care, finances and bureaucracy-skirting.

The whole business remains unresolved. I will not sign the contract. I will leave at the end of the year.

The next day I have another visit from Dean Miao. He asks, as always, if I have any problems with my living conditions. I want to seize the time but remind myself that it is not polite in China to plunge right into a subject. I chat about the conveniences, the luxuries, the views, about how much I appreciate the university's concern for my comfort and well-being, about how much I love teaching at Zhe Da. But beating about the bush is not my strong point, and I finally blurt out that I came here not only to teach but to learn something about China, that I cannot justify to my husband my separation from him if I am but dallying with Japanese businessmen and American tourists, and that confining me here not only isolates *me* but limits the access of teachers and students to my expertise and to out-of-class conversation practice. I recognize that many Chinese families have been waiting a decade or more for an apartment, and that I will be delaying their move, but I will be in China so short a time—by the time I leave the new guest house will surely be built.

As always, Lao Fan translates with such verisimilitude of tone and gesture that I have to laugh at myself as I watch him. Dean Miao sits thoughtfully for a minute, then urges me to write a letter to Vice-President Liu Dan including all the points I have just made.

I do. And as busy as Liu Dan is running a university and preparing for the upcoming Provincial People's Congress, he responds almost immediately, ordering that I be moved to the university and provided with whatever amenities I require to live there comfortably. Amen.

Bearing large notes with official seals that remind me of Alice's White Rabbit, seven of the scientists come to pay a sick call. After the tea and chit-chat about my cold and the weather, I ask them to tell me something about their families, their hometowns, their institutes.

Things are vastly different from the Gang of Four days, they say. Another great mountain has been lifted off their backs (imperialism and feudalism, at least in their grossest forms, went with Liberation). But a lot seems to depend on the particular cadres in charge of their institutes, and the various levels of party and government bureaucracy above those cadres.

But what, concretely, does all this mean? "If you have criticisms of the way your institute is run," I ask, "of policies that limit your productivity as a scientist, do you make them?"

I get three emphatic "no's"; three say they speak out again and again, but to no avail; the seventh says the new, free exchange of ideas has created good conditions for change, but that it's very complicated to restructure an entire institution after all those years of chaos.

"If someone criticized you unjustly," I ask, "would you protest and stand up for what you believe is right and just?"

"What would be the use?" asks one. No one contradicts him.

"Wouldn't your comrades stand up for you if they knew your suggestions were correct, or the criticisms against you were false?"

"No," they agree. People might jeopardize their own positions, so they'd keep their mouths shut.

"Would *you* stand up for a colleague whom you knew to be unfairly criticized?" Some stare, others drop their chins. Only Mr. Liu offers a firm "yes"; he would do so regardless of the consequences.

"What might the consequences be?"

No one expects to be beaten or sent out to raise pigs anymore, but leading cadres control work assignments, housing, salaries, promotions, even the right to attend courses such as ours and to study abroad.

"Can China modernize if cadres are not responsive to people like you?"

"As much as I wish it to be true, and as hard as I will try all my life," says one, "I don't believe China can ever modernize and catch up with the Western world."

"Oh, that's not true," says another, "though it will certainly take more than twenty years."

"But it is true," says a third, "that cadres will have to learn to listen to those with expertise. Some of our cadres are corrupt and use their positions for privilege and power, but most are good 'reds,' people who came up through the ranks of the army and the party. All their lives they have taken orders from those above and given orders to those below. They don't know how to function any differently."

"That's a good way to win a war, but a poor way to run an institute," someone adds.

"What we need is cadres who are themselves expert. How can even the most well-meaning revolutionary fighter with no background in science know how to run an institute?"

"I'm not sure you have to be a scientist to be a good administrator," I suggest. "Can you give me an example?"

Mr. Liu smiles. "I'll tell you a story," he says. "I believe you will like this." I listen attentively. This man's warmth and openness, humor and intelligence have won my heart.

"A good man, a virtuous old revolutionary, was put in charge of an elementary school. Believing strongly in the slogan 'Learn from the Masses,' he often went out amongst the school children to find out how they were doing.

"One day he came across a youngster studying his English book. 'How many characters have you learned?' he asked the boy. 'Twenty-six,' the boy answered. 'Two years of study and you've only learned twenty-six characters!' said the old cadre (who could not himself write twenty-six Chinese characters), 'I will see to it that your teacher is removed from his post.'"

We all laugh. This "red" vs. "expert" business I've heard about for so many years is a little clearer. No one wants to address the question of cadres who are expert but *not* red. "Aren't you afraid the winds will shift, that things may get bad again?" I ask.

Opinions differ. One fears it will, others that it is possible though unlikely, still others that what was could never be again because young people have learned to ask and think and not follow mindlessly whatever party leaders say.

"We'll have no more Gods for leaders," one person concludes.

"We'll see," says another, "We'll see."

*November 28*
*Another miserable letter from N. Jesus Christ! Sick in bed, plenty of time to think, anger rising rapidly to the surface. The three-week chasm between the time a letter is written and the time it is read is nerve-wracking. I feel schizophrenic. Life here is productive and happy, yet our relationship disintegrates daily. Can't go home, yet can hardly handle the pain.*

*December 8*
*Lying on cement at railroad station. Sobbing. Not in color—stark black and white like some old Yugoslavian movie. She rushes to station to meet him—frantic movement, wild pacing, knocking into people with children, chickens, baskets, carrying poles. Alone. Scared. Will he come? Train—strains to pull it in, hurry, hurry. Long train—could be anywhere. Runs from car to car through mountains of goods, hundreds of people squeezing onto train, pushing, jostling, blocking her eye, bombarding her ear. He stretches, cranes, lunges from window to window searching, calling her name amidst the cacophony. "He hasn't come"—aloud to no one. "She hasn't come"—wailed to all the world. So he doesn't get off, she doesn't get on. Train puffs, wheezes out of the station slowly, faster, faster, and then he sees her, she sees him. Too late. It's too late.*

Lao Fan returns with a contract for me to sign. He is pale and stooped. I think he's ill, but he won't admit it. He puts in more hours teaching and preparing classes than anyone in our unit; he tutors the children of friends and colleagues preparing for college entrance exams; as Ming teaches in an elementary school an hour and a half by bus from here, he does most of the housework—I often chide him for spoiling his son, who hardly helps—and as ground pipes are being laid and there's little or no water, he either pumps it into pails that he carries to his fifth floor apartment or stays up til one or two in the morning when the gurgling in the pipes tells him he can fill the tub for tomorrow's water needs. Above all, I sense that he's disturbed by memories of his mother, who died last summer.

And then there's me. Poor Lao Fan is solely responsible for my every need (real or perceived). I'm sure that there have already been innumerable meetings about this apartment business, and that he's been burdened with most of the details.

He hands me the contract, a six-page document on re-recycled papers in pseudolegalese:

### CONTRACT

Zhejiang University (hereafter referred to as Party A) has engaged *Ms.*     *NAOMI WORONOV* (hereafter referred to as Party B) as a teacher of *,English*   , the two parties having in a spirit of friendship entered into the present agreement.

I. The term of service is   *two*   years, that is from   *Aug. 20th*   to   *August 20, 1981*           *1979*

II. During his (her) term of service Party B will undertake work of the following character:

   1. Conducting   *English*   classes, taking up out-of-class coaching, correcting students written work, and advising students on extracurricular activites;
   2. Training teachers *of*      and research students, and attending to their questions;
   3. Compiling teaching materials in his (her) charge;
   4. Giving     lectures to the teachers and students;
   5. Making tape-recordings of lessons and texts and of other teaching materials;
   6. Accepting other work connected with teaching entrusted by Party A.

III. Party A shall pay Party B a monthly salary of Yuan (RMB).

IV. Party B shall work six days a week, eight hours a day, shall give 18–22 classes a week . . .

And on it goes for several pages. The contract is generous with regard to vacations and travel subsidies, but the work load is staggering and there isn't even a salary figure—what would Mother say? A person would have to be out of his (her) senses to agree to this vagueness, but here is Lao Fan, so wan, so worn. He is my "handler," sent here to handle me, to get me to sign this thing. If I don't he may well be subjected to reprimand, and will certainly suffer through endless hours of discussions about what to do with this impossible foreign woman.

"Don't he silly," he says to me with undisguised impatience. The contract was sent down by the Foreign Experts Bureau in Beijing. Every foreign expert signs it. Has the university ever mistreated me? Has he? But Suzy Fast's face and fury loom before me. I don't want to make trouble for Lao Fan or in any way alter our relationship, but I also don't want to be "handled."

We compromise. I will keep the document and rewrite it in any manner I deem reasonable, and he will submit my version to the authorities. "O.K.?" he asks. "O.K."

I have to give so many lectures, I'm beginning to repeat them. This week I did my slide-lecture on New York City at Hang Da. Hang Da (the liberal arts college down the road from Zhe Da) has a real English department, so the response was much livelier than it is here. I showed the World Trade Towers, the Statue of Liberty, the United Nations, universities, museums, parks, theatres, churches, and some of the beautiful apartment buildings in Manhattan, along with slum housing, the porn district where I teach (48th and Broadway between one skin-flick house and another), and the men and women, black and white, old and young, living and dying on the streets. Toward the end of a lively question period, someone asked me to clarify a point: Were these pictures of "olden time" New York? "Sure," I said, "last summer before the Revolution."

This week in class we discuss holidays East and West. I explain at length about Thanksgiving. They are incredulous, nauseated. "Turkey? You eat turkey?" Turkeys are funny-looking creatures that strut about in zoos. No one eats turkeys. This from the folks who love snakes, dogs, and sea slugs.

We go on to Christmas and New Year's. I tell them about resolutions, parties, hats, noisemakers, Times Square, and football games, and they tell me that in some areas at Spring Festival a fish was put on the table but not eaten, for the word *yu* means both "fish" and "good fortune"— you wouldn't want to eat up your luck for the coming year. (Today, I'm assured, the fish is eaten.) Up north, on the first day of the New Year, you can use neither knife nor broom, for both have worked all year and need a rest (unlike the lady of the house); furthermore, money is brought into the house on New Year's day and you wouldn't want to sweep it out accidentally. Also up north, where *jiaozi* (dumplings) are the traditional New Year's meal, you can't say that a *jiaozi* has a break or hole in it, but must observe that it has "opened its mouth." And here's my favorite: on the last day of the old year you eat glutinous (i.e., very sticky) rice and feed some of it to Buddha so when he makes his annual ascent to heaven his lips will be stuck together—your year's misdeeds remain secret.

Customs die hard. While several layers of clothing help handle the cold, the ears and face of the bike rider require attention. Downtown, I stop in the hat store and buy myself a warm, wooley hat with a little peak in front. This modish article can be folded down into a face mask, the slit where the peak comes through being the eye hole. The next morning I merrily make my warm way to school in my new hat. Well. Such stares! Such remarks! I have purchased a *nan lao ren maodzi*, an old man's hat. No one can refrain from enlightening me on this point, or from offering advice as to where I might buy a perfectly lovely lady's hat. It amuses me that the same people who urge me to dress "Western" (whatever that means) are alarmed at the sight of a "lady" in an old man's hat. (I'm reminded of a day, perhaps ten years ago, when I wore a Saks Fifth Avenue pants suit to work. No one, but no one, could resist some remark about a woman coming to work in pants.) Well, I see longish hair and bobbed hair bouncing around the streets of Hangzhou now, and I even saw a woman wearing lipstick at the New Year's Eve dance. Heavens! What next?

*December 26*
*From N, brutal, tearing letters, then sweet, tender ones, and then yesterday, just minutes before I was supposed to go off to Ming's Christmas goose dinner, more vicious, cutting words.*

*So my "Dear Everybody" letters are "disgusting," "boring," "shallow." I have been in China but a few months and he wants profound treatises on the nature of the Chinese universe. From every corner of America I get notes thanking me for my letters, encouraging me to write more. People seem genuinely interested in such mundane matters as orange peels. If his intention is to get even with me for going away, he's even.*

*January 2*
*Cold and lonely Sunday morning. N writes that he didn't mean all those terrible, terrible things. Too numb to feel any sense of relief. Off on a lark to Shanghai and Tianjin—to hell with suffering. Think I'll frame Ruth's New Year's telegram: "LOVE AND STRENGTH FOR THE NEXT DECADE!"*

# 8
## "Dark Willow: Bright Flower"

West Lake in winter wears a gloomy aspect, the watery greys of trees, lake, mountains, and sky washing into one another, obscuring meaning. But, oh, those days when the sun wins out! I sit in bed and watch the great fire rise in the East and sing aloud: "Red is the East, rises the sun, China has brou-ought forth a Mao Zedong . . . ." I sing quietly, you understand, as this is not a popular tune nowadays. By seven a.m. the sun is up, and if I happen to be working at home on such a day, I can watch it arc across the lake, changing the scene so thoroughly I think myself glancing up now and then from a train window. Toward evening the red disk slides down behind the mountains to the West, the birds sing, the lake is still and lovely in the moonlight, and the stars are ever wondrous to a native New Yorker.

I suppose I'm crooning about the beauties of Hangzhou again because I've just returned from my trip to Tianjin and Beijing and am rudely reminded how lucky I am to be here.

Ellie and Joan, who teach up at Tian Da, came through Hangzhou and invited me up for a visit. Why not? I ask the Foreign Affairs Office to secure a second class ticket for me. They will not. Only twice-the-price first class for the likes of me ("for your comfort and safety," says Madam Lo, assuring me that second class is neither clean nor private). So I ask George to help me order my own ticket from China Travel—no English spoken.

The train trip is fine and fun, but Tianjin is dreary and depressing. The three of us—quite a spectacle—bike through a city still dotted with mud and brick shacks with cardboard windows and tarpaper roofs. About four feet high and less in length and width, these crude shelters were thrown together after the July 1976 earthquake that killed an estimated 240,000 of Tianjin's 7.5 million people. Humor has it that the shacks remain (despite a 1978 law banning them) because couples can send their children there to play while they enjoy a bit of privacy at home. Rubble still clutters the dusty streets; I must concentrate to avoid being thrown from my bike.

We dine at the Kiessling, an old German restaurant that's been around since long before Liberation. Dinner conversation, after-dinner conversation, and all the next day's conversation centers on ex-husbands, ex-lovers, current prospects, future prospects, etc. I have much to contribute.

In Beijing I find that everyone I know is, as I am, out of town, but an acquaintance puts me up in her French Embassy residence. While Yvette works during the day, I shop and sightsee, and I'm pleased to find I now know enough Chinese to ask directions, order meals, and get myself a ticket to the circus, though the man in the box office has difficulty believing I want but *one* ticket—who would go to the circus alone?

At a bus stop, I queue up behind people who stare at me and whisper to one another. I'm used to that, but then the conductor bars me from the bus. Too crowded for me, I guess. This happens again. I'm furious, convinced this is gross discrimination based on race, color, and place of national origin. But a woman finally manages to get through to me that I'm standing not at a public bus stop, but one designated for factory buses taking local residents to work.

An hour from the city center is the embassy neighborhood. It's another world—suburbia with walls and PLA guards. In Yvette's three large, bright rooms, no antique table is without some objet d'art to touch or turn (carefully) in the hand, no wall without hours of serene contemplation of cherry blossoms and misty mountains, no inch of floor uncovered by exquisite Chinese carpet. In the kitchen, an old-fashioned oven with four burners on top and a refrigerator stocked with all the cheeses I'd salivated over in my dreams. In the pantry, a separate freezer stacked with steaks, chops, bacon, and sausages flown in from Hong Kong and Europe. In the living room, a liquor cabinet to satisfy the most exotic taste. I refrain from nothing and soon find myself sunk deep into the pillows of a sumptuous sofa, singing with Yvette sad songs of the wayward ways of the male of the species. This is not what I had in mind at all; this is not it at all.

I return to Hangzhou, rejuvenated neither in body nor in spirit, but glad to be home.

It's March. March is doom and gloom. I hear there's an apartment for me on campus, but no one will show it to me or give me a moving date. Maybe it's time for me to go home anyway: I was lecturing on transportation the other day and heard myself say that all American emergency vehicles have "silens." And I have bronchitis. I ride over to the hospital with Lao Fan. The doctor looks no older than I am (though you never know in China). "Do you feel tired and run down?" she asks. Yes. Very. "Have you ever had bronchitis?" she asks. No. Never. "Have you ever been sick for this length of time?" she asks. No. Never. "Well," she concludes significantly, "you're getting old."

At dinner I repeat this story to Bunny, whose flaming red hair above fair, freckled face do not for inconspicuous make. Bunny teaches English in Beijing; she's down south on sick leave because of *her* chronic bronchitis. But the rest of us are still teaching, so we excuse ourselves after dinner to get back to work.

"Hey, where's the action around here?" she asks.

Paul smiles. "There isn't any action around here."

"You mean you guys don't do grass?"

"No," Paul answers quietly, "we guys don't do grass."

"How the hell do you keep going down here in the boonies?"

"What do *you* guys do up in Beijing?" George asks.

"Oh, man, the stuff is everywhere." Bunny extends her arms to express the concept "everywhere." "I mean we do it in window boxes, but it's all over the countryside. Don't kid yourself—peasants know a good thing when they see it. I can show you guys how to do it," she offers.

"Thanks just the same," says Paul.

Fully aware I'm making an ass of myself and sounding like somebody's old maiden aunt, I lecture Bunny on China's drug history, the Opium War, the astonishing success of the Communists in the fifties in eliminating drugs, drug addiction, and, when necessary, unrepentent dealers—

"Opium, shmopium," Bunny interrupts. "I'm just talking grass, a little harmless grass. Life is too boring in China. The kids who come to my room really love it."

George and I gossip about Suzy, who recently departed for the States. She and Paul have split. She blames all things and people Chinese for the disintegration of her marriage. What most irked Suzy about Chinese behavior is what she called lieing—and it's true that, from a Western perspective, the Chinese do lie. You might ask, for example, to visit some town or village. No one will say "no" or "that's closed to foreigners." They will tell you that the matter is under discussion, and when you ask again they are indeed sorry but the roads to that town have been washed out by the rains. If you're brazen enough to point out that it hasn't rained in three months, you will be committing a dreadful faux pas: you are expected to understand this is a face-saving lie. This sort of thing is infuriating because it's so hard to interpret the signals: "No, there is no bus to that place" may mean "You, foreigner, should pay 15 yuan for a cab to take you where a 10-fen bus would get you," or it may mean that there is no bus to that place.

This indirectness has many ramifications. A Zhe Da scientist writes a letter to an American professor and brings it to me to correct. In wildly flowery language, the first three pages sing paeans to the professor's work, inform him that his papers, translated into Chinese, won high acclaim at a recent conference, and offer endless accolades for his contributions to his field. The last paragraph mentions in passing that this scientist would like to study in the United States and hopes this professor can secure for him a visiting scholar position at his university along with travel, research, and living funds. The man wrestled with this letter for weeks—go explain to him how it would be received! We compromise by devising a thesis statement, noting in the opening paragraph that the letter is written to ask a favor as well as to express admiration for the professor's contribution to science.

### March 4

*It's the Year of the Monkey and I've sure made one out of me, the sweet, understanding woman writing reams of sweet, understanding letters to N. Am I not to blame at all for the mess we're in? Yes, for this: Though I have struggled mightily with the Angel in the House, that woman Virginia Woolf describes as "intensely sympathetic," "immensely charming," "utterly unselfish," guilt has restrained me from evicting her. Enough!*

*What can marriage mean to him? To me? He's right to say I really want a friend, someone to rely on to give as well as receive comfort, encouragement, affection. A friend considers how his friend will feel about the words he pours out on a piece of paper.*

*Does he, after all, want a woman to cater to his needs, lick his wounds—oh, and how convenient if she also earns a good living, and how nice if she's educated enough to be a sounding board for his literary theories.*

*For centuries women have sat about in their chastity belts weaving tapestries and mending socks while their menfolk roamed the world. Choose, damn you: Say that you want a woman like me—that you want me and are willing to wait—or go out and find yourself a nice wife!*

### March 8

*First snow of the year. Fat flakes swim down and settle clumsily on the earth and in my heart. Would that I hadn't called him. Oh, well, at least*

*I know where things stand now. In August he loved her—but not enough. In September, more. By the end of October, enough to marry her. And by the fall of the first frosty flakes, it all dissolved, a sugar house melting in the first tears of hurt pride.*

*International Women's Day. Ironic! I sound just like something out of some Victorian diary.*

March 8 is International Women's Day. "How nice!" I comment when Yao tells me that during the Cultural Revolution women were given half a day off. "Great!" she responds sarcastically, "We got to sit in boring meetings and listen to deadly political speeches," so no one wants to hold any more meetings or discussions on "the woman question." But we still get the afternoon off—and what an uncommon pleasure it is for me that "we" is this time inclusive (we women) instead of exclusive (we Chinese and you foreigners).

Here in Hangzhou there's a week-long film festival to celebrate the occasion. More than a dozen of us, including the four women scientists from my class, Li Xumei's young niece, and Zhang Chefu's granddaughter, crowd into the packed theatre to see "Dark Willow: Bright Flower," a dramatic film about the weal and woe of a beekeeper during the Cultural Revolution. The title is from a poem that describes how, when one reaches the end of the longest river or the foot of the steepest mountain, and it seems there is no way forward, no way out, there suddenly appears a turn that could not be seen before, and beyond it a road leading forward.

My friends are deeply moved by the film. They argue that the story is so true, yet far from the worst that could be told. All the way home they trade stories in the way that American men at bars tell war stories, with an air of black humor that allows them to handle the horror.

Li and Yao come home with me for tea. I ask what happened to all the ordinary people who committed such unspeakable acts during that period. Some have been sent to labor camps, but in every institute people who beat each other up now sit across the desk from one another. Everybody knows what everybody did. Most understand fully that what they did was wrong, but some are still "in their hearts" followers of the Gang of Four. And here? At Zhe Da? My question is side-stepped.

I've had an exciting half-holiday, but one discordant note keeps ringing in my ears: International Women's Day, just thirty years after the founding of the People's Republic of China, has focused on the evils of the Cultural Revolution, not on the status, role, progress, or problems of women. Li and Yao remind me of the brutal oppression of Chinese women before Liberation. I'm convinced that if I took a poll of Chinese women and men, young and old, in and out of the party, I would be regaled with pre-Liberation stories and assured that urban women have achieved equality.

They haven't. But the middle-aged intellectuals with whom I work will not be the ones to raise the issues. Still mindful of the not-so-distant past, still stinging from the Cultural Revolution, thoroughly engaged in their work and family affairs, and with virtually no party leadership on the question, these women are not ready to focus on the subtler forms of sexism and discrimination distorting women's lives. It remains for the next generation to do that.

# 9
# Lao Fan—His Story

Panoramic fields of brilliant yellow rapeseed alternate with tall, green winter wheat and long brown rows of beans and sweet potatoes. A picturesque canal, no more than ten or twelve feet wide, meanders beside the fields and under quaint old wooden bridges. Slightly stooped human figures, reminiscent of Turner's gondoliers, jab long poles against the shallow canal bottom to push along their cement boats.

Cement boats? "Nonsense," I say to Liang and Liang and Liang, who sit behind me in our bouncing bus. "You can't convince me those boats are cement. Common sense tells me a cement boat cannot float."

The three Liangs laugh, and soon all twenty-two scientists trip over one another with words about the displacement of water; I swear to myself that I will never again so much as snicker at a Chinese student unable to fathom the mysteries of English tenses or adverbial endings.

Lao Fan, who loves to tease, has not even looked up from his seat beside me. He stares out of the window.

"Are you O.K.?" I ask.

"Look, look over there," he says, grasping my arm and pointing at I'm not sure what.

"The mountain. Look at that mountain." I look at the mountain. I see nothing particularly interesting or beautiful about it, yet Lao Fan is agitated. His eyes dart about from me to mountain and back again. Suddenly the words rush from him: "That's where my mother's ashes are buried."

I'm startled. This is a very personal revelation, and it's difficult for me to find an appropriate response. One day soon after I arrived in China, I met a colleague whose mother had recently died. I knew she had been bedridden and in pain for years, so I said something about how sorry I was, but that perhaps, given her suffering and his own, it was for the best. His face assured me I had said precisely the wrong thing.

Visual proof that cement boats do float.

But there is no need to say anything. Lao Fan cannot long sustain such sad memories on a bus that bounds about on the road like a frisky elephant.

We clunk on to Shaoxing, about 70 kilometers from Hangzhou, where we're greeted by a China Travel Service guide hired—for my benefit of course—by our university, which has arranged this outing, provided us with elephant and driver, and called ahead to Shaoxing for all our tour and luncheon arrangements.

We name the guide "Mr. Tape Recorder," for he's learned a long spiel about this town with its 2,400-year history, its population of 1,900,000 on 70 communes surrounding the town, its 1,500 square kilometers, its more than 100 factories (there were but two before Liberation), its world-famous Shaoxing rice wine factory (four qualities in different shades of gold), and its three exhibits (house, primary school, and museum) dedicated to China's famous and beloved revolutionary writer, Lu Xun. If you interrupt our poor guide with a question (and we do), he has to (and does) begin all over again. I'm afraid we're all terribly giggly and rude to him.

But China Travel, as usual, gets even with me. At lunch time Mr. Tape Recorder seats me at a table for ten in a dining room that would easily accommodate 200—all by myself.

I go on strike. Refuse to eat. I can live and work and teach and learn and travel with Lao Fan and my students, but cannot have lunch with them? No way! The two waiters assigned to me are intensely distressed by my refusal to eat (and, no doubt, by the resultant loss of the ten *kuei* the hotel would have charged me for the same meal enjoyed by my companions for one *kuei*). They finally relent and bring me into the "Chinese" dining room where I'm greeted with cheers from the students.

We have a tasty lunch spiced with spirited conversation, and trot off to the Lu Xun exhibits. At the site of Lu Xun's primary school, Da Liang asks me to take her photograph in a doorway flanked by two long, delicate works of calligraphy. She visited Shaoxing during the Cultural Revolution but was warned that photographs taken here might be used against her by one or another Red Guard faction. She poses, we pose together, and on the bus back to Hangzhou I promise to give her these precious photographs as soon as I get them back from Kodak in Hong Kong.

For several days I search for some interval in our work, a time long and quiet enough for Lao Fan to make a quilt of the multiform segments of his life I've collected over the months. I'm simply curious, for I have no notion how extraordinary his story will be, nor does it occur to me that he, too, might be looking for an opportunity. But one afternoon after class Lao Fan invites me to lunch, and as we chop vegetables and mash ginger, light the coal stove and set the table, eat our meal and retrieve slick, salted peanuts with our chopsticks, Lao Fan speaks long into the afternoon of his mother's death, her life, and his own.

"I came back to live in Hangzhou in July of '78, and began teaching the very next day. I had no vacation, no time to spend with Mother though at last we lived so near one another. In August she had a heart attack. She had had emphysema for years, but this was serious—she was hospitalized for fifty days. After work Ming and Fan Ming and I went to the hospital to care for her—we took turns.

"She recovered very quickly; we were so happy. She even quit smoking—oh, yes, Mother used to smoke quite a lot. She soon resumed the community work she'd taken on after retirement, and got up very early in the morning to go to market, and do this and that as usual.

"Because I was so busy, I visited her infrequently, but I thought she was quite all right. We stayed with her for several days during Spring Festival, and it seemed she gained weight and was healthy and happy.

"In March, she suddenly fell sick again. She was in the hospital only four or five days before she passed away. I was with her that night. She talked to me. Then she fell asleep. At four o'clock, I sensed she was breathing her last, so I called Ming, and the next morning she died.

"We sent her body to the funeral home here in Hangzhou. The

service was very good. I had her photo enlarged, framed, and placed above the coffin. I said a few words and several other people spoke including the principal of the school where she had been a teacher. Some of my students came, and some of mother's friends and colleagues. Maybe there were more than fifty people.

"After the funeral, her body was displayed so everyone could have a look and pay last tribute to her. Then, of course, the body was burned— uh, what's the word? Yes, cremated. The box I bought for her ashes was kept in the funeral home for a year—actually, we had paid the funeral home to keep the box for six years, but one night Ming had a terrible dream: she saw mother standing in a pavilion with no windows, no doors, and the wind was howling and she was shivering with cold. Ming said we should go to the home to pay respects.

"We went the following Sunday—no box. We searched the funeral home for hours, and when we finally found it Ming insisted we should bury the box during the April Qing Ming festival."

"Is it customary to scatter the ashes?" I ask.

"No," Lao Fan answers, "you leave the ashes in the box, and then you bury it. I wrote to my cousin in the countryside and asked her to buy some mountain land for a grave. I took the bus and arrived on Qing Ming, carrying the box with Mother's picture on it. It was drizzling that day, so it was hard to dig a hole large enough for the concrete container that holds the box. We sealed it, put soil on top of it, and erected a headstone bearing her name, the date of her death, my name and Ming's, and Fan Ming's."

"Do you say anything during the ceremony?"

Lao Fan looks amused. "My cousins said quite a lot. I just said 'peace to your ashes' or something like that, but the family said *quite* a lot, and they burned paper money to pay Mother's way to the next world."

"Is that Buddhist?"

"Hm, yes, Buddhist, I think. Perhaps this is just customary in the countryside."

"Do they do it because it's traditional or because they really believe in it?"

"I think my elder cousin is religious because on Spring Festival when I climb the mountain with her to pay respects to Mother, she murmurs something or other.

"After Mother's ashes were buried, we felt all right. There is a Chinese saying, 'It is natural for leaves to fall to the roots; it is peaceful for the dead to be buried in earth.'"

Lao Fan slowly turns to me as though ascending from past to present. "But I feel very sorry for her," he says, "because I'd only been back from Beijing a year or so before she died. After her death, I began to lose my hair very rapidly."

"I heard you were pretty sick then."

"Yes. As soon as I closed my eyes at night, images of Mother swam about in my head."

"Had your mother suffered a good deal?" I ask.

Lao Fan stands and stretches, pushes aside our greasy bowls, and pours the sweet, yellow rice wine of Shaoxing into our jigger-sized cups. He sets the dish of peanuts and two pairs of chopsticks between us on the table, settles himself in his chair and says very slowly: "Suffer. Hmm. Suffer. Yes. I'll tell you about it.

"I was born in Hangzhou in 1935. My uncle was happy to learn that I was a boy baby because he had two daughters, and there was no boy in the family. As Father was away in the army, Mother took me to her family in a small county called Xiaoshan—remember, we passed it on the road to Shaoxing last week. My grandparents had a bit of land and a house; we lived in a house across from my four uncles and their families.

"Because Grandfather lost his job as a clerk, Mother had to support the whole family. Though she was only nineteen, she taught elementary school while Grandmother looked after me. Grandfather was a rather enlightened man who sent his sons *and* his daughters to school. Of course, schools were not like the ones we know; there was one room with one teacher of classical Chinese. Mother only finished elementary school, but my uncles had high school educations. My grandfather was a scholar, you know. His calligraphy used to hang in several Hangzhou temples.

"Two years after I was born, the Japanese war broke out. One day the Japanese started bombing our area. When they heard the sirens, the teachers rushed the students out of the school building. Mother was the last to get out, and it was hard for her to run because she was pregnant. The bombs fell. She was badly wounded—in fourteen places—but still she walked home. They put her on a—what do you call it?"

"Stretcher."

"Stretcher. They carried her all the way to an army hospital in Shaoxing. When the doctors operated to remove the bomb fragments, they found the baby dead. Hmm. Yes. At the beginning of the Japanese war."

Lao Fan sits very still, staring off into space. I, too, sit quietly, twisting the tiny wine cup between my fingers.

"After the Japanese invaded our town, Father came home, and we moved together to Longyu on the other side of the Qiantang River, about five hours by train from Hangzhou.

"We had hard times at Longyu because Mother was pregnant again and had no job, and Father stayed at home because we had to hide ourselves in the daytime; the Japanese would go from house to house taking whatever they could find, and looking for young men to serve as coolies.

"Mother gave birth to a girl. When we went to hide in the woods during an air raid, we had to climb over very high walls and haul the baby up in a basket with a rope, hand over hand, like this. There was so little food, and conditions were so harsh that the baby soon got sick and died."

I open my mouth to speak, but there is nothing I can say.

"One day Mother and Father were hidden and I was with an old granny when the Japanese came to search our house. Because I had long hair—I was only four or five—the Japanese took me for a girl. One tall soldier wanted to rape me, but when he found I was a boy he was disgusted and let me go.

"A few months later, the Japanese discovered Father, and ordered him to be their guide. He refused, so they put him in prison. Mother was very sick at the time, swollen all over from some—what do you call it?— yes, liver or kidney ailment. And she was pregnant again. A few days later one Japanese and one Chinese man came to our house. Mother gave them money to let my father go, and went to the prison with food and blankets, but Father was nowhere. Nowhere. So that's the end of the story."

"The end of the story? You mean you never saw your father again?"

"Never. The Japanese said they had killed him, and we believed it because if you refused to work with them . . . ." As his words trail off, Lao Fan gnaws his lip and stares down into his wine cup; it is considered unseemly for Chinese to show strong emotions.

"Mother soon gave birth to another girl and we became—what do you say? Vagabonds? She wrote to her father in Shanghai, and as soon as she received a reply we set out on foot. We wandered along the road, had little to eat, no place to sleep. I still remember we had two small suitcases. I looked after the suitcases and Mother carried the baby, but the baby was very sick, could hardly breathe, so Mother left her in an infants' box along the road."

"An infants' box?" I ask.

"Yes. Outside the Christian churches were wooden boxes where poor people could leave babies they couldn't care for."

"So people left their infants in these boxes?"

Lao Fan is defensive, feeling perhaps that I'm accusing him or his mother of heartlessness. "Yes! We couldn't afford to take her to the hospital and she was dying, so we thought maybe someone would take her and look after her. I don't know what happened to that sister. Perhaps she's alive, though it isn't likely. So that's my brother and two sisters. Only Mother and I were left."

Lao Fan turns and looks directly at me. He looks tired, drawn. Our eyes meet, and I wonder if he can see in mine the struggle to grasp the full spectrum of his family decimation. He pours wine, twists his chair to sit astride it, folds his arms across the back, and rests his chin on his hands.

"Mother's father worked in Shanghai, but he had no place for us to live. Mother was young, still under thirty, but this big family had feudal ideas so they wouldn't let her remarry. They decided to solve the housing problem by placing my cousin and me in an orphanage.

"In the orphanage, from eight to eleven in the morning, we were supposed to study. In the afternoon we knitted bags. We slept on the floor in a big room, two or three hundred of us. For breakfast you had maybe one small sweet potato; if they gave you rice, you had to pick the stones out and by the time you finished there was nothing left. The older boys teased us and sometimes played tricks on us, so we young boys often went hungry." He looks up and laughs: "It's just like that Dickens' book I once read."

"You mean *Oliver Twist*."

"Yes," he says, and adds as an afterthought, "Maybe this place was Christian. I remember they told us to pray, so my cousin and I obeyed."

"How old were you?"

"Let's see. This was in the early forties—the Japanese surrendered in '45—so I was eight or nine. One day my aunt came to visit. I pleaded with her to take me out to visit my mother, and they allowed me to go. I told Mother I would never go back to that place: 'I hear that I have an uncle in the countryside,' I said. 'How about sending me to my uncle?'

"Mother's mother moved back to Hangzhou, so mother lived with her and taught elementary school there while I lived with my uncle in the countryside and went to a one-room, one-teacher school. I went with my two new sisters—my uncle's two daughters. They're still living.

"When I was ten, Mother was made principal of a school run by a friend of my grandfather, and I finished grammar school there. Then my uncle sent me to a boarding school in Hangzhou."

"By 1949, you were about twelve or thirteen. Did your life change much after that?"

"In 1949, my uncle's life changed quite a bit. During land reform, he was classified as a poor peasant and allotted a house and some land. But before Liberation I was forced to quit school."

"Why?"

"Because you paid tuition in rice; they didn't accept paper money as inflation was so serious."

"So you would get rice from your uncle and take it to school for tuition?"

"Yes, but in the fall of '49 the Qiantang Bridge was blocked by Nationalist soldiers, so I couldn't go back to get rice and my uncle had no way to get it to me. I stayed with my grandmother, but I had to earn my living." Boyish enthusiasm lights his eyes: "I sold the *West Lake* evening paper, rushing from hotel to hotel and restaurant to restaurant yelling 'Evening paper! Evening paper!'

"When Hangzhou was liberated—I think it was May 8, 1949—I saw the Red Army in the streets, and then we had a new life in New China. In the fall I went back to boarding school. There was no tuition anymore; I just had to pass an exam. Mother could no longer continue as the principal of the elementary school—"

"Because she didn't have enough education?"

"No, no, no," says Lao Fan, now rushing headlong in his story. "Because she had been appointed by this and that, so they wanted someone new. She came back to Hangzhou and found a job in a tea factory picking twigs out of the tea, earning just enough to buy vegetables for the family—about five *mao* a day. Later she found a job in a school, and taught there until the Cultural Revolution. After the Cultural Revolution she retired—"

"Wait a minute. Hold it. Who are 'this and that'? What happened to her during the Cultural Revolution?"

"Uh, yes, well—that was all very sad. You see, Mother's village school had been donated by local landlords. The school building was actually the clan temple where everyone with a common surname—say, Wang or Li—keeps the spirit tablets. You see, the soul was thought to reside in these tablets, so they were worshipped along with icons of the gods. Anyway, during the Cultural Revolution, they accused Mother of being a 'second landlord,' a rent collector, when she was simply collecting donations for the school.

"They investigated, interviewed her colleagues and cadres during land reform, and finally decided she was no landlord, just an ordinary teacher. But her pupils were young and innocent; because she was labeled a landlord, they abused her, searched her house, and took the ink stands and Grandfather's calligraphy—she had so little—and made her sit at home for months writing self-criticisms."

"She must have been bitter after all she'd suffered."

"Yes: when you make a criminal of an innocent person, that's too bad, isn't it? It's too bad. When Mother retired, she got 75 percent of her salary—35 yuan—enough to get by on."

Lao Fan reaches for a little box of green tea, pinches two fingersful for each of us, pours boiling water from a thermos, and places lids on the cups. Clearly there's more, much more, but he cannot bring himself to tell, and I cannot bring myself to ask.

"Where were you all this time?" I ask to change the subject.

"I went to the Number One Middle School of Hangzhou, a good school, a sleep-in school. When I was a senior—it was 1953 and I was seventeen—Beijing Commercial Institute sent down two recruiters who selected fifteen students to take the national entrance exam. I was admitted, but Mother wouldn't permit me to go so far away from her." There's a long pause. "Well, I just had to go."

"Did you fight with your mother?"

"No. We just had some long discussions and she finally relented; she prepared my clothes, packed a suitcase, and found an overcoat for me. But she cried a lot when I left. I felt very bad because her life had been so difficult and so lonely.

"They assigned me to study English and business procedures, and I graduated in 1957."

"In 1957? During the anti-Rightist movement?" I had heard from several sources that Lao Fan had been in trouble during that period.

"O.K., I'll tell you about that. We sometimes had discussions about international affairs in our political economy course. Some students said Yugoslavia was a revisionist country, and the teacher agreed. Some—maybe just a few—said no. I voiced my view that when we look at a country, we have to look at who owns the property. Now in Yugoslavia the working people and the farmers collectively own the property, so according to our textbook, it's a socialist country. Later we talked about democracy and elections, and I said that electing persons we think worthy to be leaders might help us avoid problems of bureaucracy. I didn't write any articles. I didn't speak during the campaign of 'Let a Hundred Flowers Blossom, Let a Hundred Schools of Thought Contend.' I just listened."

Lao Fan startles me by jumping to his feet and addressing me—in the present tense—as though I were participating in the insanity: "But here's the ridiculous part. There's a quota—5 percent of the institute's students and faculty must be labeled Rightists."

"Who fixed these quotas?"

Lao Fan is furious. "I don't know. I don't know. It's just ridiculous. The second Party Committee secretary, an old Red Army soldier who worked in Yan'an, refuses to agree to percentages or to label us Rightists. He says we are young and have a good feeling for socialism, that the party has brought us happiness and served us since our childhood—and that we are well aware of all that. So the first secretary accuses *him* of Rightist tendencies and sends him to a party school to study."

Lao Fan sits down, looks at me, and smiles self-consciously. "O.K. But that didn't last too long. I didn't get sent away to any labor camp.

They just assigned me to work in the English department compiling a textbook. By 1959 it was all over and I was reassigned to teaching. They didn't say they'd made a mistake; they just said that your background is good and you're from a poor peasant family and your mother is blah blah blah. I look at it this way: Sometimes a child is blamed by his mother without reason. That does happen. Afterwards, the mother admits she made a big mistake, and the child can understand that."

"Do mothers often say that in China?"

"Yes. It's quite understandable. To myself I used to say, 'let bygones be bygones.' Since then I've been well-treated and well cared for, so that's that."

"That's that, huh? What happened after 1966?"

"Oh, well, in '66 the Cultural Revolution started—out of the frying pan, into the fire." Lao Fan chortles as he often does when he puts another notch in his idiom belt.

"When it first started, I didn't understand the real purpose. I thought the idea was to rid China of bourgeois ideas, of the danger of going back to the old society—like in the Soviet Union. They say there's an elite class there, and that people are oppressed."

"Did you see that happening in China?"

"Well, not exactly, but—I thought that the Cultural Revolution aimed at giving people more freedom and democracy, at teaching people to be bold, to speak out and air their views."

"Which, after your '57 experience, seemed right."

"Oh, yes. But I didn't talk. I kept silent. And I didn't join either of the two big factions."

"What were the two factions?"

"One faction wanted to protect the old cadres, like the leaders of the Commerce Ministry, the other to attack them, so the first faction was considered conservative and the other radical. I just studied Chairman Mao's works and various documents and did whatever I was asked to do, until one day I was shocked by big-character posters repudiating Zhou Enlai. About that I couldn't agree. Aiya! But still I said nothing."

"Why?"

"Because I didn't belong to any faction, so there was no forum for me."

"So unless you belonged to one of the factions there was no way to express a view?"

"None. I just argued with my friends and roommates, and finally came to understand that the Cultural Revolution was entirely rotten. From the day I saw the *dazibao* against Zhou Enlai, in '67 or early '68, I knew the whole thing was wrong."

"So for a year or so you just watched it all go on?"

"No. I stayed in Hangzhou for four months in 1967, entirely away from the Cultural Revolution."

"Away? But they say that Hangzhou was one of the worst places during the Cultural Revolution."

"Yes. But I didn't know much about all that. There were two factions, and fighting was going on here also, but Mother and Ming belonged to the same faction so they didn't have any argument. Usually in one family the husband and wife or the mother and the daughter or the father and son had heated debates or even fights."

"What faction did they belong to?"

"The radical group. They had their own views. I just kept silent because I didn't know what was going on in Hangzhou. You know, 'No investigation, no right to speak.'

"When I returned to Beijing in 1968, the Commerce Ministry had been asked to make severe cuts in personnel. So a large number of staff members, cadres, and teachers were sent down to the countryside."

"Didn't you once tell me you were sent up north to a lumber camp?"

"It wasn't a lumber camp; it was a May 7th Cadre School set up by the ministry in Jilin province, north of North Korea. When we arrived in early May the ground was still frozen. We worked in the open air felling trees, carrying logs, building houses—but it was wonderful because way up there you had nothing to do with the Cultural Revolution. Oh, once in a while we had to read something, but most people slept on their cots through the study sessions."

"Who ran this May 7th School?"

"The ministry itself. It was a far-sighted strategy to preserve the teachers and cadres, to put us out of harm's way."

"Do you think Zhou Enlai was behind this?"

"I'm not certain, but the commerce minister was firmly supported by Premier Zhou, who knew how hard it would be later to replace people educated and experienced in international business matters.

"After a year or so, the ministry set up another school in Henan province, and I went there. There was rice there—how hard it is to live without rice! In 1971 the ministry began sending me to the Guangzhou Trade Fair. I stayed in Hangzhou for two months in '73, and then they asked me to go back to the institute to teach. I was worried because I hadn't had much English practice; we were only allowed to listen to Radio Peking, read the *Beijing Review*, or read novels for one hour a day."

"How come *you* were allowed to read English but the English teachers weren't?"

"You mean the English teachers at Zhejiang University? Oh, that's another pair of shoes. Zhe Da was run by the brother of the provincial military commander—nobody dared to breathe here. Every institute, every university had different rules and regulations. But I belonged to the Commerce Ministry. They knew how to take care of their interests and their people.

"In 1973, I returned to the institute and started to teach again. Ming was fed up with this endless separation, but she and Mother didn't want to move up to Beijing, and the institute wouldn't let me move down to Hangzhou. They said it was too difficult to train someone else to teach all the courses they offer. But finally I got a transfer to Zhe Da, which was badly in need of English teachers."

Lao Fan yawns, stretches, and checks his watch. The afternoon is gone. It's time to begin the washing, chopping, cooking cycle again. "But that's another story for another day," he says, seeking my approval for his accurate use of yet another cliché. I smile, thinking that Lao Fan's life, though painfully typical of Chinese intellectuals, is no cliché. Lao Fan hands me some bamboo shoots and a little hatchet, and I gladly turn my energies to this labor.

# 10
## High Nose in Hangzhou

Rain and tears. Walls of water without and within. Only here have I begun to notice my susceptibility to subtle changes in weather, spirits warming with an open swatch of sky, dampening with drizzle and fog.

The Ides of March: Here I am at last in my new apartment, and I'm crying—not in harmony with the spring downpour that obscures all beyond the window pane, nor for the comforts I've left behind in the "imperial palace." I cry for the wretch I've become. I stand among boxes, bags, and books scattered on bed, desk, and floor, and I see Liang Tai whom I have left standing in front of the Hangzhou Hotel with *my* bamboo bookcase mounted on the back of *my* bicycle. I see him standing there as I stand here, watching the downpour, wondering if it will ever abate.

Four of the scientists came to the hotel this morning to help me pack my clothes, cameras, books, papers, typewriter and assorted Chinoiserie. I bustled about giving orders: hand me this and get me that; pack this here and put that there. Zhang Chefu patiently packed and repacked the car to accommodate goods and people. We secured the bookcase on the back of the bike, and I asked Liang Tai to ride it back for me. He agreed, of course, and the rest of us climbed in the car and drove off in the rain—*in the rain*—giving not a thought to Liang Tai standing there in front of the hotel with *my* bamboo bookcase perched on the back of *my* bike.

Three hours later. I stare out of the bedroom window of my new apartment, waiting out the torrential spring rains like a character in some exotic tropical novel. Where is Liang Tai? Is he still standing there waiting for the rain to let up? He is Chinese and will not be permitted inside the Hangzhou Hotel to sit it out over tea in the Cafe Straight Ahead. Nor would he leave my bookcase and bike untended. Has he ridden back in this pitiless rain, or, worse, walked the bike back so as not to lose my bookcase off the back? I can see him splattered with mud by passing cars and buses, unable to see, not even a free hand to wipe the water from his glasses.

What shall I do? If I go out to find Zhang Chefu and ask him to go to the garage to get the car to pick up Liang, then I'm asking this kind old man to get drenched, and I don't even know if Liang Tai is still standing there. Oh, for a telephone. What a wretch I am. How did this happen to me? How did I get like this, so concentrated on *my* needs, so absorbed in the logistics of moving *my* belongings to *my* new apartment? Me. Me. Me.

When I came to China, I refused to be pushed to the front of the line at the bank, the post office, the noodle shop; now I smile politely and take every advantage I can of my position as foreign professor. I can see how foreigners come to be so awful in Third World countries where everyone and everything seems to be at your service, where your every need is met and you come to view the world as revolving around your desires, to view people as the instruments of your satisfaction. No wonder the Chinese call us foreigners *gao bidzi* or "high nose." It's lots more than a physical description.

I will apologize tomorrow, publicly, in class. I will lose face in hopes of making amends.

In the morning I catch Liang before class. His anger is expressed neither in face nor in tone, but in the simple, uncharacteristic act of telling the truth. With the idea of taking the bus back to the university, he had tried to get someone at the hotel to take responsibility for my bookcase and bike, to lock them away somewhere. No one would. He had tried to have tea in the hotel's *Chinese* dining room. He was not permitted in. Finally, after an hour or so, he walked back to his dorm room, pushing the bike with one hand, balancing the bookcase with the other.

In class, I muster up the courage to apologize. The students can see that I'm upset by the incident, and assure me later that it wasn't my fault, that I was excited about moving, that it was only raining lightly when we left the hotel. But it's all nonsense, and I'm deeply grateful for Liang Tai's honesty.

With a little help from my friends, it doesn't take long to settle into my new apartment. It's designed for a family of four, but I'm assured that I need extra room because I will have many visitors. Because I feel claustrophobic with so much massive furniture in the bedroom—double bed with head and foot boards, six-foot high wardrobe, dresser, desk, chair, and bookcase—we move the wardrobe and dresser out into the hall. I know this is considered gauche, but too bad. The living room has

My kitchen with its new tile table.

more of the same heavy, blond wood pieces: table with four chairs, credenza, large, comfortable chair, coffee (tea?) table, end tables. Funny how different are our needs: I could do without most of this stuff, but find inadequate the two sweet little lamps with their 25-watt bulbs and the desk that's hardly large enough for a typewriter and a piece of paper.

The kitchen is white tiled from floor to waistline, with a tiled counter running from the cement sink to the window. A two-jet burner is attached by a hose to a large gas tank. I'm taken with the easy-clean design of the cement floor that slopes ever so slightly toward a small hole, but there's no storage space, no cabinets. Confusing.

I have three requests: another table for the kitchen, a much larger desk, and a heater because I'm so cold I want to spend my life in bed. Here I go again: I argue fiercely how I can live under absolutely any conditions, then immediately begin to complain that the desk isn't big enough, the lamps are inadequate, the kitchen facilities won't do, I must have a heater. Foreigners! What a pain.

There's a problem about the desk. The Dragon Lady is concerned about the time and money it will take the furniture shop to make a new desk to match my other furniture. Since I cannot transport her to my apartment in New York, I spend hours convincing her that an existing, unmatched desk will do me very nicely. Several workers transport to my house a large, beautiful desk (from some university storage room I'd adore to rummage through), and place it before my bedroom window. From here I watch my neighbors go about their daily lives.

Then comes the question of a kitchen table: four—count them—four workers in grey uniforms squeeze into my five- by eight-foot kitchen. When I leave the house at 7:15 a.m., the two women are beginning to mix batches of cement, and the two men are preparing tiles. When I return at 7 in the evening, they are still at it. No, the Foreign Affairs Office couldn't just give me an old table and, no, the workers aren't paid an hourly wage. In fact, Lao Fan says that only for me would the workers work overtime to get the job finished in one day.

And then there's the matter of the heater. There has been only one snowfall this winter, but the early April temperature still lingers in the 30s, and the dampness creeps into your bones. A radiator-sized heater arrives in my bedroom but cannot be plugged in. Permission must first be granted by some municipal office for additional electric lines to the university. Then come the electricians, two cheerful women who spend a week installing an auxiliary heavy-duty wiring system in the building as well as appropriate plugs in the bedroom.

The heater is wonderful. I turn it off at night, wake at five, turn it on again, and jump back under two heavy cotton quilts and a soft, warm, woolly maroon and white blanket. When the room heats up, I get out of bed and warm each layer of clothing on the heater: underwear, long-johns, Danskins, thermal socks, wool pants, light sweater, heavy sweater, hat and gloves. I even turn my fuzzy boots upside down on the heater to warm the insides. But leaving the bedroom to go to the toilet is traumatic, cooking dinner in a down jacket is no mean trick, and I haven't learned to cook with gloves on as yet. To wash my hair, I bring two tin basins into the bedroom, along with two thermoses of boiled water and a pan of cold water. I mix the hot and cold water, pour some into each basin, wash my hair in one, rinse it in the other, and then use my hair dryer.

But how do the Chinese manage? They, of course, have no heaters or hair dryers. The answer is layers and layers of clothes, only the top one or two being removed at night. The big problem for students and teachers is how to use their hands without getting chilblains, painfully cracked and sore fingers and knuckles which are all too common. My colleagues sit at home each night with hot water bags on their laps, rotating their hands, palms up and down on them, until they're warm enough to write their lessons. Lao Fan says it's literally impossible to type. I asked him how, without a hair dryer, he and Ming manage to wash their hair without catching pneumonia. He shrugged.

Despite my experience with Liang Tai, it doesn't seem to penetrate how much trouble I'm causing. More dissension occurs over the assignment of an *aiyi* or maid. *Aiyi* means "auntie," but "auntie" is nineteen-year-old Little Flower, who seems to know as much about housekeeping as I know about nuclear physics. She is a cadre's daughter, and she already has a job as a typist at the university. It is too difficult and time-consuming, I'm told, for me to do my own shopping, cleaning, cooking, and laundry. Thus the need for an *aiyi*.

The Dragon Lady insists I need her full-time; I counter with two hours a day. Oh, no, she says, you need her at least half a day. O.K., if you want her here half a day, it's O.K. with me. So Little Flower works for an hour or two and then sits in the house studying English. I wouldn't mind, except that now I'm told that I'm to pay her wages, 20 yuan a month. Twenty yuan is no big deal on my salary of 650, but I feel cheated because I've just saved the university about 1,200 yuan a month by moving out of the hotel. Furthermore, *they* insist I have an *aiyi*, so they can pay for her. But they don't. I do.

The truth is that Little Flower is a joy to me, and very quickly becomes my *xiao meimei*, my little sister. She does all the work that needs doing, and speaks Mandarin as well as *Hangzhouhua*, so she has as much to teach me as I her. Why, then, I ask myself, am I behaving so strangely with regard to her services?

One problem is that I don't understand that her strange housekeeping habits are not the results of her inexperience but mine. Only as I start visiting my neighbors do I realize that everyone stores the morning's vegetables on the kitchen floor, that everyone scrubs clothes in cold water with large bars of coarse soap, that everyone cooks with great globs of thick rapeseed oil.

Second, I don't yet understand that Little Flower is not simply another foreigner privilege. To my surprise, maids are common here; many busy households, especially those with children, hire a full- or part-time *aiyi*. They are paid at least 40 yuan per month, about as much as an elementary school teacher—not bad by Chinese standards. Most, of course, are older women, not blossoming nineteen-year-olds.

Finally, there's the spy question. George and Jack assure me that I'm paying Little Flower to spy on me, to read my letters and keep notes on who comes to visit. One of the younger English teachers tells me I've been moved next door to the Dragon Lady for the same reason—so she can keep an eye on me and anyone who darkens my door. Now this teacher is the most cynical person I've ever met, and he has a reputation as a doer of evil deeds during the Cultural Revolution, so his word is not necessarily worth a lot. But Li Xumei gets wind of all this and is so distressed that I might think I'm being spied on that she brings over a small corps of vice-presidents to assure me it is not the case, that I was moved next door to Madam Lo because she will be so helpful to me.

It is certain that the Dragon Lady has no interest in helping me with the time of day. It is my upstairs neighbor Sally (Chen Xiaoli) who tells me how to peel strange vegetables, which parts to discard and which to eat, how to distinguish and where to dispose of different kinds of garbage according to what the peasants collect to feed to the pigs.

As to spying, I guess I'll never know, but I do know I feel conflicted when Little Flower turns up after class with a much-needed umbrella, or spends hours searching for some item I've idly expressed a desire for. I've come to look forward to our English/Chinese lessons and our language-limited chats, and think now the Foreign Affairs Office really was thinking of my interests and not its own when they chose her. But I still have a lot of trouble with the idea of having a servant.

Ho, ho, ho. How I laughed at people who used their nice new bathtubs as water reservoirs! Now I fill up the tub at the first sign of water, even if the little gurgling sounds alert me after midnight. Now, too, I feel pained watching Lao Fan carrying buckets of water up to his fifth-floor apartment, and I recognize yet again how selfish I've been in assuming that so much of his time and energy were at my disposal.

As for baths, there are public bath houses. I'm told they're crowded and not exactly immaculate, but that's not what stops me. When I go to town on my bike, five hundred pairs of curious eyes are glued to me; the idea of displaying my Russian peasant body in a room packed with tiny Chinese women is just too much. So once a week, I return to the Hangzhou Hotel on my bike, borrow a bathtub from one of the foreign experts or tourists, and take a long, leisurely bath in a big tub of luxuriously hot water.

The apartment complex is like the projects in the United States, but on a much smaller scale. The buildings are a block long and five stories high, divided into three sections of fifteen floor-through apartments. Each, of course, has a balcony.

The apartment buildings that line the road leading to the school gate are just like mine, but they all have storefronts: the post office, the bank, the department store are now quartered here. The population of vendors and craftspeople has multiplied. They sit behind their shoe repair or sewing machines, or, like my friend Mr. Woolworth, squat near a sheet spread with pins, ribbons, shoelaces, and notions whose function I cannot even guess. Refreshment stands are also popping up with cakes, pastries, candies, and cookies. (Soon, you can be sure, the notion of dieting will make its way to China.)

There's a new bakery stall that makes fresh loaves daily on the waste heat from one of the university-run factories. The bread is extremely popular; all rank is forgotten as student, teacher, and foreigner alike push in to order either *tiande* (sweet) or *xiande* (salty). But I cheat: I've arranged to advance order several loaves, which they will save for me. Yesterday, however, there was no bread because "it's too cold for the dough to rise." Today people are lining up to sell old paper, bottles, and orange peels for a few pennies per *jin*.

From wheelbarrows and carts people sell plants and flowers, ice cream pops and cookies, a particular crop of vegetables or fruit. Now and then a small truck parks by the gate loaded with notebooks and pads of scratch paper. You can hardly get near it, or near the occasional book or calendar table. Inexpensive and superb reproductions of Chinese paintings of every variety and period make calendars the most popular form of household decoration. Popular, too, are those with full-faced, pink-cheeked, large-eyed children. I was recently presented with four seasonal calendars: full-length portraits of sleek, silk-robed women with flirtatious eyes, coquettishly cocked heads, and elaborate hairdos and makeup. These are China's famous "four beauties," women who prostituted themselves to the enemy—my phrasing—to save the empire. I, for one, prefer the robust women workers with picks and shovels of the Cultural Revolution days. More Western work has appeared: the Mona Lisa and Winged Victory, on the one hand; on the other, vintage forties girlie calendars displaying blond-haired teens in one-piece bathing suits or off-the-shoulder prom dresses.

Peddlers and repairmen add tune and color to the neighborhood. They sell eggs or peanuts, sharpen knives, restrap beds, or repair bamboo items. They carry their goods or tools on shoulder poles or bicycles, calling out or singing simple songs that identify their trade. The children often follow and mimic them as they move from lane to lane.

Morning has its special sounds: the scraping of bamboo brooms on sidewalks, the beat of kitchen hatchets on chopping blocks, the scratching of clothes brush bristles against stone slabs. At 6:00 a.m. the muzak starts over the loudspeaker, ranging from standard Chinese schmaltz to "Lady of Spain I Adore You." At 6:15 comes eight minutes of the music for Chairman Mao's Four-Minute Exercise Program; serious-faced people on balconies, front stoops, or out in the street bend and stretch, making me feel old and brittle. Hundreds of runners and joggers jam the roads from 5:30 to 7:00, when bikers take over.

Little by little, the rock-strewn dirt patches in front of each building are giving way to rock gardens, flowers, vegetables, bushes, or tiny trees, all tended with great love and care by the families, the children helping to look for stray stones and weeds. Chickens walk about freely, puck-pucking most aggressively, I think, in front of the signs that say that chickens aren't permitted in these nice new housing projects. The

Hangzhou street with wash slabs out front.

signs are quickly torn down. Moral: If the masses don't like the line they just don't implement it.

And of course there's the laundry. Ground-floor residents get the gardens and large spaces to wash, dry, and air the endless rounds of family laundry. Along with babysitting, these tasks seem to fall to grandparents, most of whom, as far as I can determine, enjoy being active and useful. But all ground-floor windows have bars, and someone has to keep an eye on the clothes line.

Speaking of which, the locksmith has just arrived. I have no idea who asked him to change the lock, but the university seems concerned for my well-being. I now have a smashing good bolt lock on my front door, but anyone who really wanted to get in could climb to my third-floor balcony and easily enter the back door. Ah, but then I could ring the secret buzzer installed in my bedroom, its thick long black wires leading next door to the bedroom of the Dragon Lady, who would, I'm told, rush to my rescue—*in case*. Though people park bikes in front of the buildings during the day, most drag them up to their apartments in the evening; when I forget to do so, Mr. Wang downstairs will bring my bike up for me. We have tea and a chat. (Given my Chinese level, these conversations must be very comical). At big events (movies or concerts) and at large downtown intersections, old men and women watch your bike for two fen.

Fried scallion pancakes for breakfast.

As I work on my lessons in the early afternoon quiet, I take great pleasure in the sounds of singing or recitation or recess play drifting over from the elementary school. One thing I've noticed is how little crying there is. Each block has about 100 apartments with loads of kids of all ages, yet it is rare, really rare, to hear any but infants crying. The children garner much affection. Tots are carried everywhere, kissed, cooed over, and passed from arm to arm. As they develop, they begin to attend to each other as their parents and grandparents cared for them. Rotund with padded clothing and burdened with heavy book bags, the school-bound youngsters manage to wind their arms around each other's waists and necks. By the time they begin school, the sexes have separated; physical contact and affection among men and among women, however, continue for a lifetime. Perhaps this explains in part why Chinese teens seem to manage better than ours without early sexual encounters.

From the school yard comes "Do Re Mi" from *The Sound of Music*. I wonder if the children know what the words mean. I wonder if they've been shown pictures of deer. Sometimes it's "Old Black Joe" (in English) right on the heels of "The Internationale" (in Chinese). Too often "Jingle Bells" (in English and Chinese) accompanies April's torrents.

On my way to class at 7:15 a.m.—oh, joy, to be able to walk to work—I get my daily English lesson. It's the British version of *English 900* over the loud speaker: "I beg your pardon, is this seat taken?" "Are you single or married?" "Would you kindly open the window for me?" I doubt that anyone pays attention to it, for the sound is often so garbled I can't follow it myself. But I think someone thinks that a process of osmosis is taking place, and maybe it is, who knows?

Before and after dinner the kids sit outside on stoops or stools and recite aloud their English lessons. I hang over the balcony outside my bedroom and help. These children are also mastering *Hanzi* (Chinese characters) one by one, pinyin (the romanization of the sounds), and *putonghua* (Mandarin—the common language from Beijing). They also speak *Hangzhouhua* (the local dialect). I'm awed.

An interruption, a pleasant one, and the real reason I moved here: visitors. As China is not a telephone society, people just drop in on one another. It drives me crazy because it's impossible to schedule my work, but I love it. After dinner two or three teachers or students knock on the door and ask if I'm busy. This is, of course, a rhetorical question. We chat for an hour or two about the weather and teaching English and studying languages. Most avoid weightier topics. I serve coffee or tea and assorted munchies. Last week someone brought me dried soybeans and bamboo shoots cooked in soy sauce and sugar, then set outside to dry for "two suns"—not two days, but two sunshiny days.

Lao Fan, Ming, and Fan Ming are my first dinner guests. They have become family. At first, I think, Lao Fan attended to me as was his duty. But now we're friends, "comrades" in the Chinese sense of the term. To "help" me, Ming comes in the morning and prepares *all* the dishes—she lets me watch—and then she comes again in the late afternoon and cooks them all. Well, I'll learn, I guess. We have coffee, Fan Ming and I play chess (he slaughters me), and we talk. I can return their friendship, but I wish there were some way I could repay their thoughtfulness and kindness.

In the late afternoon, I ride the ten miles around West Lake or out to the zoo or the Six Harmonies Pagoda near the Qiantang River. The air nips at my nose, the trees grow like teenagers, the sun shines through the branches, calling every bud and leaf to life.

It is surely because of my relative language deprivation that I've grown so attuned to my environment, but it's partly, too, because I'm a city girl and the sights and sounds of country life are wondrously new to me. In a brief span of time, the whole color design of the world changes. Soon after the trees begin to green, bushes abound in tiny, bright yellow forsythia blossoms the Chinese call "first sign of spring flowers." They disappear quickly, followed by the pink-tinged white of the magnolias whose lovely scent lingers everywhere. They, too, die swiftly, tossing their rosy petals upon the ground.

And then the rapeseed comes up—magnificent. From my apartment or classroom window or, better yet, gliding through local communes on a bike, I'm dazzled by Van Gogh canvases of brilliant yellow alternating with forest green and dark brown, but before this lazy lady can get her camera out, it's gone. The peasants work like mad for two or three days stripping the rapeseed tops for vegetables and oil, and turning under the stems for fertilizer. The fields are left to green and pale yellow wheat. After the rains, the rice crops grow out of silvery mirrors.

What pleasure I derive from living here and watching Chinese life flow with the seasons. If ever I write a book about all this, I'll call it *China Through My Window*. It's late afternoon and the sun is sliding down behind the classroom buildings. Out front children are weeding the gardens and trying patiently to dispose of the leftover rubble from building bricks and cinder blocks. The wash is coming in off the lines. Grandpas are strolling about after dinner, little ones in their arms, chatting amiably with neighbors as they go by. Some kids set up a string for a volleyball net. Tots try out new tricycles while their papas try to get them to stay still long enough for pictures.

Yesterday, however, this was no scene of tranquillity and harmony. It started around noon. Some workers had set up a well-shaped brick stove to make lime or some witches' brew of a building material. The stove belched out huge white clouds of noxious fumes and, as the workers chose to set it up right in front of someone's house, the dust and fumes invaded the nostrils, saturated the wash and the food. There ensued a long, loud argument with shouting and arm waving—no fisticuffs, though at times someone gently tried to calm one or another of the angrier parties. The result? This afternoon the workers dismantled the stoves and hosed down the yards.

It continues to rain a lot, making mud of most everything. It's still chilly, even on sunshiny days, and downright cold at night. But, oh, the nights! The nights are star-splendid. Bundled up in layers of clothing, I stand out on my balcony and nestle in the warmth of the stars. TVs go off, voices are muffled, bike bells cease their clamor. It is deliciously quiet.

Sunday morning. 7:30. Through my window I watch people gather for a neighborhood meeting. Up to my balcony bound the sounds of a lively discussion, but I can't make out what it's about. One woman has drawn the neighbors around her and is addressing them ardently. People point up at parts of buildings or down at the patches of mud that pass for yards. The faint hint of spring in the air creates a light, restless mood. Girls swing intertwined hands, boys hang over one another's shoulders, women poke and joke with one another, grannies shuffle after toddlers. Some decision has apparently been reached—though about what I have no idea. As my new neighbors disperse, many look up at me and wave or smile, while children say "gooda bye" and giggle. "Gooda bye," I respond, waving back. If there is hostility toward a foreigner moving into their midst, I certainly can't feel it.

At 9:30 sharp, as though a bell had been rung, everyone reappears with brooms and shovels and pails and rags. So that's what the meeting was about—community spring cleaning. I grab a jacket, collect my new broom and dust pan, and run out to help. What an opportunity to show I'm no "high nose."

It's no use. In a friendly but firm manner, my implements are removed from my hands. No argument will do. "You are a foreign guest," I am told. "You are a foreign friend." I'm hurt and confused. Is this really politeness or were people coerced into this clean-up because I've moved here?

I go back to my apartment and stand on the balcony feeling pained and angry, feeling very "high nosed" indeed standing up here above the people below who are busy sweeping, tidying, and polishing. Funny. We Americans would have handed a stranger a broom and set her to work. I like American inclusion better than this "guest" business, but then I'm a new phenomenon around here. It may take people a while to get used to the "foreign friend" as neighbor. It may take forever.

It is now, at this moment, as I stand on my balcony feeling so estranged and isolated, that a small fleet of carefully constructed paper airplanes and missiles lands on my balcony, on them crayoned, in Chinese and in English, the words "friend" and "comrade." The children will never know how much this gesture means to me.

# 11
# Buttons

I admire Cai Ping, but I'm not sure I like her. Her English is quite good so it's easy for us to communicate, but there's an odd sharpness in her manner. She doesn't go through all this "I very bother you" stuff, which is, on the one hand, a relief, but on the other seems so brusque here in China. I'm perpetually murmuring the word "sweet" in regard to my students; Cai Ping is not sweet. She's a solidly built, hard-nosed, hard-working woman with an unsentimental personality, though she clearly takes genuine pleasure in her scientific work and her English studies. Cai Ping has just turned fifty; as she often tells me, she lost her "ten golden years" as a scientist. Perhaps she feels she has no time to fool with formalities, or perhaps she doesn't have to any more, like the old women who smoke in public and don't give a damn what anybody thinks.

How different she is from her contemporary Xiao Liang. Though trained as a scientist, Xiao Liang works primarily as a lower-level administrator in her institute. She has applied for membership in the Communist Party and bubbles with the very spirit of Lei Feng, whose whole history she imparts to us during the three-hour train ride from Hangzhou to Shanghai.

"Learn from Lei Feng" is the current party campaign aimed at prodding youth toward the selfless service to the people that character-ized the post-Liberation years. In the early fifties, Lei Feng traveled about the country doing good deeds under the cover of darkness: in the morning a peasant might find his field plowed; a child his toy repaired; a mother her fuel supply cut and stacked by the doorstep. No one knew what wonderful ghost had lightened daily burdens.

Next to me Cai Ping looks out the train window, but since the Lei Feng lecture is for my benefit, I must listen attentively to Xiao Liang's lengthy tales of the much-sung hero. I do not tell her what I think—that this whole "Learn from Lei Feng" business is silly and counterproductive. I do not tell her what undergraduate students have told me—that they see this as a "do as I say, don't do as I do" campaign concocted by certain cadres who "got off the bus," that is, have given up revolutionary goals and gone in for personal gain. First of all, campus bulletin boards crowded with photographs of Lei Feng doing the good deeds he did secretly in the dark of night inspire little but cynicism; second, the early eighties are simply not the early fifties—altruism is hardly in fashion now.

When Xiao Liang finally takes a w.c. break, Cai Ping turns to me with a sly smile. "Well, at least this one doesn't have any numbers attached to it," she says.

"Numbers?" I inquire.

"Yes," she says, "you know in the fifties we had the Three-Anti and the Five-Anti campaigns—something about corruption, waste, and bureaucracy—that's a laugh—and the five against bribery, tax evasion, fraud, and things like that. Then with the Socialist Education movement came the Four Cleans and the Twenty-three Points, then the Sixteen this and the Eight that—"

"Why do the Communists love all these numbers?" I ask.

"Oh, no, no," Cai Ping says. "The Communists didn't cook up all these numbers. Remember Confucius and the 'three obediences,' and the 'ten great follies' that brought about the downfall of the Qin dynasty. No, we Chinese seem always to package our axioms in numbers. But the Communists have certainly made numerous contributions to the list."

"Mind-boggling," I comment. Cai Ping immediately takes out her notebook and asks me to spell this marvelous mouthful.

Xiao Liang returns and resumes her narrative. Her enthusiasm is refreshing, and I'm grateful to both women for arranging this weekend in Shanghai. "You need a broke," one of the students had said. And so I do.

Cai Ping's Shanghai apartment consists of two furniture-packed bedroom-studies for the family of four, the standard coaldust-decor kitchen, and a large hallway that serves tonight as a dining room for five women: Xiao Liang, her younger sister Li Mei (who happens to be in Shanghai on business), Cai Ping, her colleague and neighbor Ma Mingshi, and me. There is no place set for Cai Ping's husband, Dong Xing, for it is he who prepares and serves, dish by dish, our most excellent dinner. Today Cai Ping has guests; when her husband has guests, she explains, then *she* cooks and serves dinner. "But you're lucky," she laughs. "He's a much better cook than I am."

Table talk centers on the new apartments that Cai Ping and Ma

Mingshi will occupy by summer, and on promotions and raises. A tiny dynamo whose active head and hands seem diminutive in her loose, grey jacket, Ms. Ma is particularly animated on these topics. Scientists will now have first dibs on the largest and best new apartments and will earn considerably more than workers at their institute or nearby local factories. "It hardly makes up for the past," says Ma, "but it's very nice anyway." I'm not sure whether "the past" refers to the Cultural Revolution years or to the irritating fact that, up to now, workers have had the choicest apartments and salaries equivalent to the scientists' as part of the rush (now seen as "ultraleft") to narrow the three great differences—between city and country, peasant and worker, and mental and manual labor.

The plum wine sings in my bloodstream, the good food settles comfortably in my stomach. I look at the other four women at the table and am carried back five years.

"On International Women's Day, March 8, 1975," I comment casually, "I had dinner with a group of women here in Shanghai." There's a sudden stillness at the table, but faces betray nothing. "Of course I had no idea what was going on," I add quickly. "We were just tourists—an American women's delegation in China for a month."

No one says anything, but all eyes are on me. What am I expected to say? I think: "Where were you on March 8, 1975?" but it doesn't seem like the moment to ask. It occurs to me to see if I can learn something from these women about my 1975 experiences, which had seemed so positive.

"That day we met with ten Shanghai women. There were teachers and workers and even housewives, but one woman was a pilot, another a high wire telephone repair worker, one a plant manager, and so on."

"I'll bet there weren't any scientists among them," Cai Ping laughs.

"None," I concur. "But it never occurred to any of us to ask why. The women were lively and seemed happy with their work and their lives. We were very impressed." No one says anything. Ma shrinks down into her padded jacket and peers out at me. "We visited a women's co-op, a bicycle assembly shop set up by a neighborhood committee. We were told that many of the women were ex-prostitutes and ex-drug addicts. They seemed genuinely grateful to be functioning wage-earners." There's silence again. I'm beginning to choke on this foot I've stuck in my mouth, but I have no notion how to remove it. It is very quiet.

"Was it all a pack of lies?" I blurt out, looking around the table from one face to another.

Li Mei opens her eyes wide and stares as though seeing me for the first time. Westerners often say that Chinese women distort their beauty with baggy clothes and soup-bowl haircuts, but Li Mei strikes

1975—Shanghai neighborhood co-op employed former housewives, ex-prostitutes, and ex-addicts to assemble bicycles for local department stores.

me as feminine in the best sense: she is gentle yet strong, a sensuous person whose beauty radiates from her intelligent eyes and open, responsive face.

"Oh, no," she says earnestly. "Don't misunderstand. It's all quite true. My husband's elder sister was sold into prostitution before Liberation. She became an opium addict. After Liberation she was hospitalized and cured. Now she has a husband and children and she works in a neighborhood co-op. No, no," she says again, "Chinese women—all Chinese women, I believe—can only be grateful for the revolution."

I find myself relieved to hear this. During a flurry of conversation in Chinese I think of "my" Shanghai of 1975: the old dock worker who wept as he spoke of food, shelter, and clothing, of what it meant to him to be called "comrade" instead of "boy" or "dog"; the pilot on the

*Whangpoo* announcing with pride that his ship was designed and built by Chinese, not foreigners; the young mill worker illustrating with her arms the concept of "walking on two legs"—women working at ancient spinning wheels next to clattering modern machinery; the toothless old lady with bound feet at the "home for the respected" secure in her "five guarantees"; the doctor humbled by emptying bed pans and washing floors once a week, and by discussing his work with nurses and patients. Oh, would that we could do that in America, I had thought then. But it hadn't crossed my mind how few doctors there were in China at the time, and what suffering must have resulted from these efforts to remold doctors' attitudes toward their work and their patients.

There had been no beggars in Shanghai in 1975; I saw none now. There had been no drug addicts in Shanghai in 1975; if there were any now, they were certainly invisible. There had been no venereal disease in Shanghai in 1975; just this year, I am told, as foreigners again flock to this great port, a few cases of VD have been detected. There were no unemployed in Shanghai in 1975—ah, but now literally thousands of youths hang around the streets waiting to be assigned jobs by the government. Back then all middle school graduates (an estimated one million from Shanghai alone) were sent to factories, to the countryside, or to uninhabited frontier communities, supposedly for a year or two. "Wonderful!" I had thought then. They would apply their book learning to practical tasks, share their knowledge with workers and peasants, and find out what it meant to grow the food they ate, to build the houses they lived in. Everyone would be better for it. I flash on the spectacular street scene witnessed from our tourist bus our last afternoon in Shanghai, that last day in China in March 1975: bright red banners rippling in the wind as apparently joyous parents waved fond farewell to their youngsters off to teach and to learn from the peasants.

I look around the dinner table again. March 8, 1975, I say to myself. Do you know where these people's children were? Remembering the October demonstrations I witnessed in Hangzhou, I dare not even ask where their children *are*.

Xiao Liang and Li Mei must leave. They have a long bus trip across town. Ms. Ma says goodnight as Cai Ping's twelve-year-old son returns from a friend's house and busies himself with his homework, while Dong Xing does the dishes. I make noises about returning to my room at the hotel, but Cai Ping assures me the institute's driver will take me back later. She and I retire with tea to her crowded bedroom where she props me up against the stack of quilts neatly folded at one end of the bed and settles herself against the large wardrobe that buttresses the other.

I admire the wooden box she sets between us and recognize the scene

Shanghai, 1975—students see classmates off to the countryside.

etched on it as Mao's birthplace in Changsha in Hunan province, a place
I visited one drizzly afternoon in 1975 along with hundreds of Chinese
pilgrims.

"I have something for you," says Cai Ping.

"For me?"

With her hand on the lid of the box she asks playfully: "Do you want
to guess?" I can't imagine. She removes the lid and spreads out the
contents of the box on the clean white sheet.

"For your collection," she says, clearly amused at the foreigner's
eccentricities.

There are dozens of them. I'm delighted. The smallest is half an inch
in diameter, a button-sized portrait of Chairman Mao recognizable only
by its resemblance to the other, larger and still larger ones just like it:
left profile, full head of hair, stub nose, and sloping collar.

Here are three Little Red Book buttons, one white, one gold, and one
red, a half inch by one inch, with the same portrait of the Chairman in a
little glass bubble and "Selected Works of Mao Tse Tung" below it—in
English, no less—and several similar ones in various sizes and colors
with Chinese titles.

I run my fingers over the smooth, two-inch ceramic buttons. Unlike
the others, these portray the young or middle-aged Mao, strong, hand-

some, bareheaded or in soldier's cap, head floating above a pale-hued impressionist rendering of that same scene of his childhood home in Changsha. There are large, ugly, metal buttons with gold heads and red rays radiating out from them. There are the same busts against red flags with trains or factories or the Great Hall of the People underneath. Some have quotations inscribed on them—"Serve the People," "Never Forget Class Struggle"; some are round, some five-pointed stars, some large rectangles with sweeping flags pleating out above the frame.

We count them. Thirty-three. I have another two dozen or so at home in Hangzhou.

"Which do you like best?" Cai Ping asks me.

"Oh, these ceramic ones for sure," I answer easily. "Look how romantic the young Mao looks. It's enough to make you run away from home and join the PLA."

"If you accidentally dropped one of these ceramic buttons and smashed it," says Cai Ping, "you'd find yourself in jail."

"Oh come on," I say, looking down at the dreamy sketches of the young, heroic Mao. "Don't exaggerate. Things were bad enough. How about you? Which one do you like best?"

"I hate them all," Cai Ping says in a sudden change of mood that startles me. I look up from the buttons and into her face. "We were forced to wear Mao buttons at every moment of the day. Whenever a new one came out you had to buy it. Some people wore several at a time."

"Who forced you?" I ask, looking at this strong, stocky, sensible woman of fifty, finding it hard to imagine her putting up with such nonsense.

"If the institute wasn't under one Red Guard faction it was under another," she says rapidly. "They were well armed, all of them. They hated each other. They were always battling for control, always spewing quotations to prove who was most loyal to God Mao. So if you wore buttons all the time you were safe with both factions—at least on that count. One big button was so heavy it tore my colleague's shirt. He took it off. Within hours a big-character poster appeared near his office exposing his 'bad background' and accusing him of counterrevolutionary activities. He spent months under house arrest, sitting in a tiny room writing self-criticisms. Of course he was one of the lucky ones."

"Just because he took the button off his shirt? Cai Ping, I believe you, but I just can't understand how people could be so silly."

Cai Ping doesn't know how to respond to me. I can see in her eyes that she's furious at my incredulity and is searching for a way to get through my thick skull. It's tense for a while; when she turns her face back to me I find a wry smile.

"You use the word 'silly,'" she says. "Did you know that in some major cities Red Guards tried to change all the traffic signals so that red stood for 'go' and green for 'stop'?"

"That's about as silly," I answer, "as the Red Guards in Hangzhou running around knocking the noses off all the old statues—"

"—and the old people, the cadres, and intellectuals," Cai Ping cuts in. That's hardly funny, but we both laugh, relax a little, and sit thoughtfully for a moment.

"Cai Ping, has something happened recently?" I ask.

"Nothing's happened," she says, "nothing new." I tell myself to keep my mouth shut; it will come. It does.

"I received a letter from my younger sister yesterday. She's ruined, you know. Not dead, no, but she—well, she's ruined."

"Will you tell me about her?"

"I don't know," she says. "I don't think you'll believe me. What happened to my sister is even sillier than going to jail for dropping a button."

"Cai Ping, I'm sorry. It's very difficult for a foreigner to understand all this, but I want to try to understand. Please tell me about your sister."

I sit quietly and wait, thinking that the presence of Xiao Liang's little sister may have affected Cai Ping this evening.

"My *xiao meimei* was young," she begins, "young and beautiful and very smart. She was a shy girl, but her teachers encouraged her and helped her and persuaded her to become a scientist. In 1967 she graduated from university and was assigned to an institute in Beijing. She had a wonderful career ahead of her, a wonderful life ahead of her, and she knew it. Those were the good years, the fifties and early sixties when we never locked a door, never hesitated to help one another, when we worked with all our hearts to build socialism. Xiao Hua, too, believed in socialism and loved the party with all her heart. She would study and do research to help China lift its head proudly among the nations of the world. We had such dreams!

"When the Cultural Revolution began, she took it up enthusiastically. If Chairman Mao called upon the people to be vigilant against the enemies within, she would try hard to do so—though she was new to her institute and didn't know who such people might be. More and more of her colleagues were said to be bourgeois ideologues, or even spies and traitors. They were denounced on big-character posters and at mass meetings. As things grew more and more confused, she retreated, said nothing. She blamed herself for being unable to distinguish right from wrong, to differentiate between a socialist flower and a stinking bourgeois weed.

"One day she received a letter from a classmate working in Kunming. She was busy at the moment, so she stuck it in her pocket and went about her business. At some point she had to go to the bathroom, which was very dark and dirty. She had nothing in her pockets at all to use for toilet paper, so she took the envelope off the letter and used that."

Cai Ping looks at me. I must look peculiar. "Yes," she says, "you're already thinking this is a strange story."

"Please go on."

"Xiao Hua had no idea there was a picture of Chairman Mao in the envelope, and she didn't see it in the dark as it fell. One of her colleagues happened to enter the bathroom behind her, found the picture, and reported the story to the institute's revolutionary committee.

"Xiao Hua was immediately labeled a counterrevolutionary. At first they simply criticized her, sat her in a room, and asked her to write self-criticisms. But what should she say? She was very confused. So they placed her on stage before all her colleagues, arms pinned behind her, head pushed down on her chest; many denounced her because they thought it was the way to save their own skins, though as power shifted from one faction to the other, few were spared.

"But denouncement wasn't enough fun for the Red Guards: they beat Xiao Hua, brutally, and in public so in case the beating wasn't enough the humiliation would be intolerable. She was locked away in a room by herself and after a while found a piece of rope and tried to hang herself. As it happened a worker came by at precisely the right moment and, knowing full well Xiao Hua was no counterrevolutionary, cut her down."

Cai Ping goes to her dresser and gets me a handkerchief. Dry-eyed and clear-voiced, she continues:

"Even this did not end her persecution, nor even the beatings. Eventually she became a little deranged. She's still a little crazy and suffers badly from nightmares. But her story is far from the worst; eventually someone married her and she now has a child and a clerical job in another city."

I feel idiotic, weeping those damned tears only I seem unable to control.

"Yes, now you believe me," Cai Ping says flatly.

"What did your sister write in her letter?" I ask, no better able to control my cracking voice than my seeping eyes.

"She wrote what she often writes—that it's senseless for me to be at

Zhe Da studying English, that I must not work so hard, that I must never think of going abroad as the winds could change and I will suffer again, that I should stay home with my husband and children as she does and never mind about science and such nonsense as modernizing China."

"Why don't you?" I ask.

"My work *is* my life," she answers. "Oh, I love my husband and my children very much, but I cannot imagine life without work. Even Ma Mingshi continues to work," she adds.

I think of Ma's face at the dinner table, and how stupid I was babbling on about "my" Shanghai of the midseventies.

"Tell me."

Cai Ping takes a deep breath. "It's a terrible story. You will cry again," she says with a faint smile.

"Never mind," I tell her. "Let me cry. It's just my Russian genes." And we both smile.

"Ma comes from a 'bad background.' Her grandfather was a small capitalist here in Shanghai, and her father was a distinguished university professor, a Harvard Ph.D. He suffered a lot. He doesn't talk about the beatings that crippled him for life but speaks bitterly of the humiliation of being paraded in the streets with a dunce cap on his head.

"Near the beginning—in '68, I think—Ma was sent up north to work in a tool factory. It was really a prison, of course. At night more than a hundred women laid out their bedding on the factory floor, and in the day they worked and ate in the same cold room. For the sake of the children, her husband soon divorced her." I must look shocked, for Cai Ping adds, "No, no. He was a good and loyal man and he loved her, but it was the only sensible thing to do. He thought it would save the children. He was sent to a May 7th Cadre School—one of those places where they 'reformed' the minds of intellectuals and cadres."

As Cai Ping pauses to refill our tea cups, I relive a bitter-cold March afternoon in 1975. We were "visiting" a May 7th Cadre School on the outskirts of Shanghai. They told us—and I believed—it was a wonderful place where people combined work, play, and study, built houses, played basketball, and studied MLM (Marxism, Leninism, Mao Zedong Thought). It seemed like summer camp—except for the cold. Our guide cracked open a heavy wooden door to reveal a room with a long table down the center, books, slates, chalk, and rags for erasers scattered about it, and a large blackboard propped up toward the far end. Around the table perhaps twenty men, towels wrapped peasant-fashion round their heads, sat on two long benches. They were, we were told, leaders of local communes and were here learning to read and to write, to add and divide, and to study Marxism.

Cai Ping sips her tea, looks up at me, and resumes her story. "Their teen-age daughter was sent with another girl to a distant commune, but her mother's background became known even there. Her friend said she withstood a lot, but when she was raped by a drunken peasant one night, she drowned herself. The younger daughter somehow survived—who knows what she did with no parents to discipline or guide her, no teacher to train or encourage her. She lives with Ma now, but she's very sour and difficult."

We sip tea and sit silent for a while. I think of the early "speak bitterness" sessions organized by the Communists in the forties and fifties where people spoke out against (and sometimes stoned to death) landlords and capitalists, pimps, brothel keepers, and dope dealers who had so long oppressed them.

"There were suicides in every institute," Cai Ping continues. "In my scientific group, five people—about five of every twenty in the institute. All over the country the story is the same. And worse: in Nanning groups of scientists were rounded up in trucks and taken to the lakeside. As they wondered aloud to each other why they were there, they were mowed down by machine-gun. Truckloads of scientists from another institute pulled up to the scene and saw what was happening. They rebelled and managed to escape, so they're alive today to tell the story."

Dong Xing enters the room and slips quietly into a chair squeezed so tightly between the wall and the bed his knee touches Cai Ping's. He is a thin, pleasant-looking man in an ordinary padded jacket and pants puffed out by underlayers. He has the standard brush cut I associate with young, innocent, ignorant American sailors and soldiers I've come across in Europe or Asia, but his eyes say at once that he is neither young, nor innocent, nor ignorant.

Cai Ping brings him a cup of tea and says a few words to him in Shanghai dialect. He speaks no English, and I'm afraid the conversation will end before I have heard Cai Ping's own story. I hesitate to ask; I know I've had enough of all this. But I want to know.

"Cai Ping, what happened to you and your family?"

"Oh, it was hard for us too," she answers, almost casually, "but I was much older than my *xiao meimei*. I was already strong and sure of myself. I, too, was labeled a counterrevolutionary and a Soviet spy—I read and speak Russian, you know. I had attended conferences in Moscow in 1958 and 1960 and had exchanged papers with Russian scientists for several years."

She turns to Dong Xing and explains what we're talking about. He nods gravely, settles himself in his chair, and warms his large hands, as we do, by wrapping them firmly around his tea cup.

"They beat me for a while, yes." Cai Ping places her teacup on the floor and moves her hands like wands above her arms and legs and torso as though to heal the open wounds. "Then they locked me up in a tiny room and left me alone. I was only frightened for the baby—I was eight months pregnant at the time. How could I have my baby here in this room, all alone? I was so afraid it would be injured in some way. I asked the young boy who guarded me with a gun if his mother had given birth to him in a hospital. He said she had. I said that perhaps, if she hadn't, he might not now be such a healthy boy, such a fine revolutionary. I went on and on, and when the day came they let me out to go to the hospital. But they wouldn't let my husband see me during all that time, or after the baby was born. That was the hardest part for me."

She looks long and tenderly at Dong Xing, and I think how hard and cold I had thought her only a day ago. I see us sitting quietly across from one another sipping tea, two middle-aged professional women, but I feel terribly young, painfully naïve. It is simply impossible for me to imagine Chinese teenagers—however zealous in their pursuit of revolutionary purism—beating up a woman eight months pregnant. What a fool I am. I remember so well my return to the States in 1975: I came home exhausted, fell into an arm chair, and turned on the radio. A newscaster welcomed me to my motherland with the story of an eighteen-year-old boy who'd raped a ten-year-old girl and thrown her off the roof of a building. It seemed to me then that I had left behind the land of order, sense, and sanity and walked into an insane asylum.

"But you are still a scientist. You write papers and win awards for your work. You study English at Zhe Da and will soon go abroad. How did you come out of it so different from your sister?"

"Yes. I'm different. I am older than she is and have always been stronger. I spent two years in the countryside and another in a factory, years of hard labor, but I didn't mind that. I learned how hard life is for the Chinese people. But it makes me even angrier that I lost my ten golden years as a scientist—no research for ten years, no papers written, nothing done to help make life better or easier.

"And I'm lucky in another way," she says, turning to Dong Xing. "I have a husband who stands by me, who supports my work, helps to raise our son, and does all the household chores without complaint while I am away studying English with my fine teacher."

Cai Ping reaches over and puts my hand in both of hers; she has forgiven me my ignorance.

I have a hundred questions. Why did all this happen, where are the people now who did all those awful things, can the winds shift, can this happen again? But it's very late and I recognize a "conversation closed" remark when I hear one. I help Cai Ping carefully rewrap the Mao buttons in newspaper and nest them safely in my pocketbook. Many months from now, when I pack to leave China, I will see each of these buttons as carefully removed from these same newspaper scraps and examined by a customs officer, a bright young thing with long braids who explains in her excellent English (she was trained by Lao Fan in Beijing) that she must make sure there are no traitor Lin Biao buttons among them.

# 12
## Gifts

"A nation has borders or boundaries," begins my lesson on Western concepts of privacy. "Everything within those borders belongs to that nation. Many a war has been fought over boundary disputes. So, too, people have private territory, and Westerners take the concepts of territoriality and personal belongings very seriously."

I offer examples: I don't open my colleague's desk drawer even to look for a pencil unless I ask first; I don't open a friend's closet; I don't go into a host's bedroom unless I'm invited. And without permission, I don't read my sister's letter, my friend's document sitting on his or her desk, or even my co-worker's morning newspaper. "The vast majority of people will gladly lend you what is theirs," I add. "Just ask."

This idea is foreign—even silly—to most of the scientists, but it's agreed that they must adhere to local custom, however strange, during their sojourn in the West. During my sojourn in the East, however, no such niceties obtain. None of my letters has ever been opened (except in Hong Kong for the insertion of propaganda in Chinese), but every telegram from abroad is handed me in a jagged-edged envelop. Furious, I confront Lao Fan:

"Who opened my telegram?" I ask.

"The Foreign Affairs Office," he answers.

"But why?" I want to know. "It's addressed to me."

"It's a telegram, so it may be something important," he answers, looking at me like I need a psychiatrist.

"Precisely, but important to *me*."

"But it may be a matter about which you need help."

"If I need help I'll ask for it!"

We stare at one another, and I am once again grateful for Lao Fan to whom I can say anything, however impolite, without jeopardizing our friendship.

Having absorbed his lesson on privacy, my student Mr. Ma does not tear open the package that was on my desk when I arrived in class this morning; he asks my permission to do so. Realizing that he's expended half this morning's concentration on this package I'd forgotten about, and wishing to prove my point that he who asks will be granted, I assent. A large crowd gathers around Mr. Ma. My sacred rule "Thou shalt speak nought but English in the classroom" is wantonly cast aside.

"What does 'kaw-shir' mean?" asks Mr. Ma, holding aloft a slim volume he's extracted from the fat book mailer.

"What does *what* mean?"

"Kaw-shir," he answers.

"Spell it," I suggest.

"K O S H E R."

I have no idea where this question comes from but dutifully offer the correct pronunciation and explain that it refers to the dietary customs of religious Jews, "actually very similar to your wife's," I add, remembering that Mr. Ma's wife is a member of the Hui national minority, which does not partake of the pork so beloved by the Han Chinese.

This seems like a satisfactory answer, and my students indicate they already know about Jews—they're smarter and richer than other people. After a brief discussion of stereotypes, attention returns to the book from America.

"I can't find 'Vaze Meer' in my dictionary," says Xiao Wang.

"You can't find *what?*" I ask.

She brings the book to my desk and, sure enough, right here in black and white in the table of contents I find "Tea Eggs Oy Vaze Meer" along with "Foh Nee Shrimp Puffs," "Far Blun Jed Egg Drop Soup," "Haddock Yen Tah," "Matzoh Brei Foo Yong," "Mixed Vegetables Hah Zah Rye," and a regular tsimmes of tsimilar delicacies.

While trying to get out the point that *vaze meer* is the Yiddish equivalent of the Chinese *ai ya!*, I'm laughing so hard I have to sit down. Then, of course, I have to explain what's so funny. God bless my colleague Ruth Weinstock with her never-failing sense of humor: at the end of a "Dear Everybody" letter I noted that I'm now doing my own grocery shopping and cooking, and have need of a Chinese cookbook—in English, of course, as you can't hardly get that kind in China. Ruth ran right out and mailed me a gift (from her own bookshelf, I'd venture): *The Chinese-Kosher Cookbook* by Ruth and Bob Grossman.

Here are "Stuffed Mushrooms Mah Zul Tuv." "Mah Zul" (good luck) I have plenty of in China; mushrooms are altogether another matter— and what kind of *mah zul* is it to have to explain all this to twenty-two Chinese scientists? I once tried explaining Murphy's Law. Only Liang Tai was sophisticated enough in English to get it. As several students walked me back to the Hangzhou Hotel one day, I'd worked hard on why the chicken crosses the road. And then, not having the sense to recognize a lead balloon when it falls on my foot, had proceeded to the fireman and his red suspenders.

Ruth's is not the only gift I receive this month. Most of the students have just returned from their New Year holidays at home. (The four who could not afford the fare or whose homes were too distant spent their holidays in the classroom huddled over books at desks pushed perilously close to the electric heater—which was provided, of course, for my comfort.)

Before vacation, the groups they'd organized early in the semester swung into action. Strangers to one another last fall, they'd nonetheless held a meeting and made "responsibility" assignments. Liang Tai and Wu Jianguo handle academic affairs: they arrange room assignments so that advanced students live with those requiring more help in English; they see to it that everyone has necessary equipment and supplies and receives copies of my lessons as soon as they roll off the mimeograph machine; they also organize regular meetings to sum up their academic progress, report to the Academy of Sciences in Beijing (which pays their salaries and tuition here as well as all expenses except food), and make suggestions to one another, to Lao Fan, and to me about changes in approach or scheduling. They suggested, for example, that we begin and end classes fifteen minutes earlier (i.e., 7:15 to 11:15) because by 11:30 there's no longer anything resembling food left in the dining hall. Of course we complied.

Xiao Wang and Ma Jinghong help with family, social, and financial problems that might interfere with studies. Here again the Western sense of privacy, of "my business—your business," holds no sway. Others take care of entertainment and travel: movies, excursions, and home travel arrangements. This time there were many problems obtaining such precious commodities as train tickets to various parts of the country, but Lao Fan, as usual, came up with a *hou men* (back door) to solve the problem.

And so they go and soon return with news and photographs of family and friends, with gossip to share, with detailed descriptions of New Year's dinners eaten, and with gifts for me—no more fans or lacquer or bambooware, but bananas and enormous *guazi* (oversized grapefruit) from the South, a big hunk of cheese from the North, a jar of Sichuan hot sauce to warm me down to my toenails, and, most precious of all, a basket of two dozen fresh chicken eggs from Mr. Ma's family. (I had commented that duck eggs don't turn me on, and that the now-scarce chicken eggs are what we Americans normally eat for breakfast.)

A gift of two dozen freshly laid eggs. And another: from his hometown in a Yangzi River valley which, in an earlier era, was all under water, our geologist Mr. Qin has brought me a piece of exquisite red/gold/brown coral he assures me is three hundred million years old.

How I love these students, these eighteen men and four women who are all middle-aged, all educated in the fifties, and have all recently returned to work after ten years of idleness, physical labor, or imprisonment during the Cultural Revolution. I had asked them to write resumes; I was deeply impressed by their educational and scientific backgrounds, and by the fact that in every case extensive publications ran through '66 or '67, then resumed in '76 or '77.

And here they are, drawn from all over China to study English and Western culture before going abroad. A central fact of life abroad is the telephone. I don't have one of these either in or at hand, and miss neither the convenience nor the noise, but my students will soon live in a telephone society, so I can't neglect a lesson on the topic. We deal with information, operators, push buttons, pay phones, and long distance. I tell them about dial-a-prayer, the time of day, the weather, and, more important, local travel information. We clarify vocabulary, go from one practice dialogue to another, and do some role-playing. And then because I'd heard of foreign teachers arriving at the Shanghai airport to find no one to meet them, I ask:

"Now, suppose you arrive at Kennedy Airport in New York City and there's no one from the Chinese Consulate there to meet you. What will you do?"

Twenty-two pens are poised, twenty-two faces look up at me. Silence. I pace the narrow space between the blackboard and the long desk that's nailed to the foot-high platform. The students glance at one another. They're not embarrassed because they don't know the answer, but because *I*, the teacher, am not providing the information for them to write down and memorize. I pace, arms folded, unable to keep from smiling at the scene.

"I'm not going to be there with you to answer questions," I say, "so I guess you'll have to use the information you already have and figure it out yourselves. We call this 'self-reliance' or 'problem-solving.'"

"Oh," says Xiao Wang, "you mean we should cough someone."

"Right," I say, surpressing a giggle, "you would call or telephone someone." I turn and write "call" and "telephone" on the board. "Now who would you call and how would you get the number?"

And from here it's easy and fun.

During the break in our four-hour morning session, some students go out into the hall to smoke, others to do Chairman Mao's Four-Minute Exercises. Whatever the current status of the Great Helmsman, the

Liang Tai reads from the telephone lesson.

exercises remain part of most people's daily routine.

Other students stand in small groups discussing the news from home or from Beijing. They dutifully begin in English, but the need to get on with the content instead of fiddling with the form soon overwhelms them, and Chinese spills out from one group after another.

"Oh, well," I tell myself, "they need a break."

Liang Tai and I lean out of the fifth-floor classroom window. From here the view is spectacular; walking around the campus, you lose the nobility of the setting, principally because there is no grass. Someone has decided that grass brings disease-bearing creatures, so the grounds are either swirling dust in dry weather or knee-deep mud in the rainy season. But from up here, the sloping roofs with ancient-style, turned-up corners dominate, and the campus is circled on three sides by low, fluid mountains. Here, somehow, you assume your proper place in the scheme of things, like the tiny fisherman at the foot of a Chinese painting.

"It's there," says Liang Tai, pointing out to me the dormitory in which he and the other male students live.

"O.K.," I say. "What time shall I come?"

"Whatever is convenient for you," he says, ever polite.

"How about two o'clock?"

"Good."

Chinese Academy of Sciences English Class, October 1979–April 1980.

Wu Jianguo, one of Liang Tai's roommates, has been absent from class for two days. This means something is very wrong, so I've determined to go and visit him this afternoon in his dorm room.

"He *is* sick," Liang Tai tells me, "but I think the real problem is that he feels discouraged about his progress in English, and his institute is counting on him to attend conferences of Western chemists in the spring."

"Do you think he's homesick?" I ask, for Wu was one of the students unable to return home during the New Year's break.

Liang reaches for his dictionary, but I hold his arm. "Put back your 'bible.' You can figure it out yourself."

"'Home sick.' You mean sick to be at home? I like that," he says. "Yes, I think Wu misses his wife and children very much."

"And you?"

"I'm, uh, 'homesick' too, but I have relatives in Hangzhou so it isn't so bad for me."

Liang Tai, a cryogenicist, lives in Beijing with his wife, a physicist, and their two children. But Hangzhou is his hometown, and I have heard that his mother is ill and that every Sunday he borrows a bike, rides into town, and does her shopping, cleaning, and other chores. This is quite a burden as classes meet six days a week, and Sunday is the only full day for study and whatever little relaxation the students allow themselves.

Liang was also elected class monitor, which makes him responsible for innumerable tasks from assigning daily classroom clean-up to chairing the monthly meetings at which the students discuss their academic progress. Such a meeting was held last night, and Liang wants to give me a report.

"Shoot," I say, and he smiles because he has recently learned what that means.

"Everyone is enthusiastic about class, about your lectures, and about the dialogues you give us every day—"

"But—"

"But we do have one criticism."

I'm astonished to find that I cannot speak, but I try to look unperturbed.

"You aren't giving us enough work," he says. "We want more reading and more exercises and more writing assignments."

I can see that Liang is offended when I burst out laughing, but I'm so relieved, and I can't help but think of my students back home whining, "Do we hafta do that?"

"I think there are limits to how much anyone can absorb in one day," I tell him. Nonetheless, I promise to review my assignments and consider whether they—or I—can manage any more.

After class I go home for lunch. For a while I tried eating lunch a few times a week in the dining hall with the students, both because they're fun to be with and because it's a good time to practice "table talk." But though I'm a dedicated teacher, I'm no martyr, and the food was more— or rather worse and less—than I could stomach.

After lunch and a nap, I get on my bike and head back to campus. I steer around chickens crossing the road, dodge peasants with "honey buckets" bobbing on shoulder poles, swing past giggling children returning to school with arms around each other's waists and shoulders, and swerve out of the path of a man who has stopped dead in his tracks at the sight of a foreigner on a bicycle.

At the university gate I'm greeted by Chairman Mao, right hand raised in greeting, standing some 40 feet high. In fact, he stands precisely 12.26 meters high, for Mao Zedong was born on the twenty-sixth day of December. The university would like to rid itself of this Christ-like figure smack in the center of campus, but the statue was so solidly built that dynamite would be required to dislodge it. It's one thing to remove the late Chairman, quite another to blow him up.

I park behind the dorm, a cinder block and cement shoe box, cheerless save for the laundry that swings from every window. The halls are dark and damp, and little piles of refuse have been swept into corners. I have heard heated debates between older and younger students, the former complaining that the latter should take more pains to clean up their living quarters, the latter arguing that the university should hire and train more janitors.

It's easy enough to find their room, for the sound of a woman's voice comes from the door. I stand for a minute and listen to the recitation of one of this morning's practice dialogues with long "repeat after me" pauses between lines:

"Hello."

"Hello. Is this Dr. Smith's office?"

"Yes, it is. May I help you?"

"I'd like to speak to Dr. Smith, please."

"I'm sorry, he isn't in. May I ask who's calling?"

"My name is Wang Dawei."

"Oh, yes, Dr. Wang. Professor Smith said he wants to speak to you, and he asked me to give you his home number."

"Just a minute, please. I need to get a pen. O.K. What is his number?"

"It's 987–6532."

"That's 987–6532?"

"That's right."

"Thank you very much."

"Not at all. Good-bye."

"Good-bye."

I knock several times before my own machine-distorted voice is cut off, and Wu Jianguo opens the door. He is smiling, but I can see that his skin is pallid, his eyes tired, and his nose red. As he starts coughing, I notice that the room is stuffed with cigarette smoke, but I decide to keep my mouth shut for a while. Wu's blue pants and padded jacket hang loosely on his slightly stooped six-foot frame. His face is not handsome but clear and bright despite his bad cold, a face that displays the character that has made him one of China's foremost chemists.

"Nan Laoshi," he says, inclining his head, "welcome."

"*Xie xie ni,*" I respond, thanking him for his greeting that always fills me with pleasure, as the students well know.

Liang Tai motions me to sit down on one of the four bunk beds that occupy at least half the room, which is about 12 feet by 14 feet, all cement—walls, floor, and ceiling. Two narrow wooden tables run down the center, flanked by worn wooden benches. There's a single wardrobe for clothes and a metal stand with rings for enamel wash basins and metal arms for towels and washcloths. In this setting, eight undergraduates live and work seven days a week, eleven months a year. As my students are older, however, they live only four to a room.

Liang and Wu's roommates, Jian and Fang, push aside books, papers, tapes, cassette players, pens, and inkwells to make room on the desk for bags of pumpkin seeds and hard candies. They wash tea cups with boiling water from thermoses filled each morning at the dining hall, and hand me a cup of tea with a little lid on it. The lids are important in winter, for we are south of the Yangzi and therefore have no heat; the lids help keep the tea warm and the tea helps, a little, to keep the people warm.

What gets to me are the bars on the window. But we're on the first floor, and even with barred windows and locked doors, someone recently stole a cassette player from this room—a painful occurrence given the scarcity of quality recorders in China, their cost in relation to income, and their importance in language study.

We tease Wu about missing his wife, and about having psychosomatic illnesses. "You'll bounce back like the *gaoji ganbu,*" I tell him. At Christmas time he gave me two small, button-nosed, round-faced, red and green straw ornaments weighted on the bottom so that when you knock them over they bounce back "just like *gaoji ganbu,*" he had told me then, high-ranking party cadres.

As always, the conversation quickly returns to the mysteries of mastering English. "Simple," I say. "Less nodding over books eighteen hours a day and more R and R."

They consider this frivolous and remind me that they lost ten years during the Cultural Revolution, urgently need English to continue their scientific work, and have no time for what I myself taught them to call "monkey business."

"Go play basketball, walk in the park, read a bad novel—do something other than study and you'll learn more in the time you do study."

They look to Liang to rescue them from this temptress who would woo them from their work. There's a heated discussion in Chinese.

"We'll pick you up at your apartment after dinner tonight," says Liang, "and take a walk in the park. That way we can combine R and R with English practice. How's that?"

That evening, several of us stroll through a bamboo forest already throbbing with early signs of spring. Wu Jianguo, smoking and coughing, struggling to form English sentences and to find adequate vocabulary, describes some of China's three hundred varieties of bamboo and their thousands of uses from herbal medicines to construction scaffolding.

As we wander ancient pathways chatting about customs and habits, Wu and I find ourselves ahead of the others. "Do you realize how long we've been conversing in English?" I ask. "Could you have done that even a month ago?" He looks intently at the ground, and pushes gently with his toe at the tiny, delicate wild flowers at the foot of a bamboo tree.

We walk on and tell tales of our hometowns and families, and I find that Liang Tai has already discussed the word "homesick" with his classmates. It begins to dawn on me—this excursion has been organized not only to combine R and R with English practice, not only as an opportunity for me to encourage Wu, but also for *my* benefit: Liang's only explanation for my efforts to extricate them from their texts is that it is *I* who am homesick.

Am I? I certainly could go for a hot corned beef on rye with mustard or a large platter of assorted cheeses, but that hardly matches up with so weighty a word as "homesick." I recall being nostalgic last fall when I caught a few minutes of Macy's Thanksgiving Day Parade on the evening satellite news, but nostalgia hardly qualifies as homesickness either.

Am I lonely? Yes, sometimes. Despite all the bitterness, I long to be with Nayim. But I've never been nearly as lonely in China as I've been for long stretches of time in New York City. How can it be, I ask myself, that halfway around the world from home, you are neither lonely nor homesick?

The answer is obvious: I feel so useful, so needed, so wanted. I have classrooms full of students like Wu anguishing over English lessons, classrooms of students like Liang deeply concerned for my well-being as well as that of his classmates, classrooms of students who offer up to me daily the gifts of respect and affection. Here I am Nan Laoshi, Teacher Nan.

# 13
# Going Home, Coming Home

*April 16*
Thoroughly confused by N's letters, must make summer plans. Fantastic to think of Grand Tour of China, but as my mountain won't come here, could go home to try to work things out with him.

I study the map with each of the students as they plan their trips home—up here, down here, over here. I go to the train station almost every day as students spread out north, south, east, and west. Ms. Hua cries. A quiet, shy woman—who would have guessed she feels so strongly. It will take her a week to get to her home to Xishuangbanna by train, bus, and jeep. Wu Jianguo (whose English is so much better now) is silent. If he says anything, he, too, may cry. I promise I'll see them soon. In their own hometowns. I promise. I cry. All this crying is embarrassing.

*April 21*
Be his "friend!" His friend! Nice to know you, honey. Why don't we have dinner sometime? No thanks!

*May 4*
Five a.m. The sun glimmers on rice paddies, puffy white clouds—picture book scene. I was resigned. Resigned. Yet here are two more letters to stir up all the old anguish. "I want you as a friend, not as a wife," he says again. What does that mean?

Today is the anniversary of the 1919 May 4th Movement. As a teacher at a Chinese university, you'd think I could think of something more important than him, me, us.

*May 14*
He's right. It is I who have been unclear. He wants me "as a friend, not as a wife." This is something momentous, for he is using the word "friendship" as I myself defined it only a few months ago. If you mean

that we can live and work and make love on a basis of equality—rather than the old sense of husband and wife—oh, Nayim, I am so ready to be your friend.

*May 26*

Telegram: N passed his doctoral exams. "Congratulations" seems so small a word for so momentous an event. Now so eager to get home. Semester ends "in the middle of July," they say—this vague Third World time that waddles into operation whenever I want something from them, but marches away to precision timing whenever they want something from me.

*June 6*

Furnace. Yes. Precisely the word for Hangzhou summer. Tried so hard to be modest and indirect in my request for a fan, but as always broke down into loud demands after a couple of weeks. So now have this excellent fan made here in a Zhe Da factory, but a fan in a furnace nought availeth.

Bit scared about going home—how much pain has flowed across the ocean, across a year of our lives. Perhaps we can go away for a couple of weeks, somewhere cool and quiet where we can walk and talk and just be together. I so long for that.

*June 26*

It's getting to me. The heat. The absurd rules and regulations. The inefficiency. Trains, planes—everything so vague. Did manage to convince them to push up my exams by a couple of days, so leave here July 11—if the new Hangzhou-Hong Kong flight the papers talk about materializes, and if I get a seat on this maybe flight. "If 'ifs' and 'ands' were pots and pans there'd be no need for tinkers."

*July 3*

Heat insufferable. Furious. Can't even tell N when due. No planes from H to HK despite touted newspaper articles—why don't *they* understand how slowly things move here? China Travel Service—service! ha!—will not reserve a ticket. I must be in Shanghai exactly two days before flight to line up for ticket. Can't run up there as this is exam time, and Foreign Affairs Office will not help. Thought I was being so nice taking RMB instead of U.S. dollars I'm entitled to by contract. Other people extract full CAAC fare in foreign currency, then make their way by train and Dingbat Airlines and enjoy the loot. I tried to do that, then felt so bad about "cheating" the university, confessed all to Lao Fan. What a jerk I am!

*July 9*

Grad students here for a visit last night. "You must be eager to go home to see your mother," one said. "My mother?!!" I blurted out, having agonized last night through a thousand scenarios of reunion with N. "Well, yes, I'll certainly visit with my mother, but it's my husband I'm eager to see." They all laughed: "We would have thought that," one said, "but would never have said it."

*July 11*
"La Familia" saw me off to Shanghai this morning, the whole crowd. People on train recognize me from picture published with article on American youth in *Zhejiang Daily*—circulation about one million. Kind of fun being a celebrity.

Lao Fan has arranged for old friend to meet me in HK. Wired N anticipated date of arrival.

*July 15*
Hong Kong a big candy store after China. Lao Fan's friend Ying sends car to airport for me, books hotel room, wines and dines and chauffeurs me everywhere. Won't know how to find anything but McDonald's when I return to HK. Hideously hot and stuffy. Fun place to visit but sure wouldn't want to live here. From fabulous mansions high up in the hills, look down at the bustling harbor and miserable tin shacks of the "masses." In China, "rich" and "poor" are not so far apart, and conspicuous consumption is still frowned upon.

*July 22*
The United States of America! New York City. Home. Home, Nayim, with you. Oh, love, here in your arms "bittersweet" has new meaning. Everything is so intense. I'd forgotten how tender you are, how much I love you. The old adage is backwards: presence makes the heart grow fonder—though perhaps it takes absence to make so meaningful the presence. And with it all I feel your hurt and anger, your silent words that say I left you, abandoned you. I think of a student years ago writing of her "crossed emotions."

*July 28*
NY shocking. Inflation staggering. Walk into supermarket and out again. Subway fare up to sixty cents. Beggars wait at turnstiles for change. Neighborhood noisy, filthy, wretched. No wonder he's been such a wreck!

*August 1*
Everyone asks questions I can't begin to answer. Hard to explain that in Hangzhou I have less access to political gossip, policy changes, struggles, than people here. Enjoying my minicelebrity status—wined and dined and viewed as "the China expert." Saw Mother. Funny to think she knows nothing of N. Imagine leading such a double life in China. She

says my niece Terry is in HK. I haven't seen her in fifteen or twenty years. Why didn't anyone tell me before? Imagine explaining our family relationships to Li Xumei. Will wire Terry before I go back.

*August 9*
Put our bikes on a bus and off to Connecticut. The Chinese are quite right in calling America *Meiguo*, "beautiful country." Endless miles of trees and grass, lakes and creeks, lovely houses tucked away on hills and mountainsides. Such peace. Such privacy. All unknown in China with its billion people settled on such severely limited arable land.

Yes. This place is right for us—a quiet, lovely, inexpensive room in an old farmhouse near a lake. The whole place is ours. We have a dear little "sitting room" adjoining our bedroom, with a brandy decanter and glasses. We bike, swim, talk, make love, again make love, and sit in the little room sipping brandy, reading stories to each other, talking, talking, relieved to exchange feelings in seconds instead of weeks. There's much gender and culture confusion, much misunderstanding about marriage and friendship and what it means at this point in history to be a "liberated" woman *or* man.

But we've both grown so much, and perhaps that's why, despite the waves of anguish rolling over a whole year of days, we love each other still: Nayim is willing and able to learn and to grow. It was right to come home. Things will be better this year. For now, the closeness is all.

*August 20*
N and I reading from *All Under Heaven*, dreadful Pearl Buck novel picked up in dusty old Conn. bookstore. Cinderella and Prince Charming—Russian-born Nadia and American-born Malcolm—meet and marry in Beijing, and live there happily ever after for twenty-five years until the Communist Revolution drives them back to America. Here they are on their first day in New York:

> They stopped a few minutes later to wonder at a shop window on Fifth Avenue, and looking at Nadia, Malcolm saw tears pouring down her cheeks. He was not troubled. Nadia had the Russian need to weep and she did so easily and often . . . " [N laughs and says, "Oh, that explains a great deal about you."]
>
> "It is wonderful to see not a beggar," Nadia sobbed. "Not one, Malcolm! Where are they? Can it be true that here is not one beggar?"
>
> "Since you do not see them, I suppose there are none," he replied reasonably . . . .
>
> "Now," she said. She wiped her eyes and laughed suddenly. "I am crying because I need not to see hungry people any more. Oh, I do love America already!"

The irony of it: Now Nadia would have to go to China "to see not a beggar" (or hardly a one). It seems to me things have deteriorated in New York in just one year. Poverty has increased, the subway is certainly worse. I'm shocked by the staggering waste of paper, glass, plastic, metals. And the prices! Embarrass N more than once by exclaiming aloud about the cost of ordinary vegetables or coffee or paper towels. "You'd think you'd been to the moon," he says. Perhaps.

The best: hot running water, marvelous Mozart, great coffee, magnificent museums, jazz and more jazz, unimaginable everything from soup to nuts—and no lines to stand in. (Beware, my dear, you're gaining about a pound a week.) Best of all, the people, the wild, wonderful parade of people of every color in every kind of dress. Told N about the albino I once saw in Hangzhou—poor stark-white woman amidst the sea of black-haired Han.

The worst: *Dressed to Kill.* Told it's an artsy satire of sex and violence films. Missed the satire for the blood, gore, disease, dismemberment, sickness and perversion that begins at the beginning and doesn't stop till you come to the end. Told N about British version of *Cinderella*—satinned, silked, and white-wigged ladies and gents of the court discourse about glass slippers in badly dubbed Chinese, then jump up on tables and burst into song in English.

*August 22*
Met today with group of Chinese scholars collecting in New York to leave for home after a year or two. Asked what advice they would offer their friends preparing to come abroad:

• Examine program content because titles differ in China (especially in social sciences), so you may end up in field not your own.

• If you pick a famous professor, he's off lecturing and his assistant is running things. You work much less with professors than expected—they may not show up at the lab for weeks at a time.

• You may find people willing to help and share, or you may find cutthroat competition.

• Try not to be so modest: If you say your English is not very good or that you are not an expert in your field, you may find yourself washing bottles all day in the laboratory.

• Postdoctorates should be clear before they come what is planned for them, or they too will find themselves sweeping floors.

• China should send more people to state universities. Not everything is happening at Harvard and MIT.

• You may find that you already know what is being taught, but the equipment here is generally much more advanced than in China; units should authorize scholars to purchase equipment.

• Not much English is needed for lab work, but if your English is good, you'll be able to attend classes and learn a great deal more.

• It is ideal if you can arrange to live with English-speaking people, but the only way to manage on $5,000 a year is for five or six to live and eat together. Food (especially rice and chicken) is very cheap, but rent is *very* expensive.

• There is much less socializing than expected. Early on, you're invited to dinner once or twice, but then you're on your own.

• Many receive letters from the Guomindang here or in Taiwan saying, "We got your letter and know how much you want to be free," etc. Don't be concerned. The embassy knows this is happening.

• We must be realistic about what we can accomplish abroad. We must not expect—and our units and families must not expect—that we will all produce Nobel-quality work in two years. We all do our very best, but there are many variables. Two comrades recently committed suicide here, one because he learned he was terminally ill, the other because he felt people at home would be disappointed in his accomplishments here. That is very sad.

*August 23*
Oh, love. How shall I leave you again? Remember: one year is easier to measure than two, and this time we're both going off, I back to China, you to the Middle East to do research and visit your family. After you return and sort through your research, it will be time to come and travel with me in China. And yet the Russian woman weeps.

*August 26*
Slept in every Korean Airlines terminal in world, I think. Lost track of hours, days. Not jet lag, but jet chasm. Terry at HK airport. Would recognize anywhere my secret sharer—me at precisely half my age. Find myself envious: she's fluent in Mandarin, learning Cantonese, knows lots of Chinese history, art, etc., travels and works all over Far East. What wonders the women's movement hath wrought, that she can do in twenties—with knowledge, language skills, strength, and confidence—what I in forties fumble about in. Now glad we haven't known each other all these years as we can be friends instead of aunt and niece (though am taken everywhere for her mother). Would be fun to travel with her in China—she'll try.

Bought: small refrigerator to be shipped to Hangzhou; classical and jazz tapes; Chinese mustard—not coals to Newcastle as no one in H ever heard of mustard even when I showed them the character in my dictionary; bales of bullion cubes and packages of instant soup, boxes of Aunt J's pancake mix and Kellogg's and Cream of Wheat, mayonnaise, salami, cans, jars, boxes, bags . . . . And I was the one to live the simple

Chinese life! T says she'll box and ship it all to me.

*August 27*
Trouble with China Travel Service. Can't get me train or boat ticket before Sept. 1, but visa expires Aug. 31. Much to-do.

*August 29*
CTS says it can't be done. Must apply (and pay) for new entry visa. No amount of hand-wringing about classes starting makes any difference. Big rip-off. Made them wire Lao Fan about the mess.

*September 5*
Pleasant pontoon trip up Pearl River from HK to Canton, but disappointed: wanted to take train across bridge into China. Canton horrendous. Not even in Shanghai are there such crowds and traffic jams. Head straight for airport, luck out on direct flight to Hangzhou.

*September 6*
Whole family at the airport to meet me. Madam Lo furious because I'm late, everyone else happy to see me again. Funny—feels like coming home.

# 14
## Changes

Like the moon, like the tide, like eternity itself, workers plod along dirt roads, harnessed before endless cartloads of soil, passing their doubles bearing back empty carts to be reloaded. Standing on my balcony, mesmerized by this sight, I feel an intruder in history, at once irked by the idiotic inefficiency of this parade, yet swayed by the ancient rhythms of the work. They come and go, all day, every day, as they have forever, as they surely will forever.

But their project is the opposite of eternity, the end of the forever that has been. I think of the old Chinese story (oft quoted by Mao) of the Foolish Old Man who believed that if he chipped away at the mountain for his lifetime, and his sons and grandsons did so after him, the mountain could be moved, the sunlight would shine in his window. Mao had in mind the twin mountains of imperialism and feudalism that sat upon the backs of the Chinese people, but I mean it literally: Day by day, *mu* by *mu*, the commune next door is being swallowed up by progress, by the need for the new, by the need for a higher standard of living for the Chinese people.

It works this way: Each patch of land grows a particular crop; as the crop is harvested, that area is filled in as the site for more university housing, an annex for the elementary school, a China Travel Service apartment building, or the snazzy pink "foreign guest" building with adjacent dining room and meeting hall now slated to open next September. (I'm glad I didn't hold my breath.)

And the peasants who have worked the land since time immemorial? The unit that buys the land must employ them. This enables the peasants to keep their own houses (at least for the present) and be slowly absorbed into the working class. Older peasants generally are given clean-up jobs; others work in one of the university's factories or on local construction sites. This all seems to be a carefully planned process, for the land purchased by Zhe Da and other units belongs to a small brigade that will soon cease to exist, while the lands of the larger, more productive communes adjacent to the university remain pretty much intact—at least for now. These communes also participate in the process, however, gradually consuming their own land with new factories, turning still more peasants into workers.

What will people eat if such good, arable land is no longer cultivated as it has been for centuries? I'm told there's a plan: production is increased on some crops while others are phased out and the land sold or developed, and all of this is done within the framework of state and local requirements for the locality (and, thus, the communes within it) to produce specified amounts of specific crops, especially staples like rice.

One evening, wandering up into the hills behind the university with some of this year's class of scientists, I stop to peer in the open door of a peasant's house to find the family just sitting down to dinner—at this time of year they work *very* long days. They insist we come in to see their new house and chat a while. I notice how easy is the rapport between the scientists and the peasants and wonder if it is the product of my students' good natures or of their years in the countryside.

The family expresses no nostalgia about the gradual loss of land. As they're in good part paid in grain, they're happy to find their income rising rapidly as family members become workers. Furthermore, factory work is easier than farming, and workers get cotton and other scarce-item coupons. (I've noticed that local peasants often come around selling eggs, peanuts, or other extra crops in exchange for coupons instead of money.)

It's been an unusual summer and fall, they tell us, cold and wet. This has had a disastrous effect on the crops. The shortage of vegetables, though hardly a crisis situation, is very noticeable, and the weather has damaged both the late spring and early fall rice crops. (Already the reduction of rice-producing acreage, so neat on paper, is exacerbating the problem.) It's going to be a hard year for producer and consumer alike—but not for me: Lao Fan has his *guanxi* (connections) and asks how much top-grade rice I'd like to squirrel away for the winter.

As we stand to leave we shake hands all around, and I, wishing to thank them for their time and trouble in proper Chinese fashion, trot out my sentence about how much trouble we have caused them. Only I get it backwards, letting them know in no uncertain terms how much trouble *they* have caused *us*. Everybody laughs heartily at my mistake.

I guess I've changed, too, mellowed some by my month in America. Though I still write long, detailed letters to friends and family, and though I still write regularly to Nayim, who is off doing research in the Middle East, I have set aside my diary, which had served so well to sop up the small agonies of the previous year.

Paul Fast has gone back to America. I miss his wry humor and disinterested observations. But there are three new American teachers now, all housed here instead of the Hangzhou Hotel. Above me lives Zang Jiemi (Jenny), a Chinese-American woman in her fifties, who had not been back to China since she left as a teenager. Many of her family members were killed or suffered badly during the Cultural Revolution; she's trying to come to terms with this, with her culture, her identity.

Darrell and Fred, who share the apartment across from hers, are like yin and yang. They've been hired through Volunteers in Asia. They aren't trained teachers (and, therefore, come cheap) but seem to be doing well in the classroom and relating well to the younger Zhe Da students. Darrell is one of those serious sorts who runs the same distance at the same hour every day, studies Chinese assiduously, won't lend you a tape unless you clean your tape heads first, meticulously cleans his apartment, and compulsively prepares his classes. He will surely be in the State Department's Far East Division one day. Fred is an easygoing, pleasant fellow who plays the guitar and suffers only from the need to remain scrupulously aloof from the lovely young female students who flock around him.

Proper conduct requires Chinese of the same surname, town, region, or province to be responsible for orienting and helping one another in new circumstances. Thus Li Xumei assumes that I, the old-timer here, will become the "responsible person" in this little foreign community. Not likely. Though even more impatient than I with inefficiency and backwardness, Jenny is Chinese-born and has friends among the Zhe Da deans with whom she attended college in the States in the 1940s. The boys, of course, are off on their own, wanting little commerce with and less advice from an old lady like me.

There have been other changes since I left here in July. We have zip codes now (though no one uses them), and Chinese-made frisbees (called *fripan—pan* meaning dish or plate) whiz about in the neighborhood, rivaling badminton as the daily outdoor sport. But best of all we have water—cold, of course, but water. Regularly. All day, every day. Will wonders never cease!

A distinctly unpleasant, in fact unnerving change is in the peace and tranquillity I so enjoyed last year. One sound is especially haunting. It seems symbolic—though in truth I don't know what it's symbolic of. There is a retarded child in the building across from mine. For several hours every day he beats on a wok with chopsticks. (This is my image; Jenny thinks it's a fork on a pot lid.) Sometimes his pace is steady and rhythmic, sometimes chaotic, frantic, driving. He sings a pathetic little song to this music, sounding as though he were in the doctor's office

Noisy stone-chomping machines for road paving.

with a tongue depressor in his mouth and gravel in his tonsils. He's supervised by a woman I assume is his grandmother. Mildly retarded people are looked after by the neighborhood committee and given whatever tasks they're able to perform. There's also a mental institution not far off.

The boy has competition from the construction site that has crept into my backyard over the summer. The building of auxiliary classrooms for the elementary school has developed apace, which in fact it should since two shifts run from 5 a.m. to 10 p.m. There's the putt-putt of motors, the clanging of pipes, the twanging of instruments on metal, the buzzing of saws, the banging of hammers on wood, the scraping of thousands of stones dropped onto the sidewalk, shoveled into creaky old carts, dumped on the roads, pushed around, then chomped up to bits by ancient stone-chomping machines. It's like living in the middle of a perpetual basketball game, for the workers use whistle signals to inform crane operators where and when to load and unload.

Then there are the human sounds: groans of workers struggling to lift immense cinder blocks on metal poles run through the centers, iambic work songs that set the pace and ease the way for men and women deftly balancing construction materials on shoulder poles, shouts and hoots and laughter and banter. I love these scenes when I pass them on the road; up close and constant, however, it's Excedrin headache #840. Saddest of all, the songs of the school children are drowned out.

I can hardly blame the itinerant workers for being so expansive during the day. Though well-paid, they return at night to their "dormitories"—long row of sleeping mats in jerry-rigged barracks. That's it. I often see the men outside the door washing in enamel basins. (What they use for toilets I haven't asked.)

No engineer I, but I'm fascinated by the "plan ahead" elements of this construction project. When I moved here there was a neat brick wall behind our complex. Apparently it was in the way of the construction site, so one day they tore it down and, the same day, built another. A few weeks later I noticed that to facilitate movement of machines and materials into the site, a huge hole was knocked right through the wall. But I guess the hole wasn't big enough, for the next day they tore down the whole wall and put up yet another a few yards away from the site of the last one. You understand, of course, that the buildings are not yet built—the foundations have hardly been poured—but there must be exterior walls. I believe that I'm witnessing the collective unconscious at work, a deeply embedded need to enclose within the family, the clan, the community, the county, the city, the nation, and to shut without all alien elements (spirit and human). For two thousand years walls partitioned one administrative unit from another, clearly delineating the sphere of influence (and graft rights) of each bureaucrat.

On our side of the new brick wall, ground-floor apartment gardens are dumps for bricks, cinder blocks, and huge cement slabs of different shapes and forms, sometimes stacked up neatly, sometimes strewn about in designs that would surely win awards in modern sculpture contests. I've thought of taking pictures, but I couldn't think what I'd say to someone who asked me why I was photographing a bunch of cement slabs.

Perhaps to compete with the general noise level, or perhaps because there are so many more of them now, radios and TVs are turned up full blast every evening. At 10, however, the workers retire, the TVs are hushed, and the world winds down for another day. Occasionally the cry of an infant is heard. At 7:30 a.m. comes bugle call for first class—sounds like the U.S. Army or, worse, summer camp.

Another sad change has occurred in my life here. This time it's my fault and I'm kicking myself for it. I've lost Xiao Zhou, my *xiao meimei*. Before I left for the States last summer, Madam Lo asked me if Xiao Zhou was good at her work. I said that I loved her dearly, but I couldn't resist the flip comment that she knows as much about housekeeping as I know about nuclear physics. Fool that I am! They sent her back to the typing office and will not reconsider their decision. I ask myself why I was so stupid, and can only answer that the idea of having a maid, a servant, was anathema to me.

If Xiao Zhou was excessive in her care and concern for me, the new *aiyi*, Xiao Tu, is dull and close to useless. She "works" half a day for Jenny and half for me. We've come to call her "Little Miss Mei You." *Mei you* means "there isn't any" or "they don't have any," which is what she comes back with whenever we send her to buy anything from bamboo shoots to toilet paper. In a way I admire her ability to do what she likes to do and avoid what she doesn't; she loves to prepare Chinese medicines and is therefore useful to Jenny, and she does like to do wash, a big help to me.

The university is certainly into *jinjinjijiao*—squaring accounts to the last fen. At 7 a.m. someone from the accounting office shows up with some unpaid fuel bills from shopping trips in town last July, and they want not only my word but receipts for every penny I spent getting from here to New York and back. I don't have receipts (though I did keep records), so they want me to return to them the difference between what they gave me (in RMB, mind you), and what I can prove on paper. I'm insulted. Angry. Consider what I saved them by accepting renminbi instead of foreign currency for my trip (which I didn't have to do), that I brought here nineteen cartons of books and never asked a penny reimbursement in any currency, that I saved them $400 in excess baggage charges from Paris, and (though this is hardly their affair) what these two years cost me in lost salary, lost pension, etc. Lao Fan mediates; we compromise.

Then I go to class where I'm interrupted by a man from the media center, which houses a sophisticated collection of high-priced, high-tech Japanese equipment someone will surely find some use for someday. He's come to tell me he'd be glad to comply with my request to show my new classes the videotape of the social customs lecture I recorded last year. But electricity is expensive; I must pay eighty yuan out of my own pocket. The man stands open-mouthed as I rant and rave at him in English, which my students refrain from translating. They gently maneuver him out the door and calm me down. Lao Fan mediates; we compromise. They will show the tape if the session is open to all university students. Fine with me.

Another sad new thing. Last week I saw three beggars in town. (So much for my plans for Pearl Buck's Nadia and Malcolm to come back to China!) I've heard there are many beggars up north where agricultural conditions are so poor. But people live pretty well down here. One ragged-looking child said his mother is dead, his father an invalid, and he needs money. Yao says she thinks it's nonsense because the father's or the deceased mother's unit would look after the family members. I have no way to know what's true.

The Hangzhou Hotel (where I still go regularly to borrow a bathtub) is in new hands. There is a perhaps apocryphal story that Mismanager Li, in his soft, subtly pinstriped Mao suits, has been kicked upstairs into a deanship at Hang Da. The hotel has acquired an automatic coffee-maker whose instructions no one can read, and in the CAFE STRAIGHT AHEAD, a small band muddles nightly through Western ditties.

My minirefrigerator arrives from Hong Kong and, with more of Lao Fan's *guanxi*, glides through customs. I am now the most popular person on campus—the only one with access to *cold* beer.

I have great plans for this refrigerator as I eagerly await the arrival of goodies Terry sent from Hong Kong. From an appliance store she got an empty TV carton, packed it, and lugged it to the post office only to be told that it was too heavy to ship. She dragged the thing home, scrounged three liquor store cartons, and repacked and hauled them back to the post office where she filled out sundry customs forms. A clerk informed her she was not permitted to send food to China. She put the three boxes in a cab and went across town to another post office where she filled out the customs forms all over again, this time indicating that the cartons contained books and other reading materials. The clerk marked and stamped and smiled and sent them off to China.

I receive two of them. The third never appears and is soon forgotten. One day Lao Fan informs me that some customs officials will "visit" me tomorrow afternoon at three. "Is that convenient for you?" he asks. What have I done now? What terrible thing has some misguided friend (or guided enemy) sent across the border?

At precisely three o'clock a jeep pulls up. Three customs officials swing out of it while I compute the cost of the scarce gasoline that brought them here. One is the driver. The second is a gentleman in a spiffy white uniform who speaks no English and, as far as I can determine, serves the purpose of protecting the female officer from dangerous foreigners. The woman is life itself: her braids shine against her vibrant face, her smile is sunshine. I think about the FBI, the old mean agent/friendly agent business. Lao Fan tells me Ms. Wang was his student in Beijing. That accounts for her excellent English.

I serve candies and cookies and tea and coffee—expensive coffee from the box of "books" from Hong Kong. We discuss the weather and the rice crop. I'm getting nervous. At last we get to the matter at hand: A package arrived for me from Hong Kong before the October Moon Festival. Yes? Shanghai customs officials wrote to Hangzhou customs officials, whose responsibility it is to settle a rather delicate matter. Yes? Well, you see, in the box is a broken bottle of mmmm . . . Yes? She tries several pronunciations, but I'm lost. She unfolds a letter and copies the word "mayonnaise."

They're really upset about it. They're worried about how they can possibly repay me for such a terrible loss. "You're putting me on," I say. "Pardon?" she says. Out of the kindness of my heart, I agree they can look on the bottle top to find the price in Hong Kong dollars, convert it to renminbi, and send it to me. How relieved they are. How relieved I am. We drink more coffee.

A couple of weeks later I get a letter from Shanghai customs; they will send me one yuan and twenty fen to compensate for the broken item, and hope that will be satisfactory. A week later I get a notice to bring my I.D. to the P.O. to pick up the money. Still no box. In November the carton comes to the international post office in town, so I have to get Zhang Chefu and pay for the gas to pick it up. In a plastic bag, customs has carefully placed the broken bottle, which has, of course, cut right through the plastic, so everything else in the box is coated Hellman's yellow and dotted with small slivers of glass. And what is this large lump of green mold? In its day, it must have been that irresistible Italian salami, and it must have cost about ten times as much as the mayonnaise.

What I'd like to know is this: Was all this customs business for real, or was it an elaborately staged means of indirect communcation with foreigners about lies on customs forms and the misuse of the PRC mails?

# 15
# Oh Dear, Ann Landers

Now I'm in trouble.

It's not *Huck Finn*. I can handle that. A new edition has just been published, and my junior students have bought out the shipment. They easily grasp the plot—which they love—and glean a good deal of the humor, but as serious English language mavens, they press their noses to their "bibles" and try to decipher every word and phrase:

> "What's de harem?"
>
> "The place where he keeps his wives. Don't you know about the harem? Solomon had one; he had about a million wives."
>
> "Why, yes, dat's so; I—I'd done forgot it. A harem's a bo'd'n-house, I reck'n. Mos' likely dey has rackety times in de nussery. En I reck'n de wives quarrels considable; en dat 'crease de racket. Yit dey say Sollermun de wises' man dat ever liv'. I doan take no stock in dat. Bekase why: would a wise man want to live in de mids' er sich a blim-blammin' all the time? . . .
>
> "Well, but he *was* the wisest man, anyway; because the widow she told me so, her own self."
>
> "I doan' k'yer what de widder say, he *warn't* no wise man nuther. He had some er de dad-fetchedes' ways I ever see. Does you know 'bout dat chile dat he 'uz gwyne to chop in two?"

Dictionaries in hand, *Huck Finn* all marked and underlined, the eager youngsters come to me asking for definitions, grammatical analyses, and textual explications.

All this is no problem. Words can be defined, dialect explained, Biblical stories retold, and even post-Liberation children have read or heard about the old system of concubinage.

But now I'm in trouble. Our junior class monitor, Qu Aimin, has come to tell me that every student knows every word of *English for Today Book IV: Our Changing Technology*, that *English for Today Book V: Our Changing Culture* has just arrived in the bookstore, and, oh what an opportunity it would be for them to do that book with *me!*

Sure. Why not? I can teach English out of one text as well as another, and if they're excited about this, why, all the better. So Qu Aimin gathers a few of his fellow students and we ride off six abreast in the misty rain to the bookstore. I ask their names: they are Qi, Qu, Zhu, Zhang, and Zhiang, but would I call them by their Western names? Oh, gladly. Gliding along on my left and right they introduce themselves: Roderick, Wellington, Rochester, Humphrey, and Heathcliff.

We arrive at a building behind the Foreign Language Bookstore on the other side of West Lake. My literati are welcome. I am not. I am a foreigner. Foreigners, says the ancient sentry at the door, are not allowed. I take out my handy dandy bright red with gold lettering two-inch-square photo I.D. book to prove that I belong, that I am not any old foreigner, that I have a work unit—the Foreign Language Teaching Group of Zhejiang University.

No good. I can buy anything I want in that store over there, but nothing in this one over here. I'm getting angry. In a most un-Chinese tone of voice, I demand, through Qu Aimin, to know what sort of silliness this is. The old man finally admits that the store is stocked with pirated editions of books of all nations; he has been ordered to admit no foreigner. True that I stand before my classes each day teaching out of pirated texts, but they must be provided by my unit.

Sunday night: Lao Fan delivers my precious copy of the book with its thin, sickly yellow paper cover. I turn quickly past the first few tissue paper pages, which faithfully reproduce all the copyright information, and come to the material I've assigned to my students—sight unseen. On the first page of the first chapter of *English for Today Book V: Our Changing Culture* I find:

Dear Ann Landers:

My step-daughter is in high school. She is only fourteen but she has the body of an eighteen-year-old. The problem is she has the mind of a ten-year-old. We have told her no dating in cars until she is sixteen, but . . .

Reader from the Old School

Oh, lord, now I'm in trouble. The junior class (the first to enter the university on the exam system after the Cultural Revolution) includes students who came directly from middle school, and others who worked in factories and fields for years, but managed to pass the entrance exams. Thus they range from twenty to thirty years of age, are unmarried, and—from all I can discern—thoroughly untutored in bird-and-bee-related matters.

My mind flashes back to the New Year's Eve dance. I arrive at "the club," a hall that seats 2,500 for lectures. People who couldn't get tickets are hanging around outside, while inside, several hundred students (three-quarters male) appear magnetically attached to the four walls. The "Blue Danube" scratches away on an old record player. No one dances. But knowing that dancing was forbidden during the Cultural Revolution, and that science students are not the most socially progressive people in town, the dance organizers have imported students from the liberal arts school next door. "Students in the Hang Da English department practice dancing every night," someone whispers to me in awe.

Indeed, they can waltz and do some fancy fox trot steps, and they do get the ball rolling; soon thirty or forty couples—men and women, women and women, men and men—are making some effort, one partner trying to teach the other the little he or she knows. Almost everyone galumphs about in layers and layers of essential winter clothing, the occasional person in slim bell-bottoms looking very risqué (and very cold). A few of the women wear dressy brown or pink velvet jackets, sparkling scarves, and beauty-parlor hair combs.

Bernard Shaw, who said that dancing is "the vertical realization of a horizontal desire," would retract his words this New Year's Eve, for there is not an alluring movement even among the technically most advanced dancers.

Now, how am I going to explain Old School and her fourteen-year-old daughter to all these sweet innocents?

Monday morning, 7:30 a.m. I look around at the thirty-five eager young faces, the crew cuts above the tidy blue and grey jackets, the pink- and yellow-ribboned braids dangling on flowered blouses.

When I published my article on American youth in the *Zhejiang Daily* last July, all references to premarital sex and pregnancy (as well as drugs) were deleted, ostensibly because Chinese youth would not understand, but actually, I assume, for fear that if Western kids did it, why, then . . . .

"Let's begin with vocabulary," I suggest, venturing timidly into the mined harbor. "Are there any words or phrases that are unclear?"

A long silence. A hand. A young man in his late twenties with the face of a fourteen-year-old stands.

"The letter is signed 'Reader from the Old School.' Can you explain what the 'Old School' is?"

Ah, good, I think, safe entry into the channel.

"The term 'Old School' suggests that there is also a 'New School,'" I remark, "that there is a gap—in this case, what we call a 'generation gap'—between the attitudes, ideas, and values of one generation and those of another."

That seems innocuous enough, I tell myself, but a queasy feeling reminds me that someone may ask just what the values of these particular old and new schools *are*.

Another hand, another earnest young face.

"What is the meaning of 'body of an eighteen-year-old and mind of a ten-year-old'?"

I glance around to see if this is a facetious question, but there are neither giggles nor smiles.

I think of Lao Fan's assurance that his son, who until very recently has lived in one room with his father and mother, knows absolutely nothing about sex.

"An eighteen-year-old, uh, person is physically matured, uh, biologically, uh, complete," I venture. Tiny smile lines appear at corners of mouths. "A ten-year-old mind, on the other hand, doesn't know right from wrong, understands nothing about the sexual implications of physical development . . . ." Confusion. Stares. I hear them thinking: "A fourteen-year-old girl? What can the professor be talking about?"

"Could you explain 'no dating in cars'?" asks another young man.

"An American can get a driver's permit at the age of sixteen. Parents may then lend their cars to teenagers when they go out on dates, say, to the movies. We even have something called 'drive-in movies' with big, outdoor screens such as you have near your dormitory, only instead of bringing stools to sit on, people come in their automobiles, park, and then sit in their cars to watch the movie."

"Is there a difference between a 'car' and an 'automobile'?" someone asks.

"No," I answer, wondering at this endless interest in vocabulary when such world-shaking matters are at hand.

"Does Old School object to her daughter seeing a movie?" asks the same young man, as though following my thoughts.

"Quite the opposite," I answer. "She objects to her *not* seeing the movie, that is, she objects to what the girl is doing with her boyfriend in the back seat of the car *instead* of watching the movie—basically the same thing that some of you might do under the bushes in the park," I add, doubting that this is accurate, but not wishing to be more explicit.

My former housekeeper, Xiao Zhou, aged twenty, maintained she had no idea where babies come from. I chose not to enlighten her.

A Shanghai friend told me she became pregant on her wedding night. Despite what her female neighbors told her that very afternoon, she made no connection between sex and pregnancy.

"Look. This is not the way to approach this matter," I say, backing the boat out to safer waters. "Let's begin with a discussion of the dating habits of Chinese men and women." The words "men" and "women" already sum up the impossibility of explaining "Old School's" dilemma, for in China men and women are "boys" and "girls" until they marry, generally in their late twenties or early thirties.

More flashes during a long silence. I call on Qu Aimin, figuring he owes me one. He maintains that college students rarely date because they are deeply concerned about their studies, and that association with the opposite sex might interfere because "one thing leads to another."

Aha! So there is some idea that "one thing leads to another"—but "one thing" and "another" remain unnamed, so I'm not sure we're even talking the same language. I try out the topic of "the good-night kiss" and am surprised by the free-wheeling discussion (though the girls don't participate):

"If the girl wants the kiss, it's O.K., but the boy can't compel her. If she doesn't want to be kissed she shouldn't let the boy pay for the movie or the tea and cakes. If he pays the bill, she should give him the kiss."

"That sounds like pre-Liberation China when women were just property. A good-night kiss is a moral question: it means 'I love you,' not 'thank you.'"

"A good-night kiss seldom happens. It depends on mutual understanding. If you like and know each other very well, there's no problem. Of course you shouldn't force her—a kiss is not a question of money."

"We have no experience with kisses, but it sounds very nice. It's true, though, that you have to be very careful because even a smile or a handshake is serious. A girl's reputation can be ruined by a good-night kiss. People will say she is 'fun.'"

"Everyone would like a good-night kiss, especially from a beautiful girl. I don't think she becomes "fun" if you give her a kiss. We should change these feudal ideas in our country."

"Kiss or no kiss, if she finds out you have no money and no prospects, the girl will brush you off."

"Some girls are like that, but not all of them. Anyway, I don't think the boy should always pay the bill. If you share, then the kiss is clear; it has nothing to do with money."

I can't help but smile—this debate is *so* fifties. It brings me back to the days when my own eighteen-year-old body of a fourteen-year-old was stuffed under my too-small school desk, my fingers stuck in my ears against the sing-song screams of the air raid test sirens warning that the dirty Commies—in my mind, bright yellow Russians with no regard for human life—were going to swim across the seas and, with their evil concept of "Free Love," destroy the American Family. Yipes!

Some days later, Nan Nan and Li Lei, two of the three girls in the junior class, stop by my apartment for a visit. Li Lei admits she has a "friend," though both girls assure me she is the only person in our class who does. And Li Lei is worried: students are not permitted to marry, and when they graduate, there's no knowing where the government might send each of them.

Nan Nan scorns her friend. From her point of view, it was stupid to have allowed such a relationship to develop. She steers clear of boys, keeping her mind on her studies and her eye on her career in high-speed photography.

"You start to think about a boy," she says, "and the next thing you know you can't concentrate on your books any more. You're thinking about when and where you can meet him again, what you can or cannot do . . . ."

"It sounds to me as though you have some experience in these matters," I suggest.

"None." Nan Nan is offended. "I room with Li Lei so I can see what happens."

Li Lei looks uncomfortable under her friend's gaze, and admits that the relationship has affected both her own and her boyfriend's concentration, and that the competition for grades is very serious because they, too, want to be good scientists at top institutes.

I try to think how to approach the question of sex, and decide on an oblique inquiry: "Do you use birth control when you sleep with your friend?" I ask.

Both girls stare at me. Li Lei turns purple, tries to imitate a turtle, and mumbles, "Oh, we wouldn't—I mean—well, he kissed me, but . . . "

Some snooping around Zhe Da turns up more campus "friendships" than Nan Nan and Li Lei implied. Yao reminds me that Chinese rarely show affection in public—only the boldest couples might hold hands down by the lake. Wu adds that the female population of Zhe Da is only 20–25 percent; if half the women have formed attachments, that's still only a small fraction of the school population. Furthermore, the rigors of scientific education militate against it.

Dating is more common at Hang Da, the liberal arts college next door, but even there things aren't likely to "go all the way." Western sexual freedom depends on mobility, on independence from family that presumes economic self-sufficiency, and on privacy—if a letter isn't private, imagine managing trysts with your neighbor's offspring or spouse.

Behavior in sophisticated Shanghai and Beijing may differ, though I believe this is mainly a "class" question, for all the wild stories I've ever heard originated with children of the highest cadres. Having more money, more access to private space, and more exposure to the freer life-style of the higher echelons, cadres' children are rumored to indulge in a wider range of activities and experiments.

I've also heard of sexual intrigues and adultery, a phenomenon surely not uncommon in a country where couples may work hundreds of miles away from one another, or be abroad for two to five years. (Would that I'd had a tape recorder on the New York City subway one night as Mr. Ma told a lengthy tale about a PLA officer who ran off with someone's wife while his wife ran off with someone else's husband, etc.—all this with great confusion of third person pronouns.)

But widespread pre- or extramarital sex presumes a philosophy un-Chinese, a philosophy emphasizing immediate personal gratification above family and social interests, personal emotional response above duties and obligations, individual satisfaction above the individual's place and behavior within a social hierarchy—a philosophy inherently dangerous to social order. (Thus the civilians in Ma's story were severely chastised, the PLA man imprisoned.) Unlike my colleagues here, I have been conditioned to be primarily (if not solely) interested in *my* love life, *my* career, *my* psychological development—in short, the pursuit of my own happiness. I spend my time and energy trying to get reality to conform to my ideal; if my ideal changes, why, then, I change my plans and pick up and go off to China, for instance, or get involved with a man of whom my family could not approve. It's my business, my life. In other words, I define myself in relation to myself—or I believe I do, anyway, as horizons shift in different periods, places, and cultures.

In Shanghai a few university women, interested not in sexual but in social reform, thoughtfully discussed with me the need to alter dating patterns. They're now free to choose their own husbands, but on what basis? If a single date implies engagement, how can a woman make comparisons or get to know a man well enough to make a sensible decision? In the countryside women's organizations still struggle against forced marriage and bride price. In the cities, personal choice of partners seems nearly universal, but Western concepts of romance are not; many people approaching thirty simply decide it's time to pair off and have that one child.

It seems ironic to us that the Chinese spend a great deal more time and care creating friendships than choosing mates, but not surprising considering that for centuries marriage has been a pecuniary institution, not an emotional matter. (I hear my mother's voice: "Naomi dear, it's just as easy to love a rich man as a poor man.") The quality of marriage in China appears as varied as personalities and experiences, but the quality of friendship seems generally more deep and abiding.

Though I have not heard this view expressed in China since the seventies, I believe late marriage is generally advantageous to women.

The marriage law of 1950—the first law enacted by the new government—sought to give women a new sense of equality. Trained to be demure and accepting, women had been subject to forced prostitution, arranged marriage, concubinage—everything and anything. It isn't a bad idea for a woman to establish her position, her views, her sense of self before marriage.

Though the Chinese live under restrictions of personal freedom unacceptable to us, they live in a society much more orderly than our own, one in which teen pregnancy and sexually transmitted diseases, for example, are not major matters. And given the Sex Tours for Western Tourists that have become the economic lifeline of several nearby nations, Chinese women have much to be thankful for. In the fifties, China virtually eliminated prostitution. Houses were closed and women were cured of diseases, trained for jobs, and reintegrated into communities prepared to welcome them as victims of the old society. It isn't clear what may happen now that China has once again opened to the West, but I, for one, hope the party keeps a stranglehold on this institution we tolerate (encourage?) in the name of individual freedom.

But what about libido? How do people manage without sex until their mid or late twenties or during long separations? Views on masturbation are again reminiscent of the fifties: men are urged to wear loose underwear, jump right out of bed in the morning, and take cold showers, while women are given no advice at all. But then my students are still studying chemistry and physics out of textbooks from the forties and fifties—why should their information on masturbation be more up-to-date? That will come. Everyone is urged to participate in sports, and Chinese custom provides for comforting and affectionate same-sex contact—hugging, hand-holding, touching—that American youth can achieve only with members of the opposite sex.

Does this lead to homosexuality? I had thought so. Arthur had me convinced. Arthur had had a serious quarrel with his lover in New York and had run off to Shanghai to teach musicology. Arthur assured me that China is swarming with homosexuals, male and female. In detail both repulsive and riveting, he described his encounters with hotel waiters and floor attendants, young teachers, and even street pick-ups. (Ethics, he said, forbade him to have anything to do with his own students.)

On bike trips to distant areas in search of privacy, he said, his young friends initiated him into the invisible underworld of elaborate codes: the color of a scarf, the unbuttoned button, the handkerchief tied at the throat. I was astonished, but each time we met, Arthur offered still more vivid descriptions of magnificently muscled body types hiding beneath baggy trousers and jackets. He spoke of his perpetual fear of detection, for he was happy here and wanted never to leave.

It was not until the week that Arthur did leave China that I learned from him that this was *all fantasy*! In fact, homosexuality is such a taboo I believe the vast majority of Chinese believe it doesn't exist or was some perversion of the old ruling classes. One evening I saw *Sunrise*, a play about pre-Liberation Shanghai in which one character was portrayed as homosexual, limp wrists and all. I asked Lao Fan if the audience understood the implications. He said that those who had grown up in the old society probably did, but the younger people surely had no idea. Whatever homosexuality now exists in China is securely bolted in the closet.

Does all this mean that Chinese sex lives are without joy, that the Chinese deserve to be sneered at as "puritanical"? I daresay no Westerner knows what happens in the "typical" Chinese bedroom—if there is such a thing—but I'd beware of labels. In China there is quite literally a time and a place for everything. In *Chinese and Americans: Passage to Differences*, Francis Hsu points out how this is reflected in literature: American fiction (like American life) is almost universally preoccupied with sex; Chinese fiction (like Chinese life) relegates sex to a separate genre. Ordinary Chinese novels generally exclude sex; pornography describes sexual pleasures in blatant detail and, says Hsu, "in no Chinese novel is sex as such ever condemned." The Chinese were never burdened with notions of sex as sin—original or otherwise. "The sexual urge," says Hsu, "leads to undesirable results or punishments only if it appears in improper places and is indulged in excessively or between improper parties."

When Americans here decide to have affairs with or to marry Chinese, their work units consider it their responsibility to debate the merits of this liaison for the two individuals and all those with whom they do or might have contact. The cadres may be excellent, well-meaning people or nasty busybodies, but to ask them to butt out is to say: "Damn it! Why can't you Chinese be American!"

Yes, it all sounds so fifties. But we should not jump to the conclusion that the Chinese either will or should leap into our eighties, "catch up with us." Whatever liberalization of dating habits may occur, no far-reaching sexual revolution is on the horizon. On one hand, the Confucian ideal of social order would not tolerate it; on the other, however repressive Chinese morality may appear to us, it is eminently practical: China has doubled its production since Liberation, but it has also doubled its population. Ronald Reagan notwithstanding, China cannot seriously improve the standard of living of the people if it does not effectively curb population. Furthermore, a loosening of strictures against premarital sex, adultery, and prostitution would necessarily result in major health hazards. The Chinese all but eliminated VD in the fifties—an AIDS epidemic in the eighties would be disastrous.

Only on one point do I feel strongly: Education must supersede ignorance in sexual matters. Modern China prides itself on its efforts to eradicate superstition, to buck the international regression into supernatural mumbo-jumbo, to establish a modern scientific nation. This cannot exclude sex education. For the reasons outlined above, Chinese need not get bogged down in the American debate about sex education and promiscuity. It would not be difficult to educate leaders of existing institutions (e.g., the neighborhood committees, which conduct very thorough contraceptive education) to teach adult women and men about their own and one another's biological needs and desires.

But China will not easily change its moral code. We would not care to conduct our social or sex lives in accordance with Chinese values, and I don't see why we should expect the Chinese to conduct themselves in accordance with ours—which tend to change rather rapidly anyway. The Chinese themselves have had sad experience trying to impose one people's ways on another. In vain have they attempted to alter what they consider the loose and lascivious sex habits of Tibetans.

# 16
## Sally's Shoes Are Stolen

Sally loves the supermarket lesson. I can hear her making her way down from her third-floor apartment to mine below, trying to keep the backs of her red embroidered slippers from clap-clapping on the grey cement stairs. She peers into the window of my next-door neighbor, Madam Lo, who, Sally assures me, keeps tabs on my visitors. But the Dragon Lady isn't home, so Sally knocks on my screen door and asks if I can help her with the supermarket lesson I've designed for the scientists; she will teach the material tomorrow to a class of Zhe Da professors (including her husband) slated to leave soon for America.

"Wow, look at you," I say, admiring her turquoise jacket, which, through the screen door, looks like something Hong Kong kids wear over their jeans in the New York subway. Close up, however, I can see there's nothing polyester about it; Sally's is an elegant—if slightly threadbare—hand-embroidered silk jacket.

"I only wear it around the house," she assures me in a tone that includes me in the circle of both her daring and her restraint, qualities reiterated in her modest but un-Chinese waves and curls.

Cheng Xiaoli has been "Sally" on and off since her girlhood years at an American missionary school in Shanghai. The name was buried, of course, during the Cultural Revolution when any hint of Western influence was so dangerous. Sally managed to conceal a few family heirlooms from Red Guard marauders, and she and her husband John (Jian) silently sat out the ten terrible years when teachers could not teach and students could not study.

"John learned to sew and cook and care for the children," Sally told me one day. "I love it. He's done all the cooking ever since."

"What are you going to do when he's in America for two years?" I asked her.

"I don't know. I guess we'll live on air fried in water," she answered.

With the fall of the Gang of Four in 1976 and the arrival of foreign teachers soon thereafter, "Sally" was resurrected, and her English and her acquaintance with things Western once again became assets. But that doesn't mean Sally loves to teach; until this week, when we got to the supermarket lesson, others had taught her classes because she developed some ailment or other and had a doctor friend say she couldn't go to work—though she certainly scurries to go shopping with me whenever the opportunity arises.

As I spread out the sale flyers and goods I recently brought back from Hong Kong, Sally fondles the jars of mayonnaise, peanut butter, and instant coffee.

"Do you get these refilled in the supermarket?" she asks, for in China you come bottle-in-hand to buy such items as vinegar, wine, and oil. She plays with the milk container, the egg carton, the paper napkins, paper towels, and Kleenex.

"You just throw away all that paper!" she says. I understand her sentiment; China could print a textbook for every child in the country with the paper daily dispensed at McDonald's franchises alone.

"This is disgusting," says Sally, fingering the Saran Wrap as though it might melt permanantly onto her finely filed fingernails.

"True," I say, "but you'll find it useful when John comes back from the States with a refrigerator." Next year John will be a visiting scholar at UCLA; Sally is already preparing the house—and the neighbors—for the refrigerator, washing machine, stereo, and color TV she expects him to buy out of the $5,000 a year the Chinese government will give him to live on.

I show Sally some sale flyers, and we get into frozen foods, Minute Rice, the astonishing array of cleaning products, the differences among crackers, cakes, cookies, rolls, and buns, the killed, plucked, cleaned, and packaged chickens (whole or in parts), and the prices of everything. Sally makes out a sample shopping list (omitting paper and cleaning products as extraneous expenditures) and comes up with a bargain:

"Dog food is much cheaper than beef and pork," she observes, "and John loves it." I explain that that's not dogs made into food to feed people, but food for people to feed dogs. She's disappointed. Then she sees an ad for "hot dogs" and I have to explain that.

Though I assure her we have a legitimate reason for being here together, Sally's getting edgy because the Dragon Lady is soon due home from work. She tenderly gathers all the jars, containers, cartons, bottles, bags, and boxes and gently places them, one by one, in an A&P shopping bag. At the screen door she peeks out, thanks me profusely for my help, and clap-claps up the stairs with her harvest of Western wonders.

The next morning Sally goes off to teach the supermarket lesson. I'm dying to hear how it went. At lunchtime, when I swing into our lane on my bicycle, I can see her waiting for me in front of the building.

I find Sally in great distress. "Did the lesson go badly?" I ask.

"No, no," she says. "It isn't that. But I had to wait here to warn you."

"Of what?" I ask.

"Thieves," she says, peering under the stairs as though there were room there for four bicycles *and* a thief. "Come inside. Come inside."

Sally takes my key from me, unlocks the door, goes in first, and peers around to make sure there are no surprises inside. She closes and bolts the door behind her.

"Sally, what's going on?"

"I've been robbed," she says in low tones, "cheated."

I sit her in a chair, pour out tea, and put a plate of cold vegetables and two pairs of chopsticks on the table between us.

"Now. What happened?" I ask.

A man came to her door selling eggs. She said she'd buy some; he gave her the eggs, but when she got out her wallet to pay, he grabbed it and ran away. He didn't have the good sense to run very far, however, and when Sally found him several minutes later selling eggs to a neighbor, she demanded her wallet back—and got it! Caught red-handed, he just turned it over to her and quickly left the neighborhood—before someone could find someone to arrest him, I assume.

Poor Sally! I understand the stomach tied in knots. I tell her about my down-and-out days in New York when, with what were literally my last dollars, I bought an electric typewriter and advertised for work in the neighborhood. My ads were noticed: twenty-four hours later the typewriter was stolen. I bought another on time and chained it to my radiator. Two days later I walked into my steam-filled apartment to find that the radiator had been torn right up out of the floor; not only was the typewriter gone, but my books and furniture were ruined by the steam.

Sally is astonished by my story, but distressed at my blasé attitude toward the robbery. "He asked me if it's true there are foreigners in the building," she says significantly. I promise to be extremely cautious. Actually, I seldom buy from door-to-door peddlers anyway because they speak only the local dialect, and I'm not sure what the prices ought to be. In the market place, the presence of onlookers dissuades anyone from cheating me. Yesterday I bought four ice cream pops for forty fen from a peasant woman who short-changed me two fen (by accident or not I don't know); the fifty or so people who had gathered to watch the foreigner buy ice cream pops wouldn't let her get away with it.

Sally leaves, instructing me to lock the door behind her. I turn to such mundane matters as lunch, nap, and work on another class lesson. (Lao

Fan and I have begun to talk about putting these lessons together into a textbook.) But my mind drifts back to Sally. I recall that when I moved here university officials were so concerned for my property and well-being they had bars placed on my kitchen window (accessible from the stairwell), a heavy bolt lock affixed to the front door, and an SOS buzzer installed in the bedroom. Like Sally, Madam Lo had been annoyed by my amusement at all this fuss, but nothing ever happened and I noticed that this year when Jenny, Fred, and Darrell moved into the building, these precautions were omitted.

I feel so secure here. When friends stay in local hotels, I spend the evening and ride my bike back through streets so black I can hardly tell where the road is. Often I can't find my turnoff and hail a passing bicyclist, who kindly escorts me through the woods to the campus. I have never felt afraid. "Frankly," I told Lao Fan, "you'd have to be a damn fool to assault the property or person of a foreigner in Hangzhou."

"Do you think Hangzhou doesn't have its share of damned fools?" he responded.

A few hours later, I'm startled by a loud banging on my (locked) door. It's Sally again. She's frantic.

"My shoes are gone," she cries in despair, "my shoes, my new, new leather shoes. I paid nineteen yuan for my new leather shoes two days ago. Two days ago!"

This *is* serious. It turns out that *two* men had come to sell eggs to Sally this morning. (She hadn't mentioned the second man earlier because she was afraid I'd be terrified.) When she turned her back to get her wallet to pay for the eggs, one of them stole her expensive shoes, then the other grabbed her wallet. Not until she went to polish the shoes did she understand the scam.

So inured am I to larceny, petty and grand, that I smile at so small a matter as a pair of shoes, but I quickly realize that for Sally, in both psychological and financial terms, this is no less a matter than my typewriter—theft is not an everyday occurrence, and nineteen yuan is nearly a third of her month's salary.

Sally has upgraded the lock on her door, added a second hook lock on the screen door, installed a lock on her bedroom door, and taken to locking dressers that contain—well, I haven't asked her what they contain.

What amuses me most is her continued adoration of the West and all things Western: I flash on Sally living in my apartment in New York, crouching behind the dead bolt, clutching the police lock, standing on tip-toe to peek through the peep hole—is it *really* John on the other side of the door?

All this suggests the topic of my next classroom lesson. Under "transportation," I talked about the necessity and manner of locking bikes. An American thief, I said, could pick a Chinese bike lock with a hair pin, and I described the tempered steel chain that protects my Peugeot at home. I thought I was very convincing—no Chinese student ever contradicts me (except on abstruse points of grammar). Then one day Li Songlin asked if he could read aloud in class a letter he had received from his wife, now a visiting scholar in Kansas City. The letter announced that someone had cut right through the lock of her inexpensive second-hand bike. The students were surprised. After class, Liang Tai apologized for not believing me earlier.

But bicycle theft is hardly the essence of the matter. The problem with a "crime" lesson is how to teach avoidance techniques without scaring people to death. Few Chinese scholars return from the States unscathed; since they're poor they live in at best marginal neighborhoods, and there is a scent of innocence about most of them that makes them ideal targets.

In my handy-dandy *World Almanac and Book of Facts* I find crime rates by state; the figures are staggering. In Detroit, for example, 58 out of every 100,000 people are murdered annually. If you applied that rate, say, to Shanghai, you'd have 6,380 murders a year; if 1 in every 50 women were raped each year you'd have—unthinkable!

Rummaging around in my books and papers, I come across a pamphlet from my local police station which I have simply because it was stuck in a pile of other papers the day I packed to leave for China. It is conveniently divided into categories (protecting yourself at home, in the street, from purse-snatchers and pickpockets). The practice dialogues are fun to write:

> [Zhu has a cold one day and doesn't go to the university. Her doorbell rings. She goes to the door but doesn't open it. She looks through the peephole and sees a woman with some papers in her hand.]
> Zhu: Who is it?
> Woman: My name is Mary Ellen Robbins.
> Zhu: What do you want?
> Woman: I'd just like to give you a message from Jesus, Miss. It's free. It won't cost you anything.
> Zhu: Thank you. I'm not interested.

In thinking out the "Dialogue Situations" (designed for classroom discussion or role-playing), I recall that last week I got on a bus with a clerk from the local branch of the Bank of China. I had often seen him on this bus, taking the day's receipts in a brown paper bag to the main

Zhe Da students study new criminal law.

branch in town. I asked him if he wasn't afraid of being robbed, since everyone knows he's the bank clerk and is carrying lots of money. "Oh, no," he said. "*Because* everyone knows who I am and that this is bank money, everyone would rush to protect me. I feel very safe."

So I ask students to imagine themselves on a subway where an elderly woman is being robbed. "What would you do and why?"

We discuss what we would do and why. Several people insist they would help her. I point out that (unlike the situation of the bank clerk on the bus) it's likely the thief has either a gun or knife, and that you're endangering your own life by coming to her aid. We go around on this for a while until someone asks me what I would do. The police would urge me to mind my own business, I say, but I might try to judge my chances of actually helping without getting myself killed. In truth, I don't know what I'd do, but it occurs to me to add this point: "You are going abroad to study science to meet the needs of your nation. I don't know what *I* could or should do in such a situation, but I believe that *you* should focus on why you are abroad and stay out of danger."

That evening, walking through the botanical gardens, the students entertain me with gory details of hometown crimes of passion, usually involving a young man or woman who, wooed but not wed, hauled off and butchered the beloved with some instrument from kitchen or factory.

As the story of Sally's shoes circulates, more crime accounts emerge. An elderly woman who usually stays at home ran out of soy sauce as she was preparing dinner. Someone apparently watched her hobbling off to the market on her bound feet, leaning heavily on her cane and stopping for breath from time to time. By the time she got back she found her apartment empty: TV set, clothes, money, coupons—even pieces of furniture were gone.

Crime is on the increase in China, and most people blame it on teenagers, on the "lost generation" reared in the chaos of the Cultural Revolution. I recently heard about a foreigner held up at knife point by kids in Shanghai, and have noticed signs in hotel rooms warning of thieves and pickpockets. In Shanghai (though oddly not in Beijing) I clutch my pocketbook under my arm as I would in New York. There's a sense of trouble lurking in alleyways that I've felt literally nowhere else in China, a sense created, I'm sure, by the teens who dress like "hooligans" (dark glasses with "made in USA" labels plastered in front of their eyeballs, leather jackets, tight jeans or bell bottoms), kids who seem to have nothing better to do than hang out. They just make you nervous. Well, teenagers, I say to myself. It's the same story the world over: the biological upheaval of adolescence, the enforced freedom of unemployment, the loss of clear social values all inevitably lead to teenage crime.

Wrong again. Yao tells me that crime in China was never a teen phenomenon until the Cultural Revolution, that even during China's opium century, drug addiction was not a teen phenomenon, that Chinese adolescents were always more influenced by kin than by peer pressure. Came the Cultural Revolution, however, bitter distrust or the removal of parents and siblings ruptured the family structure, often leaving children to fend for themselves in the streets. When schools were closed, some thirteen million young people roamed the country wreaking havoc on the population in the name of destroying the "four olds" (old ideology, thought, habits, and customs). Many beat, raped, or killed; many harassed their victims to suicide.

I remember a disagreement about teen crime and punishment when Suzy Fast was still around. Not long after we witnessed the demonstrations of youths wishing to return from State farms to live and work in Hangzhou, Suzy and I visited a local turbine-engine factory that has thousands of workers—*almost* all of whom belong to the union. Chinese unions do not negotiate for wages and better work conditions but rather function to help increase production, administer workers' welfare funds, etc., so why, I asked, would anyone not belong to the union?

The young leader of the factory's Communist Youth League answered that a few workers are denied the right to union membership because they have committed crimes and been sentenced to work under the supervision of the masses—their fellow workers and neighbors.

What sorts of crimes are we talking about?

"Perhaps someone got drunk one night and punched someone," he said. "Or maybe he hit his wife, or caused a big traffic accident, or stole something from the factory—things like that."

Suzy was upset. She maintained that it was unfair for criminals to be working while thousands (our demonstrators) dreamed of living and working in Hangzhou. Why not put the criminals in jail and give the jobs to these exiles?

The cadres couldn't follow her point about fairness. "We have here two separate questions," argued the leading cadre. "Unemployment is a national problem that only the central government can and will solve step by step—more than eight million youths have been given jobs this year." The unemployment problem was created by "economic misman-agement and the political chaos of the Cultural Revolution, and it has to be tackled in a well-planned, systematic way. But the question of *our* workers is *our* problem. We hope that by providing structure—a job, an income, peer guidance in solving the problems that led to criminal behavior in the first place—we can help these young people and prevent them from falling into worse crimes."

"Of course," the Youth League worker added with a shy smile, "much depends on the 'masses' under whose supervision delinquents are placed. Long lectures about serving the people are no more likely to win the allegiance of young people than stories about 'when I was a boy.'" We laughed and assured our friends that this, at least, is cross-cultural, but the leading cadre stood up so suddenly it seemed a little barb had hit its mark.

Suzy remained unconvinced, repelled by such an invasion of privacy, by the spector of meddling busybodies—the "granny police"—implied in the concept of "mass supervision" (though supervision by jailers didn't seem to bother her much). Like most American journalists, Suzy saw workplace or neighborhood committees as elaborate spy systems for the Communist Party. I have no doubt they are, but they're also China's social work organizations. Neighbors keep an eye on one an-other (especially on trouble-prone unemployed teenagers) and try (with varying degrees of success, no doubt) to occupy idle hands and minds, and to prevent family or neighborly squabbles from escalating into full-blown feuds or fisticuffs. And if the party uses this system to its own advantage, it certainly didn't create it; for centuries Chinese law has depended on "the doctrine of mutual responsibility."

Most American parents retain sole responsibility for their children. When they are too young and inexperienced or troubled to maintain control, there's often no one and nothing to hold the reins until something terrible happens and social agencies step in. In China people have always been expected to know what their family members and neighbors are up to, and to try to prevent crimes before they occur. Parents share or even abandon control to grandparents, in-laws, uncles, aunts, teachers, or even neighbors when necessary. What makes this possible is an almost universally shared, family-centered value system canonized by Confucius. How many Americans would willingly abandon their children's moral and ethical training to relatives, much less to strangers?

As I talk over these issues with my students and colleagues, I come to see that the difference between an Eastern and Western approach to crime and punishment is something like the difference between inductive and deductive logic: In America, public debate on the causes of crime, the propriety and effectiveness of various forms of punishment, the role of laws, courts, jails, etc. begins with *me*, with *my* right to life, liberty, and the pursuit of happiness. In China there is no debate. The starting point is the well-being of the whole, the maintenance of harmony, an orderly universe wherein individual interests are, a priori, secondary to duties and responsibilities. For us the purpose of the criminal justice system is to punish someone for infringement on the rights of someone else. Crime in China is seen in a broader context: not only is another person harmed, a family is damaged, the family's community, workplaces, and schools are disrupted, the engine of the nation is thrown off track.

Rarely do I hear Americans argue that "the system" or the government is at fault for murder, rape, robbery, teen pregnancy, or drug abuse, but in China disharmony implies the inability of the ruler or ruling party to rule. It is not the purpose of a trial to establish the innocence or guilt of the accused—that's pretrial police work. The trial simply removes the social impediment and, by example, discourages others.

One evening several of my students arrive at my apartment with an issue of *Time* magazine devoted to crime in America. They are utterly dismayed by the "crime clock," which vividly illustrates that in the United States a rape occurs every x minutes, a murder every x minutes, etc. Why, they want to know, don't we execute the criminals? I try to explain our sense of justice, our abiding concern that a person might be unjustly accused and convicted—it happens. "When you see truckloads of criminals, heads lowered, placards about their necks, paraded through the streets, taken to mass rallies and then publicly executed, aren't you concerned that some of them are innocent, while the well-connected, say, the children of high-ranking cadres, have gotten away with their crimes?" I ask.

They note that people live in small communities and work in small units where everyone knows everyone, so it isn't difficult for investigators to determine who has committed a crime, but they admit that people who hold grudges against others do lie, that the police may frame people simply because they have to blame someone for crimes or lose face, and that justice varies considerably depending on the cadres in charge in a given time and place.

Nevertheless, while Westerners agonize over capital punishment for religious, social, and political reasons, every Chinese person I've talked to is certain that capital punishment is an excellent deterrent and entirely justified for the restoration of social order. Dead people don't commit crimes. Errors may be made and innocent people executed, but how many equally innocent Americans are harmed by those who *are* guilty and not executed? By sheer numbers, they maintain, you would be "executing" fewer people.

"Just because we don't execute people doesn't mean we don't punish them," I argue. "There are some 700,000 people in prison in America." They, in turn, refer me to the *Time* discussion of plea bargaining, diverse sentences for similar crimes, the insanity plea, and, worst of all, legal loopholes for people known to have committed very serious crimes. This dichotomy between what is clearly right and "the letter of the law" makes no sense whatever to them. Evil-doers should be punished, and if they commit serious crimes or persist in criminal behavior, they should be eliminated from society. Period.

Li Xumei reminds me that the Chinese legal system needs much improvement and is being revised right now. "We need to make great strides in protecting the rights of people falsely accused, especially by those in power. But crime is increasing in our country. We must also work harder to prevent crimes and to punish those who commit them. Feudal law is certainly out of date, and though we have much to learn from American law, it is not a system we would or could emulate."

Go argue with that. First, it's true that our own judicial system is a bundle of contradictions and can hardly be defended as a model of success. Second, it always comes back to the same premises: We worry about *a person*, while the Chinese worry about *the people*.

And though crime is on the increase in China, it is, by our standards, minimal. As long as China can manage to keep drugs and guns out of an increasingly open nation, and as long as loyalty to the unit—family, school, community, nation—remains above loyalty to self-interest, crime will never take on the proportions or the terror it has in America.

Sally may have to protect her own and her family's shoes, but she isn't likely to fear for their lives.

# 17
# Visitors

Sea crabs are too salty, but hoorah for lake crabs! Served with soy sauce seasoned with vinegar, rice wine, and lots of finely chopped ginger, they're simply wonderful. Wonderful, yes, but they have to be cooked. Miss Mei You brings home a mesh bag full of desperately flailing claws, deposits the black creatures in a lidded pot, and puts potatoes on top to keep them from crawling out. I slide the lid off just a sliver, just enough to tip in the water kettle spout, but two crabs scramble out and frantically scratch toward the darkest corners of the cement floor. Here I am, a full-grown adult, behaving like a comic book female confronting a mouse. I can't leave them there and I won't pick them up, so I decide to pour boiling water over them right there on the floor until they die agonizing deaths.

As I lift the kettle to do the deed, I'm stayed by a loud rapping at the door. What a surprise! It's Xiao Tu and his new bride, Mei Mei. I must look rather wild, for they ask immediately if I'm all right. I explain my silly dilemma. Xiao Tu grabs a crab with each hand and restores them safely to the fold. I use the boiled water for tea.

The newlyweds are beaming. Was it our teasing that made them go and tie the knot? He blushes. They had a grand, three-day wedding in Mei Mei's hometown and have ten days off for their honeymoon. They have been to Huang Shan, China's (perhaps the world's) most magnificent mountain, are in Hangzhou for a few days, and will then go up to Shanghai, mostly to shop.

But what then? Isn't Xiao Tu preparing to spend two years in America? He was, but that must be postponed now for they have each put in for transfers to the other's locale. Mei Mei works for an import-export outfit in Wuhan, while Xiao Tu is an astronomer hundreds of miles south in Kunming. Transfers take time—a year, two, maybe more in their case because Mei Mei is very good at her work and speaks fluent English, so her company is loath to part with her, and while Wuhan

164

Every feather, every drop of blood is useful.

boasts many scientific institutions, it's no place for an astronomer. But this is no time to talk of separation; they are in love and having a blissful honeymoon in Hangzhou's fine fall weather.

Fall reaches deeply into winter now, but still the autumn dominates with tints of yellow, brown, and green. It all seems especially beautiful, despite the increasing cold, because it isn't raining—we've had our forty days and forty nights, I guess.

Bundled up in winter layers, I work with the windows open (it's just as cold inside as out) and savor, through the din of construction noise, the off-key voices from the schoolyard.

But soon wretched screams obscure the children's voices. Sally and Miss Mei You are executing the chicken. On a back street in town I came across peasants sitting on the sidewalk slitting the throats of chickens and ducks. The smell, ugh!, the blood spattered about, the feathers flying, the squawking and yelping. The blood is saved for soup, the feathers to make feather dusters or to stuff clothes or quilts. Nothing is wasted. So when my former student Da Liang writes to ask if she can spend a night with me on her way to do research in Hungary—all that English and they send her to Hungary!—I think of making honest-to-God chicken soup.

They hack it up, bleed it, pluck it, clean it, and remove the head, heart, neck, feet, and liver of this expensive guy. "Expensive" and "guy" are to be taken literally: this scrawny five-yuan purchase is a castrated cock, theoretically more tender than its mate. I'm glad I didn't have to deal with that operation.

The sounds of slaughter have not been conducive to work, but I must knock out another lesson for the scientists. At my urging, Lao Fan has contacted a publisher interested in turning the lessons into a textbook. I draft each lesson with a series of practice dialogues and discussion questions, scrawl corrections all over the typed sheets, and hand them to Lao Fan, who magically interprets my scribbles, adds Chinese notes on idioms, retypes the whole thing, and hands it to the school typists who cut stencils and send them on to the duplicating office, which runs off precisely twenty-five copies—one for each of the students, one for Lao Fan, and one for me.

No matter what we Americans say, the duplicating office refuses to make more than twenty-five copies *or* keep the stencils. Each of us has repeatedly offered to show them how to keep the stencils in old newspapers for reuse next term, but they maintain that their stencils are too fragile and it can't be done. Nonsense: their stencils are precisely the same as ours, and it's infuriating. The two English-language typists are overburdened to begin with, and this means they must retype all of our lessons again each semester.

The duplicating office is off limits to foreigners. One day I say in jest to Li Xumei that the Gang of Four has been sent down there to do manual labor. She makes all sorts of denials, so many that I judge I may have accidentally hit on some truth, that is, that people who committed serious crimes during the Cultural Revolution may well be "under the supervision of the masses" in that mysterious den.

Inspired, no doubt, by the chicken, I'm working on a chapter on eating in restaurants, with dialogues about buckets of Kentucky Fried and Big Macs—my mouth is watering all over the blank paper. As I type I find my fingers so numb I must resort to my electric heater. Hangzhou Time is Magic Mountain Time, calculated not by the calendar but by subtle alterations of flesh and bone that lead to adjustments of clothing, behavior, and attitude.

In minutes the heater swallows the chill. Layer by layer the clothes come off. Soon it's warm, cozy, so warm and cozy it's hard to concentrate. Warm. Cozy. Sleepy. The knocking is so far away, so dream-like, it takes me a while to realize that someone's at the door.

It must be Da Liang. I rapidly don my coat, hat, and gloves and fly to the door. A stranger, holding a young girl in one arm, begins explaining something to me in rapid Mandarin with accompanying gestures. I make of all this that he comes from Anhui province, that something (sand? money?) has run through his fingers, and that he needs—what? Money? Food? Coupons? I feel confused. He and the child appear well enough dressed, but he's begging, and I don't know if it's a con or not—Sally has made me paranoid. He didn't seem in the least surprised to find a foreigner at the door. Did he come to rob me? Or did he come for coupons—I'm the perfect person to ask for coupons since I can get as many as I wish.

They look neither ill-clad nor ill-fed, I tell myself. I apologize perfunctorily and close the door. But now I'm unsure. Why didn't I just give them some coupons? Or some food? Maybe he and the child are really hungry.

In the warm bedroom I peel again and settle down on the comfortable chair cushion Sally made for me—she considers it unseemly to sit on a bed pillow. Once again I try to bend will to work, and once again there's a knock at the door. Is it the same man? What shall I do? What if it's a different one? Perhaps I ought not to answer the door at all. Why am I making such a big deal about this? Probably, I decide, because of Sally's robbery.

But this time it's Da Liang, her breath forming little ghosts as she hops about before the door.

In the bedroom we remove our outer garments and settle ourselves next to the heater, but remembering the tea things, we dash into the living room, grab the freezing thermos, tea canister, and cups, and run back into the heated room. Chinese thermoses are remarkable: when we uncork this one, the steam rises from it.

Da Liang's exuberance charges the air. This is her first trip abroad. Will anyone in Hungary know English? She shows me the new sweaters and Western-cut grey suit and slacks she has had made with her 300-yuan clothing allotment. She was instructed to buy "high heels," so she clunks about my apartment in her new 1-1/2" inch black pumps of Czechoslovakian leather. I think of the days in New York when I got dressed to go job hunting: girdle, stockings, three-inch heels, suit, blouse, pocketbook, gloves, hat. I would invariably trip and fall, running the stockings and splattering the clothes with mud, then go home, massage the indentations left by the girdle bones, and postpone job hunting until my scraped and bloodied knees were again presentable. May Chinese women forever be spared such misery!

Da Liang talks of her family, I of Nayim. I play tapes of Middle Eastern music and show Da Liang the two pairs of soft, warm Danskin tights Nayim sent for my birthday. Why, she asks, have they no toes or heels? I tell her of Xiao Tu and Mei Mei, and of their happy marriage and honeymoon and their efforts to obtain transfers.

"It shouldn't be too difficult for them," she says, "because they both reside in populated cities."

I don't follow. Da Liang explains that every citizen is registered where his or her mother resides. If mother lives in a populated area, you can easily transfer to a less-populated city or town, but not to a larger one. Without a residence permit, you can't get a job, an apartment, or necessary food coupons.

"Do you remember my classmate Pu Yaping?" she asks, "the hydro-biologist from Guangzhou?"

"Long Pu?" I answer laughing. "Of course I do." From childhood he had been "Long Pu" because of his long, thin frame, his long, dangling arms, his long, gangly legs, and his long, sad, sallow face.

"Mr. Pu was sent to a tiny pig farm during the Cultural Revolution. There he married a peasant's daughter and they had two children. After the Cultural Revolution, they returned Pu to his institute, but his wife and children could not obtain residence permits in such a big city, so they were left behind. Pu was never much in love with her—he really wants an intellectual woman who can share his interests—but he is proud and loyal and refuses to ask for a divorce.

"But he is also, well, you know, a man. So he brought his wife and two children to Guangzhou anyway. They all now live in the one room assigned him by his institute; as his wife cannot work, they all live on his salary and his allotment of coupons."

"That's outrageous. Why would anyone, in China of all places, create such an antifamily policy?"

"For good reason," says Da Liang, amused at my hot-headed-ness. "Without controls, people would flock to the cities. Even now housing and jobs are such a problem, and crime is on the rise. What would our cities be like if people could move anywhere they wished?"

That isn't difficult to imagine, but I argue that, as always, China has built no flexibility into its policy for cases such as Mr. Pu's.

"That's true," says Da Liang. "We are always that way. If Chairman Mao says grain is the 'key link,' then everyone everywhere abandons all crops and plants grain. I don't understand why we're like that," she smiles, "but we are."

It occurs to me to ask Da Liang about my recent visitor, the beggar from Anhui province.

"There was a terrible drought in Anhui recently." (Aha, I think, that was dry soil running through his animated fingers.) She explains that when this sort of thing occurs, the government gives the peasants free train travel to other provinces to look for food for themselves and their families. People give them money, but it's a lot harder to get grain coupons. Seeing the look on my face she adds, "Never mind. You couldn't have known all that."

"But where do they live? Can he get a job?"

Da Liang says they generally stay with relatives, and that he can't get a job because he doesn't have a residence permit. The government doesn't want him to go hungry—but it doesn't want multiples of him to move into Hangzhou either. "So there's a little flexibility in the system, after all," she concludes.

It is time for us to sleep. Da Liang is amused that I remove all my clothes at night and get into a full-length flannel nightgown; she wears her underwear (boxer shorts and undershirt). Lying in the big double bed, we laugh at each other's habits. She tells me that when a Chinese woman has a child or an abortion, she stays indoors for at least a month wearing long-sleeved and long-legged garments regardless of the weather. The pores remain open after childbirth, she says, so if even the tiniest breeze brushes the skin you will surely catch cold. I insist this is a *bubbameise* perpetuated by women who aren't eager to go back to factory or field, but she has a friend in Shanghai whose mother permitted her to go out and she did and got very sick, and that proves the point. Well, it's a good thing Chinese women get fifty-six days paid maternity leave (seventy-two for twins).

Two days later, Lao Fan and I take Da Liang to the train station. I'm sorry to see her go, but I must get back to my lesson on eating out. No sooner am I at my desk than I have another visitor, a girl so beautiful, with a smile so sweet you could never forget her. I haven't forgotten her exactly, but I can't put a name to the face. She has by the hand a bubbly boy of nine or ten with the standard Chinese brush cut.

I know I know her. Surely she must be the daughter of one of the English teachers. Who else would come on a Saturday morning to chat—in Chinese—for a couple of hours? Her name is Lan—no bells ring. I later describe Lan and Little Ho to Lao Fan, but he can't place them either.

The following cold, drizzly Saturday, I get up late, futz around in grungy dungarees, and finally settle down to work when pretty Lan appears again. I explain that I'm too busy to talk today. She says her family is waiting for me. For me? Yes, you said you'd come to dinner today. Uh-oh! Often in the flow of Chinese I nod my head and agree to all sorts of things I don't understand. This afternoon? I ask. Nine o'clock, she says. Tonight? I ask. No, now, she says. Well, there's nothing for it. I throw on a sweater and grab a bag, figuring we're just going around the corner and—damn it!—never think to take my camera.

We walk down the street past the teachers' housing and come to the bus stop. I rummage through my mind: which teachers live in town? By the time we resolve the standard dispute over who will pay the bus fare, it's time to get off, turn down a dirt road into a small commune, then navigate across a muddy one-foot-at-a-time lane between vegetable rows.

Lan leads me into a ground-floor apartment of an old two-story row house. In the kitchen, black with coal dust, Grandma is already cooking for you-know-who. How do you do, how do you do. I won't see Grandma again for three hours. We squeeze through the middle room, hardly bigger than the double bed it holds, and into a bright, comfortable sitting room with desks, chairs, and a red plastic couch that serves as a bed. I spy more bedding folded away on a high shelf. Mama, Papa, Grandma, Lan, and Little Ho live here.

Mother offers a warm welcome. I have never laid eyes on her before. She goes out to join Grandma, and that's the last I see of her until lunch. We examine the photos under the table glass; I recognize no one. Out come the candies, peanuts, shrimp crisps, and pumpkin seeds. Now, I just finished breakfast, and I've seen what's coming for lunch, but it doesn't matter. I must eat.

We examine the collection of gold figurines and pastel animals in an old wooden cabinet with glass doors. We teach each other the names of animals in Chinese and English; I write my name, they write theirs; I pretend to like the Peking Opera screeching from the radio; we eat candy; I think of all the work I'm not getting done.

I call Little Ho "Little Ham." He rolls on the floor while his sister jerks him up by the arm. "Are you an Englishman?" I ask him. "No," he says, opening his eyes very wide. "Are you a Frenchman?" "No." "American?" "Japanese?" I've run out of countries whose names I know in Chinese, so I have to end the game: "Oh, I know," say I, "you're a *houzi guo ren*" (a monkey-land person). This brings on great squeals of laughter.

At long last Papa arrives. Papa is a dead-ringer for a middle-aged Henry Fonda, only smaller in build. Neither his facial features nor his hair seem Chinese. Papa is a railroad engineer. I'm bewildered: who is this girl and what am I doing here? In case I'm getting hungry, Papa forces an apple on me.

A modest man with beautiful, deep eyes, Papa seems to sense my frustration and assures me that an English-speaking neighbor, Mr. Xu, will join us for lunch. In the meantime we go through the utilitarian "How many people are there in your family?" He names them, including a brother in Shanghai, the girl's uncle, the uncle she was going to visit when I met her on the train. The train! The girl on the train to Shanghai. Last July. It all comes back.

Last summer, when the provincial newspaper *Zhejiang Daily* published my article on American youth (along with my photo), it caused quite a stir. An article by a foreigner hadn't appeared in the paper since Liberation. On the train from Hangzhou to Shanghai to catch my flight for Hong Kong en route to America, a China Travel Service translator recognized me and asked if I had a copy of the article with me. Of course I did. When I produced it everyone had to read and comment. Lan, who was sitting across from me, was so excited she asked me to give her the paper, which I did, along with my address and an invitation to come and visit when I returned to Hangzhou in the fall. So that explains why I'm sitting here now.

With the arrival of Mr. Xu, who studied at the University of Michigan in the forties, the seven of us squeeze around the dinner table. There are (count them) fifteen dishes ranging from minuscule shrimp to duck soup with a whole duck in it. They pour beer, wine, more beer, more wine. I'm getting tipsy and clumsy. I drop food on my pants and on the floor, spill wine on the table. Polite as I am, I cannot eat unshelled shrimp, so I amuse them all trying to shell these tiny mollusks. A month's salary has gone into this single meal, hours and hours of female labor have been expended, but I'm becoming ill. They comment on how little I eat, while Little Ho goes on stuffing his funny face just to prove, it seems to me, how much I really could eat if I wanted to.

At last it's over, but for the tea and a big pan of hot water with washcloths—a wonderful custom. *Now* we can talk. Lan takes out my article, carefully preserved in plastic. They have all read it and are especially interested in one point. I can guess. Every person I've encountered seems interested in the same point: the independent thinking of American youth, the willingness to work hard to attain and maintain independence. I try to explain how difficult it is to generalize about Americans, try to show both sides of the story, even emphasize the negative in an effort to cut into the "nirvana" view the Chinese have of our world. But it is this characteristic, independence, that fascinates my readers.

It occurs to me that this is a great opportunity. In my bag I have one of several letters written in response to the article. I've been meaning to ask Lao Fan to translate, but we've been too busy. Mr. Xu is delighted. It comes from a commune in a distant Zhejiang county.

Dear Nan Huamei Laoshi,

How are you? We read your article in *Zhejiang Daily*, studied it, and had a discussion of it. Following are a few points we would like to discuss with you.

1. You mentioned that we mustn't take the material wealth of Americans at face value. We must also look at the quality of life. What does that mean? Aren't the goods owned by the people the criteria by which to judge the living standard?

2. Some youth growing up in such a society depend largely on grabbing others' material goods. They live in misery and their lives are extreme. Is this due to the nature of the society? How does their behavior affect others?

3. You describe some youth looking for jobs, trying again and again in vain, giving up and living on whatever the government gives in welfare. If they have spent all that money, does the government give them more? Is welfare given monthly? What's the percentage of their salary?

4. You mentioned that many Americans have their own houses, cars, etc., which are bought through loans from banks. If they lose their jobs and cannot pay the bank, do they keep the houses and cars? Is their life "comfortable"? Is this the middle class?

5. What is the standard of living of those people who fall below the poverty line formulated by the government?

6. You emphasized that you love your country, that most people work hard and struggle for the improvement of their material well-being, and that many even sacrifice and fight for the rights of others. Will you please give us one or two examples? We would like to hear these stories.

7. We are very much interested in the independence of American youth. You said most youths become independent and earn their own living when only in their teens. How do they become independent so young?

8. You say that in American society there are classes. We wonder if this term is commonly used in the U.S. As far as we know, this is a Marxist concept, so it is very hard, we think, for Americans to accept it. Is this true?

After our discussion, all of us think we are most interested in these basic characteristics of American youth: diligence, independent thinking, sense of justice, search for meaning in life. These are the points we should learn from. Only in this way can China ultimately realize the four modernizations. But our strong will to learn from them is rather abstract; it's very hard to integrate theory with practice. Could you please write some other articles to explain the ideas of independent thinking and how, through hard work, young people become useful and contribute to their society?

We also think there is a weak point in your article: you have emphasized the gloomy side of American society more than the bright side. Yet as we are ordinary Chinese peasants, and our newspapers and magazines don't normally print such articles, we seldom read material describing the life and economic conditions of people in other countries, so we consider your article the fairest and most all-sided we've read so far.

Nan Huamei Laoshi, we have taken too much of your time to read this letter and also it is extra work for the translator comrade. Forgive us. Many thanks. We wish you health.

I try to explain some of the points raised in the letter, but as the sun begins to set we are still stuck on the phrase "quality of life." Lan and Ho escort me home, where we have still more tea. The day is gone, a strange, exhausting, exhilarating day, certainly not the one I had planned.

I give serious thought to answering the many letters that have come, but the complexity of our "quality of life" discussion makes me realize how much time it would take to do so. Instead I write and ask to be invited to visit their units; I would be happy to talk with them and respond to their questions. The brigade tries hard to get permission from the local authorities for such a visit, but finally writes that they cannot. I'm inclined to think there were many more letters addressed to the newspaper that never reached me.

It's December and I want a Christmas tree. Last year George went up in the hills and cut down a lovely fir. Of course it's illegal to cut down a tree—as well it might be, for slash-and-burn operations have resulted in tragic floods even in recent years. We foreigners, however, have a strong tendency to consider ourselves, if not above the law, at least exceptions to it.

"Do Jews celebrate Christmas?" a student asks.

"No," I answer. "Christmas is the celebration of the birth of Jesus Christ."

"Then why do you want a Christmas tree?" A logical question. I explain that since America is a predominantly Christian country, Christmas is a national holiday with decorations and parties and ornamented trees everywhere. For many, like me, there is a festive holiday spirit having no religious significance.

The students are determined to meet my whim, but it isn't easy. Finally (unbeknownst to me), they ask the Foreign Affairs Office for help. (I can imagine the Dragon Lady's reaction to this one.) Someone in her office dials who-knows-who who calls who-knows-who who says you have to have a note signed by who-knows-who. It works. Armed with a little note with a big red seal we set off to find the university nursery. They suggest we walk around campus until we find what we want; they'll cut it down for us. We look and look—too big or too small. But at the foot of a huge cedar Mr. Ma asks if a branch would do. Ingenious. He also suggests I offer some cigarettes to the man who cuts and delivers my "tree," which reaches almost to the ceiling.

Jenny, Darrell, Fred, and I trim it with improvised objects and real lights purchased in Shanghai last year. Jenny cuts a white star out of an old box. My students soon pile in with ornaments ranging from miniature Chinese lanterns to cigarette-paper-covered triangles. They've made a red star for the top. We put up both stars—one for the Nationalists and one for the Communists, Fred quips.

On Christmas Day I anticipate many visitors, so before I ride across town to the post office to pick up gifts from home, I wrap little animals and candies for the children. As I place them under the tree I recall the first time I gave a gift to a Chinese child. He said "thank you" and slipped it in his pocket. I was insulted that my gift received such short shrift, but learning that it's the custom here not to open gifts in the presence of the giver, I now marvel at the child's discipline.

I, on the other hand, tear open my packages right outside the post office and find an Aretha Franklin tape, coffee, books, and, from my colleague Micky X, a pair of hand-knitted booties. Micky writes that she was moved by my descriptions of the cold.

I ride carefully through the Liberation Road traffic: bikes, pedestrians, carts, pedicabs, three-wheelers, minibuses, buses. I'm pulling in to the right of a bus as it pulls up to a light when a man whizzes by, knocking me off balance. My left hand scrapes against loose metal pieces on the side of the bus as I go down.

The man stops for an instant, then speeds away. He should have stopped, of course, but I guess he saw I was a foreigner and had a swift image of the consequences he might face if I were hurt. Truthfully, I can hardly blame him. Several people stop to help. One woman presses my glove against my bleeding hand, a young man takes my bike, and another my bag. (Try that in New York.) Another woman stops a bus that gets me to the nearby No. 2 Hospital, which is, fortunately, the best medical facility in Hangzhou.

In the emergency room, people squeeze together on a bench to make room for me. I look around this wretched, crumbling, dark, cold, room crammed with people covered with coats and cotton padding, lying on quilts or blankets or homemade cots that serve as stretchers borne long distances down dirt roads and through the busy streets by friends or relatives. Others stand or squat or sit on stools or benches. There is an eerie quiet. An old woman whimpers. The two women try to distract me with friendly questions.

I'm soon given four shots on the inside of my right arm just above the wrist, then taken into a back room—which doesn't stop people from coming in to stare at me. Two bus conductors are here, one from the bus I hit and the other from the bus that got me here. Two cadres from the bus company arrive. Here comes the corner traffic cop, and here's a fancy-dressed cadre who says he's the father-in-law of someone I'm supposed to know at the university. Everyone is filling out accident reports in duplicate and triplicate. Doctors and nurses mill in and out examining my hand. Dozens of people who have nothing better to do wander in to peer at the foreigner.

I manage remarkably well in Chinese, making myself understood and understanding maybe half of what's said to me—I think—though when the nurse who gave me the shots says something about twenty-five fen, I rummage in my bag with one hand and give her what I assume to be a twenty-five-cent registration fee. She laughs and points to her watch: I have to wait twenty-five minutes for the tetanus shots to work. The words (even the characters) for cents and minutes are the same. My two companions escort me to the X-ray room, and within a few minutes I'm presented with what looks like a negative photocopy of my hand—nothing broken, no bones damaged. I'll just need several stitches.

We pass again through the emergency room and out into the old grey courtyard where people are lined up before the apothecary's window. What will the operating room look like? They guide me in and out and around corners. Like a mirage, right there behind the old hospital, appears a sparkling, nine-story, turquoise-tiled building. It is the new hospital, so new it is not yet in use. I will be its first occupant.

Dr. Wang walks me through the empty corridors to the Chinese-style bathroom, opening the pin that holds my pants because I lost the button. Embarrassing! The operating room is as modern as any I've ever seen, but the new hospital has no more heat than the old one. A little coal stove is brought in, and I'm covered with my jacket and wads of cotton padding that look like the insides of quilts. Dr. Wang wants me to take my pants off so she can sew a button on, but I refuse because I'm cold and because it seems absurd. She wins: she sews the button on while I lie there waiting for Dr. Li, reputed to be one of China's best hand surgeons. Another young doctor gently rubs my uninjured hand to warm it. I swear I would marry this man no questions asked, such tenderness is there in his touch.

The anesthetist probes the area of my collar bone. I jump. Do I have pain in my hand? No. I have pain where you just put your finger (I half say and half mime), so she agrees to give me a general anesthetic. Just before I fade out, I look up at a white gown and mask from which emanates the muffled voice of Lao Fan making cracks about Christmas day. It's too late for translations, but I'm very glad he's here. The room begins undulating wildly, just like in the movies, and I float out into the universe in my yellow submarine.

I dream in Chinese while another part of my mind finds that amusing. We're all sailing around in space in huge styrofoam boxes, weightless, free, joyously free amidst the blues and greens, the boxes outlined in yellows and reds and oranges the way we used to dark-outline in coloring books when we were kids. I struggle to determine what's real and what isn't, believing at each stage that *this* is reality and the last part dream. When the intense glare of turquoise tiles and white gowns and the hazy rainbows in the operating lamps come swirling into focus, I recognize the source of much of the imagery.

I stagger into the car and am hardly in bed before the "get a good rest" hordes begin pouring in. The story, much embroidered, has spread like prairie fire. Lao Fan posts Miss Mei You at the door so I can sleep, but I do have a big argument with Ming who insists on washing my feet for me. I cannot imagine allowing someone to wash my feet. These strange Orientals. Ming cannot imagine a person getting into bed without washing her feet. These strange *gao bizi*.

By the following evening I'm fine. Lao Fan and Ming and all the students come for a grand Christmas party with singing and storytelling and general good humor. They won't let me go to class on Friday, but on Saturday morning I show up with my bandaged hand covered by a large easy-tie mit Yao sewed for me to keep my hand clean and warm.

An old Chinese saying has it that if you have a small incident of some kind at the end of the old year, it will keep you safe and sound in the year to come. Amen to that.

# 18
# The Sorry History of Lin Feifei

One evening Lao Fan and Ming drop by to chat. As I'm making coffee (instant American) there's a knock at the door. Lao Fan goes to answer it. He comes back with a tiny, grey-haired woman in her mid-fifties.

It's impossible to tell much from her appearance. She tells us she lives in a small village not far from Hangzhou, but she has nothing of the peasant about her. She stands very straight, and her skin is not leathered by endless seasons of sun and wind. She is aggressive and confident, but not in the manner of an intellectual, and she speaks no Mandarin (as most intellectuals do) but only a local dialect I can't understand a word of. Fortunately, Lao Fan was brought up in a village not far from hers and is able to translate easily.

"My life is an extraordinary one," she says, then rapidly switches to the requisite apologies for having disturbed us. In fact, she doesn't seem in the least sorry; Chinese courtesy requires several cups of tea and intolerable amounts of chit-chat before the point of a visit may be made clear, but it takes Lin Feifei about sixty seconds to blurt out that she has come to tell me her life's story. "My life has been so miserable," she repeats, "I have suffered so much."

Her wide, lively eyes take in everything about her, testing, perhaps out of habit, like a bird tests for a nest. But she clearly fears nothing, not even, it appears, that I will refuse to hear her out. After all, she has relatives in America and knows that all Americans are kind, and she has watched me come and go and chat with neighbors. She knows she has at last found her audience.

And of course she's right, for she has precisely the effect on me that she intends. The stage is set. The four of us make an appointment for two nights later: Lin Feifei will tell us her life's history, Lao Fan will translate, and Ming and I will listen.

The next day I'm out. When I come back Sally tells me that a stranger has left me five loaves of bread, a six-pound bag of apples, and a letter. Sally translates the letter for me:

My Dear American Professor,

Last night I took the liberty to visit you at your home. Thank you so much for your hospitality. Before I went to see you I was a little worried about what you would think of me, but since we have met I am now very happy. In all my life I have never visited any foreigner's home and I am very lucky to have found your kindness and warm enthusiasm. Thank God. May God bless you, protect you, and favor you. Visiting an American, especially you, makes me feel so much closer to my father who is still in the U.S. I don't know why, but for some reason I want very much to see you every day. But it is a pity I don't speak English, and I don't want to give you too much trouble.

You love flowers, yet I don't know how to grow anything. I shall go to town to buy books and read them so as to help you manage your plants. I saw someone yesterday with a little bowl of flowers in his hand. When I asked him where he got it, he said there is a small flower shop near West Lake. I'll buy a little flower plant for you to put on your table.

Yesterday I saw in the shop some new foods and I bought some for you. I put them in my room. Later on I went out and bought five loaves of bread and a bag (about five *jin*) of apples and I brought them directly to you, but you were not at home. It doesn't matter. I'll ask somebody else to bring them to you. After all, it won't be too long before we see each other again.

I wish you good health.

Lin Feifei

Just as Sally finishes the letter, Lin Feifei shows up again, this time with big bags of cookies and candies and a miniature rock garden in a Chinese-red bowl. By this time I'm really upset about all these gifts, and try to get her to take all—or at least some—of them back. As politely as I can, I explain that in my culture it is improper to accept such lavish gifts from strangers, for by Chinese standards her gifts are painfully extravagant.

We go back and forth on this for a while, and I finally ask Sally to make a stab at it as my Chinese is so minimal. She does. Lin Feifei begins to cry. Oh my God! I have never seen an adult Chinese person cry (except at the movies), and I'm completely befuddled as to the proper response.

Finally, I agree to accept her gifts if she agrees to bring no more. This makes everyone happy. She leaves another letter dripping with sentiments about Americans and about how God will bless me for being so kind. (I'm reminded of students at home who put "JMJ" [Jesus, Mary, and Joseph] on their compositions in hopes of improving their grades.)

The next evening she arrives precisely on time, but not alone. "This is my son," she tells us, gesturing toward a lanky boy in his early twenties. The boy had not written to her, but simply arrived—after many years—and knocked on her door.

"I didn't recognize him," says Lin. "The neighbors were surprised that a mother doesn't recognize her son, but I explained that my case is rare, a case of suppression by the Gang of Four. He was only a boy when I last saw him. That was ten years ago."

And he has shown up today, of all days. I don't relate very well to quirks of fate; I'm always suspicious that the director or the stage manager has arranged them. But the whole business is so strange, so theatrical, that I suspend disbelief, arrange five chairs around the table, pour the tea, and turn on the tape recorder.

"Maybe it will take a year to tell my story," Lin begins, "but I'll try to give you a brief version. Their father never told this story to my children. This is the first time my son will hear of my miserable life." The boy nods but says nothing. He sits very still, staring at his mother.

"When I was six my father forced my mother to get a divorce. How should I know that I must suffer the same fate in my marriage? Several years after his divorce, my father went to France to study. As a 're-turned student' he was soon appointed private secretary to Chiang Kai-shek and was made director of the President's Confidential Office in Nanjing. Then in 1948 he resigned—the resignation was carried in all the papers—and he went to Hong Kong to do business. Before Liberation he remarried, and he and my stepmother went to the United States, taking my stepmother's children with them. We were left here. If she were *my* mother she would have taken *me*. That's the fate of Man, isn't it?"

Lin speaks in a deep, quiet, forcefully subdued voice. She sits very straight and still in her chair. Now she spreads her hands before her on the table, palms upward, then lifts them dramatically as she curses the fate that led her father to flee the country, taking his second wife's children to America, to Nirvana, and relegating Lin Feifei to a life of suffering.

"I had a brother and two sisters," she continues. "Before Liberation my brother enlisted in the KMT [Guomindang] Air Force Training Academy. He became a pilot in the KMT Air Force and then went to Taiwan. He is now flying passenger planes for Taiwan that will soon fly directly to New York, so he and my father will often see each other.

"I also had two sisters. We were born into a big feudal family. My grandparents, of course, liked boys better than girls, but my mother had three daughters and only one son. We were very badly treated, so in 1950, after Liberation, my sister and I ran away and joined the PLA [Peoples Liberation Army], leaving our youngest sister at home because she was so frail. She was forced to do all the housework and was always ill-treated. Even when it was learned that she had TB, they never gave her enough to eat. Mother died, and life became even harder and sadder for my sister, so one day she went out and jumped into the well and drowned herself."

Lin begins to wander off, her sister's suicide apparently a vivid and painful memory for her. I wonder if she feels guilty because she and her sister ran off and left the youngest behind to suffer as she herself had been left behind to suffer by her father and stepmother.

"But I want to go on with my story," she says, snapping back.

"In such a feudal family, one must give total allegiance to one's elders, and we were therefore always terrified of them. We were looked down upon because our parents were divorced and we had no mother to look after us. I was so ill-treated and so oppressed I developed a very peculiar disease: I began to wet my bed or my clothes very often. For this my grandfather gave me daily beatings. Finally, they got fed up with me and sent me to boarding school.

"But for some reason I was always rather stupid in school—perhaps I'm just not very smart. Though I worked very hard, didn't play with the other children, and buried myself in my books, still I always got low marks.

"Finally, I ran away and joined the PLA. I had no experience of life. I was delighted when I was recruited by the army. I thought only that the Communist Party is good, and I thought women were emancipated, liberated. Those post-Liberation years were the only happy ones of my life. I believed everything, everything we were taught by the party, and I was wonderfully happy.

"After a year in the army I came to know the boy's father. He was much older than I, but he wanted to marry me. I had absolutely no experience—I'd never even had a date—so at first I didn't agree because of the gap in age and because he was a battalion leader and I was just a new soldier. I wanted to work and study hard, for I was so young and aware that I was terribly naïve.

"But then party leaders urged me to see that most of the battalion leaders were rather old, and it really was time for them to marry. I reasoned that since he was a battalion leader and a long-time party cadre, he must be very moral and very good. So after a few months I agreed to marry him."

Lin smiles wryly at her own naiveté, and I myself cannot contain a smile because her face has the slightly comic elasticity of a mime, while her son sits stiff and still as though the slightest movement would shatter his bones.

"Afterward there was gossip in the army, and gradually the boy's father came to look down upon me because I was not very capable, and because my family background is rather bad—though everyone knew those things when they all wanted so badly for me to marry him.

"When the Korean War started, we both signed up to go to the front. I stayed until 1955, when I had the boy. I didn't know the boy's father very well, and I had the boy in Korea so I named him Hu Zhongchao [Hu China Korea].

"After I gave birth I returned to China, but the boy's father stayed on until 1958. His family wrote him saying that my background was bad and would adversely affect his ability to get promotions." (Here Lao Fan and Ming glance at each other and nod.)

"Gradually my husband treated me worse and worse, and finally put forward the question of divorce. 'After a divorce,' he said, 'we'll arrange your life and personal affairs.'" Lin snorts and again twists her mouth into an ugly, ironic smile.

"So I ended up with the same fate as my mother. In 1968, the third year of the Cultural Revolution, I was forced to divorce him. At that time my four children were very young. I had one girl and three boys, but the second boy died. As my husband started to treat me worse and worse, he egged the boys on to treat me as he did by offering them coins and candies and toys. The boys were only children, and naïve, of course. When I asked them to do something, like housework, for example, they told me they didn't have to obey me, that they didn't like having me around, and that I should go away."

Still the boy says nothing, but his chin sinks down on his chest and the corners of his mouth turn down; it's clear Lin is telling the truth. "Then, of course, as the Cultural Revolution heated up, I was not only viciously oppressed at home, but publicly attacked as well. Big-character posters went up in every street and lane about people with bad family backgrounds. So the father asked the boys, now in their teens, to read Mao's quotations saying that those the enemy opposes, we cherish, and those the enemy cherishes, we oppose. I, of course, was considered the enemy.

"At the time of my divorce the youngest child was only three years old, so I had to concentrate my efforts on him. He got pneumonia and was hospitalized. I stayed in the hospital with him for several weeks, but when he came out he was not fully recovered. I wanted to buy good food for him, but my husband took away my bank book and my money and the accountants would give me none of his salary. Within a year, the boy died. I haven't worked since 1955. I became a housewife, so I was entirely dependent on my husband. No woman should be in that position.

"At one point my husband told the boys that if a child under sixteen kills a person, this case will not be brought to court. Then I told him that I can't endure this any longer; if I'm oppressed this way I'll have a nervous breakdown. He said 'That's fine. If you have a nervous breakdown, I'll just send you off to an institution. Let them keep you. Good.'"

The mother smiles again, but the son looks pained, rubs his temples, and turns down the corners of his mouth as though struggling against tears.

We try to stop for tea to give Lao Fan a rest and to relieve the tension, for despite her ironic smiles this story has little comic relief. It's no use; Lin cannot stop the flood, so we let her go on.

"My husband had spread so many vicious rumors about me that I couldn't speak to anyone. So when he went to his office I tried to cope with my loneliness and misery by writing things down. One day I was writing and the boys were playing downstairs. When my husband returned he asked the boys where their mother was. I was scared to death."

Lin rises, pushes back her chair, and enacts the scene before us. My heart starts to beat wildly, and I notice that Ming is clutching the edge of the table.

"When he came into the room he wanted to see what I'd been writing, but I wouldn't let go. We were struggling over the paper while we were going down the stairs. I shouted 'Help! Help!' because I wanted the neighbors to hear me. 'What I have written is for the leading comrade's eyes, not for yours,' I told my husband. The neighbors gathered and the leader came and I gave what I had written to him before my husband could stop me. Ho ho—he was certainly afraid of that."

Suddenly conscious that she is standing and performing, Lin glances at her son and at each of us in turn, then sits down and resumes her story, hardly missing a beat.

"The leading comrade decided that it would be impossible for us to live together any longer, so he phoned the provincial government, and they agreed that we must divorce. By June of '68 I could endure no longer; I left and went back to my home village, leaving all my children with him—I had no choice. As soon as we got divorced, he remarried, so it seems there was another woman all along."

Finally, much to my relief, the silent boy can no longer contain himself. "Our stepmother also treated us very badly," he says. "She had two children of her own to care for, and father is an army division chief, so we were afraid to speak out."

"No," says the boy, in response to my question, "I never heard this story before." I start to ask him another question, but Lin does not wish to share the stage even with her son, and lurches on in her narrative.

"Since we were divorced, he had by law to give me support money. After much bargaining, he gave me 2,000 yuan including travel money— something like a bride price to set himself free of me. In the army, of course, our wedding had been very simple; I was just given to him for nothing. I had several thousand yuan in savings, but he got it all away from me. I was so miserable and suffered so much, especially during the six months before our divorce, so I thought O.K., just give me the 2,000 yuan and let me go.

"When I got back to my home village here in Zhejiang province, the villagers thought my husband had divorced me because he didn't want me any more, so everyone looked down on me. And of course this was during the Cultural Revolution; because of my family background, I could not get a job and soon spent all my money.

"In my village I suffered deeply from loneliness, but I did not dare write my uncle in Japan or my father in America. During the Cultural Revolution they suspected me of being a spy or secret agent, and even my own sister didn't want to have any connection with me as she was trying to hush up her own origins. That's a big question, family background, so my sister was afraid that any connection with me would reveal her secret, and open her to scorn—or worse.

"But after the fall of the Gang of Four, I felt I could make contact with my father at last. Back in the days when I was in the army, of course, it was impossible to write to him, and at that time I even cut ties with relatives in my home village.

"When a person has a good and high position," Lin philosophizes, "he is praised and given many gifts. But when a person has a big heart, no one will take care of him or give him anything. When a person suffers, even his relatives will not help him out. May I draw this moral: Most of mankind is selfish; only a few are not. Well, no," she says, reconsidering, "perhaps that's not entirely true. No, I will not talk about others, just my relatives—most are selfish. But my relatives abroad are quite different. Take my uncle in Japan, for example; after I wrote to him he sent me money. He is a Buddhist, a kind-hearted man, and my father also sent me some money this year and some old clothes."

At this point, much to our astonishment, the boy rises to leave, explaining that he must catch the last bus back to the home of a friend where he is staying. I'm deeply disappointed for I've been waiting for an opportunity to question him. I ask him if he will just tell us, before he leaves, what he thinks about all this. He does so, very briefly, with Lin Feifei interrupting him throughout.

"For a long time now I've been feeling very sorry for my mother. I often wanted to write to her, but my father wouldn't allow me to. Once my sister wrote her in her village, but father has connections there and they wrote and told him. When he found out, he wouldn't allow my sister to enter our house. Father is now retired from the army, but he has the same salary and political status, and he continues to try to prevent any ties between us and our mother. I really never knew before tonight what caused the divorce. Recently my sister went to mother's village to see her. Mother had left for Hangzhou, and my sister found her and came back and told me her address, so I left home without telling my father, and came here.

"Maybe now father will not allow me to enter the house either. But it doesn't matter any more because I have a job. In a couple of days, I'm going to take mother back to her village, but I won't take her to the house, only to the station, because if I see any of my relatives in the village I will suffer the same fate as my sister.

"But I cannot get started talking now," he says. "We must leave immediately or I will have no place to stay."

Lin speaks again. She must have the last say: "In a word, my husband has no heart, and my own heart has been broken. If I were not so strong in spirit," she says, standing very straight and proud, "my bones would have been crushed long ago."

We shake hands all around, mumble a few politenesses, and they leave, disappear, just like that, just the way they came. As swiftly and unexpectedly as the curtain had risen, so it fell. I want to hold back the players, to call out to the playwright and say "Hey, wait. I'm not clear yet. Is this tragedy or melodrama? There are too many contradictions, too many loose ends. I want to know . . ."

Lao Fan and Ming and I stand by the door.

"Do you believe her story?" I ask.

"Oh, yes," Lao Fan answers.

"Isn't it possible that she was really an agent or a KMT spy or something?"

Lao Fan translates for Ming. They smile at each other and I feel very silly. No, Lin Feifei is no spy.

"Do you pity her?" I ask.

Of course they do. Lin's sorry history is a common story made unique only by her personality.

Later, as I crawl under my warm cotton quilts and close my eyes, I can see Lin Feifei alone in a country hut repeating her story over and over to the four mud walls, savoring it, retasting and reseasoning it as the years provide more ingredients, more salt. She seems so unreal to me, like an actress so enthralled with her character that she lives the role, Stanislavsky-fashion. She had had, I was certain, a thousand dress rehearsals for tonight's performance, but she had waited all these years for the right audience, a foreigner, an American. And she had found me. If the play was not completed to *my* satisfaction, it was, no doubt, to hers. It occurs to me how Fox Butterfield found so many dreadful stories to publish in the pages of *The New York Times*—every Lin Feifei in this vast country must seek out people like us, breathless listeners to sorry histories.

I try in the next few days to find Lin again, but to no avail. "Nuts," I say to myself, "making such a big deal out of a divorce case." Oh, it's sad all right, but in the year and a half I've been in China I've heard enough Cultural Revolution horror stories to make hers seem rather tame. I'm angry with Lin Feifei, angry that she married the guy in the first place, that *she* didn't divorce *him*, that she'd allowed herself to be treated that way, that with all her apparent consciousness of "emancipation" she remained a vulnerable housewife, that she'd made herself into a stereo-typic Mother Martyr, boasting that if she weren't so strong in spirit, she'd have been crushed. Well, what was she?

Perhaps it's the theatricality of the scene that cloaks its significance for me. Or perhaps it is that I, a Westerner, cannot begin to grasp the plight of a fifty-year-old Chinese woman divorced, disgraced, and bereft of family connections. I'm angry with Lin because she isn't some kind of ideal late-twentieth-century American feminist or, more to the point perhaps, one of the heroines in Agnes Smedley's *Portraits of Chinese Women in Revolution*. Here I am, I remind myself, an American wom-an of the 1980s battling for my own liberation—who am I to condemn her!

Again and again I've been told that New China emerged out of feudal/colonial China, that the struggle against pernicious feudal ideas and customs will continue for a long time to come. This sort of talk always seemed so abstract to me. But Lin's story, I realize, is a concrete example of history at work—and a beauty at that, for behind her actions and those of her husband lay centuries of feudal ideology and practice, a whole host of Confucian tenets.

No, Lin Feifei was not carried off in a sedan chair to the house of a total stranger. Her marriage had not been arranged by a father in complete control of her destiny. Instead, she (and thousands like her) was exhorted to marry by the party on whom she was just as dependent as any girl ever was on her family. Her grandparents inculcated in her the proper submissive behavior of a woman; surely it wasn't difficult for the party to convince this twenty-year-old girl that her "revolutionary" duty was to marry and care for this middle-aged leading comrade—even if she didn't much care for him. The party needed her to keep this important man happy—wasn't it bourgeois to put self-interest above the needs of the party? "In our socialist society the interests of the individual and those of the collective are unified" she heard again and again.

It seems to have vaguely occurred to her that she had the right to say no; perhaps it flashed on her that "emancipation" implied freedom of marital choice, but where was the support structure needed to take such a bold stand? The party "discussed"; there was likely little more support from the women in the upper echelons of the party than from the men (if, indeed, there *were* any women in high ranks in her army unit).

Furthermore, though happily out of reach of her awful family, she was no doubt a scared and lonely girl as well, secretly relieved to be taken under the wing of a man—a high-ranking party and army cadre at that. She was pitifully unsure of herself, lacking ability and skill in any area, and without a base from which to assert her rights. And because she'd joined up at the age of twenty in the year 1950, she had neither proved her mettle nor been tempered in pre-Liberation struggles. The poor girl had no cards to play.

Although the Confucian hierarchy of unconditional obedience among family members stressed the behavior of inferiors to superiors (sons to fathers, younger to elder brothers, wives to husbands, daughters-in-law to mothers-in-law), superiors were obliged to be benevolent to those whom they ruled. This orderly arrangement of human relations extended to the ruling class as well. Thus the party and its army were judged in part by their behavior (which was in many ways exemplary), and in part by their position in Confucian tradition as benevolent rulers. It isn't difficult to imagine that Lin, trusting the leading comrades, would believe that her husband must be, ipso facto, a benevolent person who practiced what the Communists preached. A 1964 article in the *People's Daily* put it this way:

> In a socialist society, love between husband and wife is built on the identity of political beliefs and on the foundation of struggling together for the revolutionary cause. The relationship between husband and wife is first of all comradely relations and the feelings between husband and wife are primarily revolutionary sentiments. For this reason a husband should take the attitude of a revolutionary comrade toward his wife . . . regarding [her] as . . . a class sister with whom one labors together in production or work, as a companion with whom one lives together at home, respecting and loving each other, helping each other, and encouraging each other in making progress together.

Ah, glorious! Little did Lin know, you can be sure, of Mao Zedong's behavior toward his sundry wives and lovers, or that of other Communist leaders—with the always shining exception of Zhou Enlai.

For his part, Lin's husband was surely saturated with more than his share of blindly held feudal assumptions:

• The "revolutionary" duty of a woman is to serve and service me, and to bear me children.

• Since it is my work that's important, if my wife proves unsatisfactory in any of her domains, I (like Mao) will simply fill in the blanks with other women.

• If my parents want me to get rid of my wife then I, as a filial son, will get rid of her. (This didn't seem like any great sacrifice as he clearly wasn't crazy about her anyway, but married whatever was available at the moment. Nor is that surprising, for marriage in China had seldom been a matter of romance, of individual love; it had been arranged by families to insure the continuation of the family line.)

• Lin is a "bad element." The Confucian tenet of guilt by family membership or association, expanded by the Communist addition of class, was all-pervasive. Lin had several strikes against her—she would be a liability to his career. He was no doubt right: had he stayed with her, he would not have ridden out the Cultural Revolution. (I have spoken to dozens of Chinese women and men from backgrounds far less odious than Lin's whose spouses divorced them during the Cultural Revolution either for their own survival or for the sake of the children.)

Had Lin been more important, a seasoned party comrade, she might have been shipped off to Moscow like the wives of other major leaders. (When Mao stood above the crowd in Tiananmen Square to announce that "The Chinese people have stood up," Jiang Qing was lying down in a Moscow hospital where she'd been sent for "medical treatment.")

But Lin wasn't important to anybody. She was sent back to her village to face the isolation and scorn heaped upon the head of a divorcée, a woman cast out by her husband. In China, a woman with no parents, no husband, and especially no children is pitiful indeed. She stands outside the basic unit of society. (When I first arrived in China and people asked if I had children, I said "No, I don't want children." Genuine shock. After a while I learned to lower my head and eyes and say "No, I, alas, have been unable to bear children." Great sympathy.)

It is likely that Lin's personality and family history contributed much to her fate, but like many other women, Lin Feifei was also the victim of a fledgling and often floundering Communist Party—itself born out of a society built on collective rather than individual responsibility, on duty rather than choice, and on a degree of male domination at every level we American women can hardly begin to imagine. The chasm between Communist theory and practice on "the woman question" was and is stuffed with contradictions.

How I wanted to believe, like Lin herself and despite all evidence to the contrary, the party rhetoric of the fifties about equality and mutual support. Like her, I was innocence abroad. Like her, I wanted the Communists to be instantly better than other people, to have sidestepped, in a matter of just a few years, many centuries of tradition.

# 19

# The Sunshine Seeker

Karl Marx created a character called "Mr. Moneybags," the evil capitalist whom cartoonists caricatured with a bulging belly, a top hat and tails, and a huge sack of money in each hand. And here I come, Ms. Moneybags, arriving at the bank each month with my wages.

The average wage here is about sixty-five yuan per month.

Under the circumstances, there is little need for bills bigger than tens. A person is handed, say, six tens and a five, counts them in two or three seconds, signs a receipt, and heads for the bank to put away, say, four or five yuan.

Now they come with *my* pay, *650* yuan, and insist that now (at this very moment) and here (in my office filled with students and teachers) I count it out and sign a receipt. No, they will not permit me just to trust them and sign the receipt, though the accounting office has never been one fen off in my dealings with them. So I sit here making neat little piles of tens and fives before the gawking masses.

When I haul this booty to the bank, another dozen people peer over my shoulder at the figures in my bank book and watch first the bank clerk and then me count out, say, four or five *hundred* yuan for deposit.

Then comes travel time and I need to withdraw funds. Only the sound of the abacus is heard as cotton-padded bodies press against the wooden counter to watch me count out a thousand or more in tens, stuff them in my bag, smile sheepishly, and walk off.

Ms. Moneybags' wad also presents a challenge for travel. Lao Fan and Ming, already deeply concerned about this impulsive foreign woman with her speck of Chinese traveling all over the country by herself, are also worried about my losing what amounts to a year's salary for both of them put together. It must be obvious to any evil-thinking person, after all, that a foreigner on an extensive trip is carrying a good deal of cash.

But my first major trip is in winter, and inside my down jacket is a large pocket with a velcro closing. I stuff the bills in an envelope, and Lao Fan pins it inside the pocket with my school identification pin, for there is also concern that someone might steal the pin (equivalent to a faculty I.D. card) to gain access to the university. The jacket is an ideal hiding place because you would never hang it on the back of a chair where someone could put a hand inside; this is not a matter of caution, but because it's bloody cold.

Lao Fan, Li Xumei, and Yao see me off at the train station and wave good-bye as though I were going to Siberia. Lao Fan gets on the train with me, explains to a conductor who I am and where I'm going, and urges him to take care of me. I'm surprised they don't pin a note on my chest and attach my gloves to a string pulled through my jacket sleeves. But it's traditional for everyone to see someone off at the station, and they are, I remind myself, unused to the likes of me and responsible for my well-being.

It was snowing when I left Hangzhou. It has been grey and sad there for weeks, and I was so sure that once I headed south I could break through to sky and a glimmer of sunshine. No luck. My spirits, too, are grey, for a long train ride thrusts upon me much time and opportunity to miss Nayim.

I'm going first to Guilin, about 700 miles as the crow flies. Would that trains were crows: it's twenty-eight hours from Hangzhou to Guilin.

There are four ways to travel on Chinese trains: soft berth, hard berth, soft seat (available on short trips like the three-hour Hangzhou-Shanghai run), and hard seat. The price differences are enormous, and so are the comfort levels. Soft berth has two plush, double-decker beds in a closed compartment, a large table in front of the lace-curtained windows, and lots of room for arms, heads, legs, and luggage. Victorian, egg-shell-colored doilies turn up under head, shoulder, elbow, and tea cup. Soft berth is for foreigners and Overseas Chinese, but a Chinese big-shot occasionally turns up there.

I like the hard berth which is a nice compromise between comfort and price. Soft berth is designed for privacy, hard berth for sociability. People sit on the beds or the little snap-back chairs in front of the window and swap travel yarns, jokes, Cultural Revolution tales, family stories, and work notes.

A hard-berth car has sixty beds—grey, metal planks with a layer of cotton padding covered with grey, simulated leather. Each bed has a sheet, a pillow, and a warm blanket or quilt, depending on the weather. There are no compartments as such, just three beds facing three others from floor almost to ceiling, the six-bed sections divided by a metal wall

People chat, read, and eat a lot on long train rides.

to which the beds are attached. A ladder gives access to the middle and upper bunks on either side of the wall. When you settle yourself in at about 9 p.m. (lights go out at 9:30) you feel like you're being filed away for the night.

There is much debate about which bunk is best. The lower is easiest to get in and out of, of course, but it's public domain during waking hours, so you can't stretch out to rest or read. The top bunk offers more privacy but is always hotter and stuffier, and I hit my head on the ceiling a lot. I reserve a middle bunk if I can, but this time I've been assigned the one at the end of the car, so just after the lights go back on at 5:15 a.m., the loudspeaker, hardly a foot from my head, blasts Peking Opera into my morning-tender ears. I hate it, but I'm sure others consider it a vast improvement over the Cultural Revolution days when everything but the Chinese equivalent of John Philip Sousa was verboten.

Peking Opera alternates with muzak (you'd swear you were in the dentist's office in Peoria), slow, soupy versions of "Whatever Lola Wants" and "Be My Love." No lyrics, of course. Relief from this swill comes with crosstalks, a form of comic folk art written only in Beijing dialect. Two characters rhythmically toss lines back and forth for half an hour, capping sections of the dialogue with punch lines. This is fast-paced, old-fashioned vaudeville, and people smile or giggle or laugh aloud all through it.

As soon as you get on the train, you take out your tea (the addict also brings her morning instant coffee) and hang your washcloth on the wire that runs under the luggage rack. Workers come through to refold each item neatly and evenly.

People are friendly and curious. We chat, to the extent of my language ability, about how long I've been in China, what I do, what I did in America, how I like teaching here, and how much the Chinese government is paying me. (That old Ms. Moneybags feeling creeps over me again.) Then we move on to what it's like in America, and the cost of a wristwatch, a TV, a radio, a car. We discuss unemployment in America, and the Chinese "iron rice bowl"—once you have a job, you need never again worry about putting food in your mouth—a condition that may soon become a fond memory in China. Someone tries to teach me the term *shui ping*; I'm confused because I think he's talking about the price of a water thermos (the literal meaning of the words), but he's using it in the sense of "water level," that is, "standard of living."

A newlywed couple (he's an army doctor and she an electrician) sit intimately on the bottom bunk, so a train worker sharply reminds them that they have paid for two bunks and should use them. From an ancient kettle she pours boiling water into the giant thermos held in a wire ring under the tea table between the beds.

The railroad workers really hustle. I've been on several lines now, and they are always kept remarkably clean by men and women in tidy, maroon uniforms on hourly excursions with brooms, mops, and buckets of boiling water with ammonia for the car's only toilet (a closet with a hole in the floor and foot rests to improve your aim and reduce your chances of slipping).

It's a damn good thing the workers clean so much as people make no effort to cover winter's endless sneezing, coughing, throat- and nose-clearing, and spitting. Even kids, so carefully disciplined by their parents to be polite and do or not do this or that, are never instructed to cover their mouths or noses. (I wonder if this isn't one of the reasons why China generally restricts foreigners to soft berth.)

In the dining car on the other side of soft berth they serve a mediocre

Western breakfast of fried eggs, toast, and dishwater. For lunch and dinner I buy the *san mao* or *wu mao fan*, thirty or fifty cents' worth of rice with a sprinkling of vegetables or a piece of pig's stomach on top, served at bedside in a small, rectangular, tin box. It is truly awful. People ask me why, since I have plenty of money, I would eat this stuff. I just want to know what they eat, and to eat with them because it's more fun. I do, however, bring my own chopsticks because the rumors of hepatitis among Westerners in China frighten even me.

Of course people eat all day long, and everyone forces food on me. All the egg and peanut and pumpkin seed shells and orange peels and candy wrappers and cookie crumbs end up on the floor, and the train workers sweep and sweep.

There are several children, but they don't bother me. They get restless, play games, move around, giggle, and have fun, but they don't fight or whine or cry as American children would on so long a trip in so limited a space. There are mothers with children and fathers with children. I am moved by the fathers' attentiveness and tenderness toward their own children and others'.

The newlyweds adorn the tea table with a prized purchase from Hangzhou where they enjoyed an idyllic honeymoon. It's a plaster bust of a girl with very white skin, very red lips, very rouged cheeks, and a very purple ribbon in her very yellow hair. Her purple dress is draped over her bare shoulders, and her budding breasts are pushing up from under it.

I sit on one of the little snap-back chairs watching the countryside slide by, and constantly pulling in my legs as people come and go to the two sinks or the toilet. The land is uneven, and the terraced plots swim and swirl into odd shapes and angles. Everywhere there are hills and mountains in the background, and a cluster of houses of mud, red brick, or cement with red tile and straw roofs nestled at their feet. I am reminded of the French impressionists as I was when I traveled this route to Changsha (Mao's birthplace) in 1975. The scenery hasn't changed since then, except for the new cement housing developments and factories that accost the eye at regular intervals.

Train station: a peasant carries at least three dozen live chickens on either end of his carrying pole; a woman hoists a large, heavily padded child on her back and skillfully ties it there with a long piece of cloth like a sack of potatoes; people hawk hard-boiled eggs, fried cakes, candies, cookies, and foul-tasting orange soda; on the platform, greetings and insistences on carrying the heaviest suitcases, and in the train, yawning and stretching and rearrangement of belongings.

The men smoke constantly. Some of the women knit. Everyone reads. They pass around a copy of *Da Zhong dian ying*, a movie magazine with a three-page photo spread on foreign actors and actresses. I recognize none of them, and people shake their heads in disbelief. Our disk jockey is now big on tangos. The brown earth gradually changes to red clay.

The red, plastic-covered "comments" notebook swings on a string above my head. I take it down, leaf through dozens of pages of freshly written, neat and messy messages, and write a note about how friendly the staff is and how clean the train. Everyone who can get near me looks over my shoulder. They ask for a translation, which I attempt to give them. Everyone nods and smiles.

As they reach their destinations, several people press names and addresses on me and urge me to visit them should I come through their hometowns. They don't seem to have the slightest concern about a visit from a foreigner.

A pleasant-looking woman of about my age settles herself in, and then occupies herself with staring at me, lowering her head only when her eyes meet mine. There's something odd about it; she seems to be sizing me up rather than just taking in a Westerner's features, but I guess I've been on the train too long and am getting giddy.

Wherever there is a foot of space on a hillside, something has been planted. Everything that can't be moved is skirted, so there are miniature rock gardens in the middle of tiny vegetable plots. When the train goes into one of the tunnels blasted through the mountainsides, people rush to close the windows so they don't choke on the smoke. The Chinese for "train" is *huoche* or "fire vehicle," and this great dragon belches huge clouds of smoke behind it, casting a science fiction atmosphere over the jagged rock formations that have begun to appear as we come within half a day of Guilin. The boulders are every size and shape, lying helter skelter, as though strewn about by some monster-sized goddess disdainful of mere flowers. The peasants have built house-high structures of wheat near the railroad tracks, and you can see the blankets of pollution settling upon them. The idea is to set the wheat out in the sun to dry. What sun? Not for a single moment have I seen the sun for weeks.

"Don't worry," says a voice at my shoulder, "you will see the sun when you reach Kunming."

It's the woman who's been staring at me, and I'm so astonished that she's read my thoughts that it takes me a moment to realize that she's speaking *American* English. Many people in China speak British English, but American accent and idiom are rare.

Delighted by her effect, she sits down across from me and launches into the who, what, where, why, when, and how of my existence. I manage to pry out of her her name, age, occupation, husband's occupation, and number and gender of offspring, but I cannot seem to turn the pages of the book.

"My turn, my turn," I insist. "I've told you all about me, now I want to know how Wen Xiaoli, aged forty-eight, engineer, wife of an engineer, mother of three teenage boys comes to be called 'Wendy' and to speak fluent American English."

She turns and looks at me carefully for several seconds. "You want the whole story?" she asks in a low, serious voice.

"The whole story," I answer.

"Well, O.K.," she says, relaxing, "but I have to get off the train in Guiyang about an hour from here, so 'Just the facts, ma'am.'" We both laugh at her terrific Jack Webb imitation. We move over to the bed. Wen Xiaoli kicks off her padded shoes, folds up the cuffs of her pants, crosses her legs, and leans her torso forward so that her face is very near mine.

"I was one of ten or eleven or twelve children," she begins. "I'm not sure any more how many. A peasant family. There was a famine in our area when I was an infant. My father lived in the bowl of his opium pipe, and my mother simply couldn't feed us. She heard from neighbors that there was a hospital in the next district where she could get food for us, so she took us there.

"The hospital was run by foreigners, a couple. He was an American doctor, she a British missionary. They had met and married in China and had lived here for many years. Well, the way they tell it, I smiled so sweetly at them day after day as they fed me that they fell in love with me and adopted me.

"My real mother is still alive. To this day she says she loved me very much and was forced to give me away because she couldn't bear to see me starve. I don't know. It's hard to say. Would I do the same with my children? It's hard to say.

"Anyway, the Morgans adopted me and we lived in the hospital until the bombing of Pearl Harbor. Then the U.S. government traded a group of Japanese living in the States for Americans living in China, my parents among them.

"Our ship took a very roundabout way to America because of the war. It was quite an adventure for me. I remember we stopped in a port in Mozambique, and I was astonished because I had never seen a colored person before. We also had a narrow escape from a German submarine, but I was too young to understand all that business.

"Mother and Dad had a terrible squabble with the immigration officers at Ellis Island because I was obviously not a blood relative. They had to leave me there for weeks while lawyers argued that I really was legally adopted even though there were no documents available. The guards on Ellis Island named me Wendy. So it was Wendy who finally got permission to go and live in an Illinois suburb for seven years. It was a difficult time, of course. I was young enough to pick up English pretty quickly, but I was neither fish nor fowl, a slanty-eyed kid with a funny accent. Probably the best thing I learned in America was to fight, to be assertive, aggressive. That's helped a lot over the years.

"Anyway, as soon as the war was over, we all came back to China. It was only then that we heard of the Communists. My parents were scared to death. They were actually preparing to leave again. We'd heard plenty in America about Russian Communists. Now, here in China, people spoke in whispers about Communists eating babies and raping girls. I was a teenager by then, so my mother was practically hysterical.

"But I had very mixed feelings. Certainly, I owed a great deal to my parents, but I thought, I'm Chinese. I love my country. How can I leave again? Who will I be, Wen Xiaoli or Wendy? It had been such a struggle for me to relearn my own language. Mother really tried to keep my Chinese alive while I was in the States, but her Chinese is so broken and painful to my ear that even as a child I couldn't stand to listen to her. I made the most difficult decision of my life—to stay in China even without them. Fortunately, the boat never arrived, and mother and dad live in retirement here to this day.

"Well, I graduated from high school, and the Communists came to the school, and they really didn't seem so terrible after all. No babies were eaten, and no girls raped, not by the Communists anyway. After 1949 the government sent me to engineering school for free—everything was free, tuition, room, board, and clothes as well as books. We were the first and the last to get all that. Today students have to provide their own clothes, books, and food. I became an engineer and was given a job, and I was very happy. But then the Korean War started. I was ostracized and isolated because I had lived in America, and America was the enemy. That was hard on me—after all, it wasn't my fault I had lived in America. But I had lived in old China too, and in the fifties I saw a new China developing and I was happy. We could sleep without locking the door, and we all worked very hard, not just for ourselves but for the nation. It was a wonderful time to be alive.

"When my husband began to court me, I was so shy and ignorant I didn't even realize it. It took me two years to figure out that I really liked him. So we got married and had three boys. It was pretty hard again during the Cultural Revolution, of course, but none of us was ever physically harmed, so I guess we were lucky.

"Today I speak my mind pretty freely, though of course there's always the lurking fear that it will be held against us in the future. I'd really like to return to America to study, but even today I think there are cadres where my husband and I work who would stand against it because of my background. But things are getting better and better, and I'm so glad to be bringing up my children here in China. More and more people are speaking out in public and in newspapers. I guess we intellectuals are happy as long as Deng Xiaoping stays in power. We hope Deng will live forever."

Moments later, Wendy and I hug each other, and she hurries to collect her belongings and get off the train before it pulls out. She waves from the platform, I from the window. "Goodbye," she calls. "*Zaijian*," I shout, and then blush, remembering her attitude toward foreigner-Chinese.

Guilin is spanking new in the center of town. There are new high-rises and stores, and lots of tiny new co-ops selling clothes, toys, food, materials. Most are run by young people waiting to be assigned to "real" jobs by the employment bureau. It makes me realize the significance of the new policy that allows them to fend for themselves in the meantime instead of "hanging out" and living off their parents.

I am no Pied Piper here (probably because Guilin is a major tourist attraction—but so is Hangzhou for that matter), but everyone is extremely pleased with my little bit of Chinese. They really struggle to understand me and make themselves understood. I'm completely befuddled by the local dialect. Of course Chinese from different areas (sometimes even towns a few kilometers apart) don't understand each other either, but they have a common written language so can communicate on paper or by writing characters with their fingers on the palms of their hands. (Actually, this is done all the time even among people who share a dialect; because there are only about 400 different syllables in the language, homophones are so numerous that people often resort to written characters for clarity.) But I've discovered how to cope. I seek out a person with a school-aged child. The person understands me but invariably responds in local dialect. I look confused, so the child translates into *putonghua* (literally, "common language"), which he or she learned in school, and then we go on from there. A little complicated, but it works. Think of it: in a generation the Chinese will have a common spoken as well as written language.

Three little girls out sweeping in front of their home don't want their pictures taken, so we do a little broom and camera dance and giggle a lot.

Guilin is grey and cold. There are few tourists here now, not only because of the weather but because the airport is under repair and tourists naturally don't want to spend so much time on trains. I had thought I'd hook myself onto a group with an English-speaking guide, but no such thing. Nonetheless, I can't miss the trip up the Li Jiang to see the spectacular Guilin scenery, so I've made arrangements to go with a Hong Kong group. On the bus to the boat, sitting right here next to me, is a young man from the Beijing Foreign Language Institute. Tang speaks fluent English and is delighted to have the opportunity to practice. He's planning to major in American studies and hopes for an opportunity to do so in the States. Perhaps because he's actually done some reading, he seems to have a reasonably balanced view of America, very different from the idealism of so many Chinese encapsulated in the young man who told me in a Hangzhou park that "America is my God." "You're in trouble," I had responded lightly, realizing only later that he might have misunderstood me to mean I would tell some authority what he'd said.

Guilin is famous for its fantastic rock configurations, and for each, large and small, the Chinese have concocted a story. Seven angels looked down from heaven and saw water so sparklingly clear they came down to dance around it. Nine horses climb the mountain, but the tenth—see?—over there with his head bowed?—he's tired and depressed. That lion is looking back at the horses. And there are chickens and monkeys and bears and gods and goddesses, each with a story.

As I marvel at the Chinese imagination, Tang tells me that Chinese lore, rich in legends woven about actual historical events, is rather poor in mythology. There are, he says, none of the lengthy episodic narratives of early Western literature. Early Chinese religion was without a priesthood, without idols, without anything resembling our notion of institutionalized religion. Later Chinese began to worship the "six venerables" (north, south, east, west, light, and darkness) and local deities who evolved out of revered historical figures like Ji, a minister who made major scientific advances in agriculture. Though these local gods were understood to serve under one God (who bore a marked resemblance to the emperor), China never even had a word for religion until it had contact with the West and Christianity, and China has never had a religious war. It's been live and let live, at least as far as religion is concerned.

As we pass from one rock formation to another, we glide past long, slim fishing boats with cormorants lined up on deck, their beaks partially tied so they can catch fish but not swallow them.

Our boat pulls into the little town of Yongsuo, where someone points up the hill to "a nun and a monk kissing each other." Yongsuo, in the foothills of the Li Mountains, is a prosperous-looking stone and stucco town. The peasants sell anything they can at the most exorbitant prices, from huge grapefruits for one yuan to tin trinkets for as much as twenty-five yuan. And you know what? People buy this junk at these prices!

The boat trip is a pleasure, including a delicious hot-pot lunch of fresh fish and vegetables (though I had a good deal of trouble convincing the staff that Tang was to eat with me and not in a separate dining area). A pot of water with a coal chimney in the center is placed on the table, along with plates of raw, fresh fish, meat, and vegetables. You pick up the pieces with your chopsticks, dip them in the water until cooked, then in one or another bowl of hot and spicy sauces. To my surprise, Tang is sufficiently Westernized to express his amusement openly at my clumsiness with chopsticks—something none of my colleagues or students has ever done.

Despite the haze and drizzle, I have a wonderful day on the Li Jiang and am sorry to leave my new friend, who must return to school. The next day I head off across the bridge that separates the new city from the old. Past the comic book rental stand where a few kids sit on benches reading, I turn into a lane to find myself ankle-deep in thick, black mud. I'm in the meat market, buzzing with Spring Festival business. The children are more raggedy than I've seen anywhere in China, and I give my bowl of some pasty-tasting dumplings to a ravenous little ragamuffin. When I later note this to a China Travel Service guide at the Guilin train station, she tells me in the most racist tones I've heard since I left the States that *these people* are minority races whose thinking and habits are backward, vestiges of the old days when the Han Chinese oppressed the minorities. "They simply refuse to be brought into this century," she concludes.

Up one muddy lane and down another, I amble by table after table of huge slabs of pork from which people carefully select the choicest chunks for the family's Spring Festival festivities. Eagle eyes check the hand-held scales that take me back to my childhood, to the diamond scales in my father's jewelry store. Pork is 1.30 to 1.60 yuan per *jin* (no coupons necessary), but a *jin* down here is twice the amount it is up north. I discover this when I try to buy a small bag of sunflower seeds and get a large bag of sunflower seeds and keep saying I only want a *jin* and the guy keeps telling me it *is* only a *jin*. The scene amuses onlookers no end. Someone who speaks Mandarin finally explains to me about the difference in weights.

On the outer fringes of the meat market fuzzy-hatted elders sell second-hand shoes, boots, clothing, animal skins, incense, fruits, and vegetables. There is a festive atmosphere. Houses are being remodeled in time, people point out proudly, for the several upcoming holiday weddings. Much is done with wood—a relief from the all-cement construction up in Zhejiang.

Nonetheless, the contrast between the modern architecture on one side of the bridge and this crumbling, pre-Liberation town is very striking. On the way back I look over the bridge railing at the pictur-esque sampans anchored near the shore. Am I really here in Guilin, or am I turning pages in some old picture book? Whole families are nestled on the sampans, rice bowls in hand, wash on the line. A passerby assures me these boats are now workplaces, that no one lives on them. I don't believe it. I think how odd we foreigners are, for I much prefer these timeless sampans and the quaint, colorful, ancient part of town. Of course I don't have to live there.

Come to think of it, I don't even have to stay here in chilly Guilin. It's time to head south in search of sunshine.

# 20
# Grandma Shen's Paradise

When Hua Ling had boarded the train in Hangzhou at the end of her intensive English training course, I had promised I would visit her, despite the distance and the difficulty. Hua Ling lives and works at the Yunnan Tropical Botanical Institute in Mengla, Mojiang, Yunnan province, not far from the Laotian border and about 100 kilometers from Xishuangbanna, one of China's few remaining primitive forests replete with wild elephants, tigers, monkeys, and boa constrictors.

To get there, you wait for hours (or days) until there isn't a whisper of a breeze either in Kunming or in Simao, then board an old Russian forty-seat turbo-prop that constantly seems about to scrape its underbelly on the mountaintops, then jeep six hours up and over and down and through lush mountain ranges.

At the Simao Airport, I'm met by the driver of a bus sent by the Botanical Institute for family members returning home for the Spring Festival holidays. Hua has asked him to look for me. He delivers me first to a spanking new hotel with such wondrous chambers as the "Woman Room," the "Man Room," and the "Drawing Hall." After a good lunch, I go to book my ticket back to Kunming, only to learn that (a) all airline personnel—including pilots—are going to *xiuxi* (rest) until February 12, (b) the last flight back to Kunming is on February 3, and (c) I cannot purchase a ticket now for that flight but must be in Simao on February 2 or I'm out of luck. And today is January 30. *Aiya!* I came all the way down here to spend several days with Hua and to see the jungles at Xishuangbanna, but there is no way I can stay until the twelfth, so I must be back in Simao by the second.

I curse out all procedures Third World and trek back to the hotel where the bus awaits me. "Foreign friend" is given the front seat next to the driver so she can see the scenery, and she is all but sorry as we careen around wild curves and roller-coaster through the mountains.

Breathtaking views bounce before my eyes; lunch bounces up behind my teeth. Within an hour of the institute we're stopped by the PLA. They check everyone's papers but mine—Hua has notified them of my arrival. Our proximity to the Vietnamese, Laotian, and Burmese borders explains the heavy security.

Hua's family lives in a new five-room apartment, one of several attached, one-story row houses attractively designed in stone and cement. The rooms are large, the ceilings high. The front faces banana, mango, and coconut trees, the back a low, blue-grey mountain range and a river. Each family has a vegetable garden and at least twenty chattery chickens, which are particularly communicative during *xiuxi* time after lunch. The kitchen sink has running water, but outside is a faucet next to a trough that carries away the dirty water. Most vegetables, dishes, and clothes are washed here, including mine, for Hua will not permit me to wash my own clothes but insists on doing it for me.

The whole place is well-designed for easy living, except that there's no toilet in the house (unlike all new apartments in urban areas). So you get up and go out to the public toilet, in this case only mildly smelly trenches in cement rooms with half-wall dividers between stalls. Hua warns me not to go out at night. I'm not sure why. She's probably afraid I'll break my neck in the dark. She's probably right. As she tucks me under the quilt and carefully adjusts the mosquito netting over the big, four-poster bed, she draws my attention to the chamber pot. Not a chance!

In winter it's cold and cloudy here for precisely half a day. At noon on the dot, as though someone pushed a button, the sun comes out and the layers of clothes are peeled off. Tropical winter is like New England summer: I snuggle under warm quilts at night, and in the afternoon, in a shed next to the house, I luxuriate in a delicious bath with separate pans of hot and cold water, sweet-smelling soap, and big, fluffy towels.

I'm happy to see Hua again after nearly a year. I feel a special warmth for her. Most applicants to our intensive English program at Zhe Da are men, and we're supposed to select students solely on the basis of grades to avoid any Cultural Revolution "backdoorism." I asked Lao Fan if we couldn't give priority to a few women whose grades were a point or two lower, and he readily agreed (though in two years I've never heard anyone else speak of any "affirmative action" plans, and two men who never even took the exams were admitted, so the back door clearly remains ajar despite the grade system).

Like her classmates, Hua could read English but had never spoken it. And she was shy to the point where she—a woman nearing fifty—sometimes shed tears when called upon to speak in class. We rarely heard Hua's voice. We worried that she wasn't learn-

Grandma Shen.

ing. We worried because she suffered so.

At one point I asked each student to prepare a brief lecture on some aspect of his or her field. Hua sat (she would not stand) and described in clear and fascinating detail the history of the "choke vine" that wraps itself around healthy thousand-year-old trees and literally chokes them to death.

"This is it," says Hua. It would take perhaps seven or eight people, arms outstretched, to encircle this tree now smothered in snake-like vines tightly wound around it. For both of us, the tree created a strange mixture of terror and pleasure, terror at the idea that such a phenomenon could occur in nature, and that at this point in history, at least, no one could either prevent or interrupt the process, and pleasure in remembering that Hua's presentation on this phenomenon was her breakthrough into the English-speaking world. And here is another phenomenon worthy of note: now Hua is chattering away with me in English, and she isn't a bit shy.

"How did all this happen?" I ask.

"I was given an all-expenses-paid tour of the major botanical gardens of several English-speaking countries," she tells me. "I went with another woman whose English was much better than mine, so at first I hardly said anything. But she knew nothing about airports and telephones and supermarkets and all the other things that you taught us about at Zhe Da, so I was soon doing the talking and my English just, well, it got a little bit better."

"A little bit!" I say, and hug her.

We bike all over the institute, stopping at various experimental fields, forests, and gardens. In one area they have developed herbs that are said to cure certain kinds of cancer. The Japanese are buying and using these herbs extensively, but they are not as yet in use elsewhere. From Turkish trees we pick coffee beans I mail off to Nayim with instructions on how to cook and grind them. I'm shown how rubber trees are tapped, and we discuss a paper Hua's husband is writing on an experimental field of interplanted tea bushes and rubber trees, producing higher quality and larger quantities of both tea and rubber. In the institute's museum they show and explain to me, stage by stage, the significance of their work in oil analysis and experimentation.

Hua's mother, Grandma Shen, smiles a lot. This slim, spry, almost toothless old lady is very happy living here. Her son-in-law, Pao, is one of the three directors of the institute, and her daughter Hua—whose primary education was secured by the embroidery Grandma Shen stitched for the wealthy before Liberation—is a major botanist in one of China's most important scientific centers.

There are six people in the family: Hua, her mother, her husband, and three children. One son is away in college, their daughter is studying for her college entrance exams, and the second son, aged ten, lives with an uncle.

"We both work so many hours a day, seven days a week," Pao explains, "and we both travel a good deal." Just yesterday, for instance, Hua received an invitation from the Celanese Corporation to come to Texas for a few months. "How could we raise our son properly under these conditions?"

"We've been talking about moving to Kunming next year to be near all the children," Hua adds. "There's a branch of our institute there, and it wouldn't be difficult to transfer."

"But Grandma won't hear of it," Pao cuts in with at least mild annoyance, "so we'll stay put." It's hard to imagine an American family "staying put" because of the wishes of an elderly relative; if they wanted to move, they'd move, and grandma could either stay or come along as she chose.

Grandma Shen treats me as both an honored guest and an old friend. As we sit down to each meal she says, in ancient Chinese fashion, "I'm very sorry that the food is not good and is inadequate."

"Oh," I say, pushing my chair back from the table, "I guess I'll go next door where the food is better and more plentiful." She loves it, and offers open laughter, culminating in a warm, gap-toothed smile.

I ask Grandma why she doesn't want to go to Kunming. "*Fengfeng diandian*," she replies, opening her eyes wide and screwing a work-worn finger around her temple.

Grandma is getting heated about a subject clearly much debated in the household. "It's beautiful here. It's warm year-round. Fruits and vegetables are right at hand. We have free medical facilities. Rent, electricity, and water are free [because this is a border area], and wages here are high. I have cared for my grandchildren here when they were young, and I will be cared for when I cannot work any longer [rights guaranteed by tradition and by law]. I will be buried properly when I die. The bitter past is gone. Only a fool would leave paradise."

Pao begins to explain that she will have virtually the same conditions in Kunming, but Hua gently lays a hand on his arm to stop him. Grandma's husband died early, and she determined not only to keep the family alive, but to educate her daughter. Pao's story parallels Hua's: poor parents, a struggle for education, and then, in 1951, a university education entirely at government expense—an echo of Wendy's words.

Some of the workers, however, don't seem as ecstatic as Grandma. "It's dull," a brick mason tells me. "There's no excitement down here, and we don't even have television."

"I'd swear I saw TV sets on sale in the local store," I say.

The mason laughs: "I asked the storekeeper about that," he says. "They get their goods from Shanghai, and the Shanghai distributor sends precisely the same goods to each and every department store, regardless of local need. Just standard bureaucracy," he adds.

Though there's no TV, there are movies two or three times a week, admission three fen. Under the glittering stars, we follow what appears to be the entire community carrying its collective store of child-sized chairs and stools befitting the contours of Chinese backsides—not mine. In a walled courtyard everyone finds a spot and chats with a neighbor until (and after) the film begins.

We see a great adventure about a teacher framed for murder during the Cultural Revolution. It's the roughest, toughest thriller I've seen in China, with a hearty sprinkling of Bruce Lee antics thrown in. We share daring escapes, ride the roofs of rocking trains, brave the crashing waves, and balance astride the camel's back, always awed by broad panoramas of the most remote sectors of this vast nation. Watching the actors slug it out in the very corner of China where I now occupy a tiny stool under a diamond-studded sky, I shudder with the thrill of my own adventures.

On Sunday morning, we walk across a jerry-rigged wooden bridge with gaping holes between the planks. On the other side of the river is a small Dai National Minority village. One of China's fifty-five national minorities, the 760,000 Dai in China are ethnic kin to the people of Thailand.

It's market day. On either side of a broad, store-lined street squat elderly women, teens, and young girls in ankle-length, intricately embroidered sarongs and blouses, with braids or pastel towels wrapped round their heads, silver earrings and belts, and multicolored, sequinned cotton bags. Their baskets are brim full of fruits, vegetables, chickens, rice, and tobacco.

"Do you think we could visit a Dai household?" I ask.

Pao stops a few lovely, round-faced Dai teens and discusses with a girl named Sari the possibility of visiting her home. Sari hesitates for a moment, looking confused and embarrassed, then smiles shyly, barely showing her gleaming white teeth as she leads us away from the market and down the dirt roads to a straw-thatched house perched on bamboo stilts. We're warmly welcomed by the family, and it's clear that Sari's father, Chumpol, is an old friend of Hua and Pao.

It's Sunday. To save power, there's no electricity on Sundays on either side of the river. Several members of the household are seated around a fire built into a large square of reddish clay and mud about two inches above the wooden floor level. With wood stacked to one side, the fire is fed continuously, twenty-four hours a day, 365 days a year to help preserve the rice, grain, and other foodstuffs stored above it in slatted wood cabinets. Around the square fireplace, people squat or sit on tiny wood or bamboo benches—an eerie sight as the fire lights faces from beneath and flickers on the deep colors of the women's and girls' clothing. The men and boys wear standard Chinese apparel.

"Is life very different from before Liberation?" I begin. The process of getting answers is difficult: Hua does not speak more than a few phrases of Dai, and Pao's English is not up to this task, so Pao translates Chumpol's Dai into Chinese, and Hua then gives it to me in English. What may be lost along the way is impossible to determine.

"Before Liberation," says Chumpol from beneath his PLA-style hat, "none of us had ever seen a pair of shoes. Now we each have at least three pairs of shoes, and today we wear better clothes to work in the fields than we wore on our best festival days back then.

"Before Liberation, we had no bowls or utensils, only a few crude bamboo items. And we were hungry. The luckiest of us had half a year's food. We knew nothing about growing vegetables, so we ate mountain roots and plants. Now we have three annual rice crops and lots of vegetables, so much that we have extra food to sell. In a year we get about 800 *jin* of rice, which is more than adequate. We also have good tobacco crops," he adds, holding out a fat, aromatic cigar in which he takes obvious pleasure.

"We are one of the poorer Dai villages, yet even here every family has a sewing machine, and every household at least one bicycle—in fact every male has a bicycle. We have three in this household." (I start to ask why only males have bikes, but a glance at the women's tight, full-length sarongs is answer enough.)

As the translation process goes on, I watch the glowing faces around the fireplace and long to take photographs, but my flash doesn't work. We sit in one large, loft-like room sectioned off without dividers into kitchen, living room, work area. In a separate room of about the same size, the six family members sleep.

"The Cultural Revolution didn't make any difference here," Chumpol says in response to my question, "probably because it's too far away and too difficult for any Red Guards to get here over the mountain ranges. So, really, our lives have just improved steadily since Liberation." I think this odd, as the Botanical Institute just across the river had been so badly threatened that Zhou Enlai himself had twice come down to restore order. Hua and Pao proudly display a photograph of themselves and their colleagues with Premier Zhou.

"Of course, during the Cultural Revolution the government and party gave us little help or guidance, so our progress was slower," he adds. "Until a few years ago there had been little contact between our villages and the institute, for instance, but then the institute built the bridge because it was too dangerous for their children to take boats across the river to school each day." (I am of the firm opinion that it's dangerous for the children to walk across *that* bridge.)

"Before Liberation not one of us had any education at all. Now every child gets at least an elementary school education, most go through junior middle school, and some through senior middle school. Thus far none of the children in our village has gone to college, but next year the institute will begin enrolling Dai students in a three-year training course, so you can see the government is now taking a more active interest in the development of our communities."

"The children will return to the fields once they've been educated," I comment. "Why are you so interested in their acquiring education?"

Chumpol leans forward and answers earnestly: "You know in the old days we had no machines and used only ancient farming methods. Now there are machines, so the students must learn how to operate and maintain them and make the most efficient use of them. They must learn about soil chemistry and fertilizers and new farming methods. Every family wants to send its children to school. We still work from sunup to sundown. Life is too difficult. The knowledge of the children can ease these burdens. Now our commune has been divided up under the family responsibility system, so people have new enthusiasm and even more hope for a better future."

Pao tells me that this village is small and poor, with 44 families and 236 people. The village has five pigs, three water buffalo, two tractors, and one rice thresher. "There's a bigger, wealthier Dai community nearby," he whispers, as though someone might understand his English, "which has better cadres, is better managed, and has a number of college graduates involved in agricultural planning."

I ask if there is any concern that the Dai language and culture will be absorbed into that of the Han Chinese, and that the young people will intermarry.

"Both the Han and the Dai cultures and customs are good," Chumpol answers quickly, but noting the look on grandmother's face adds that there has been some intermarriage and that the older people do worry that Dai language, dress, culture, and customs may perish.

"Our cadres are all Dai people from this village. Some of them are in the Communist Party and some aren't. All the cadres were elected by the people here. We have elections every five years. I've been chosen as a cadre six times since 1965. I don't like it, because cadres have to work so hard, attending meetings and working out problems besides all the daily work in the fields. But the people keep electing me, so what can I do?"

"Are any of the cadres women?"

"There are seven cadres in this village," he says, "and two are women. In the old days, women washed clothes, fed the pigs, and cooked while men went to the mountains to fish and collect wood. But now the men also look after the children, and men and women share both field work and house work."

I want to pursue this question, but it's nearing lunchtime, and Pao and Hua indicate that we must take our leave. We rise and warmly thank the family for their hospitality, and Chumpol for his patience in answering my questions.

An elderly woman is preparing lunch on the front porch above the chickens that bump freely into the bamboo stilts that keep the house clear of the damp earth.

On the way back to the institute in the brilliant noonday sun, we pass through the now empty market street and chat about the habits of the Dai and other local minority groups. Pao tells me that Dai people bathe every morning in the river, regardless of weather, and that they have historically picked up the entire community to follow the riverbed when its water supply dwindled.

We talk easily, but I'm troubled by one point and try to figure out how to phrase it politely: How come, of all people in this Dai community, we happened to come to the home of a leading cadre and party member?

"Was it a set up?" I finally get up the nerve to ask.

"What do you mean?" Pao asks.

"I mean I thought we were going to talk to some plain, ordinary Dai citizens, and we end up talking to Chumpol, who must of necessity present the views of the party. He's not going to tell a foreigner what's really going on."

Hua and Pao are genuinely puzzled. "Do you think something is wrong in the village?" they ask.

"No. I didn't mean that," I say. "I just don't know. But if there is, he wouldn't tell us—me—about it. He paints a very rosy picture, especially of the new family responsibility system."

"We chose Sari's father precisely because he is a cadre, because he knows about the affairs of the community as a whole and not simply his own household, because he would be able to give you an overall view and to express things coherently," Pao says, and I can see through his forced calmness that I have offended them with my Western suspicions and don't know how to get out of it.

It was not until a year or more later, when I was back in the States discussing the family responsibility system with old China hands, that the many contradictions and potentially serious problems inherent in Chumpol's enthusiastic reception of the new system came into focus.

First was the question of mechanization, which seemed so essential to the Dais: If they divided their land into one-third-acre segments, they considerably reduced the potential for machines, which work much more efficiently on larger areas.

Then there's the issue of the effect of this policy on population control. The more children you have, the more labor you have for your piece of land. In fact, the rural population is increasing again, as are incidences of female infanticide. A rise in population absorbs any benefits reaped from the increased productivity associated with the new system.

The effect on women has yet to be determined. When the family again becomes the accounting unit, instead of a larger collective body, male domination of the family is strengthened.

Finally, there's the issue of the reintroduction of hired labor. A family may now legally hire up to six workers to increase the productivity of its land. (Rumor has it the figures are *much* higher in many places.) At present, these hired laborers like the system as they are doing well, but in the event of a bad crop, a flood, a drought, the laborers could become beggars and start the old Chinese rich peasant/starving peasant cycle all over again.

Grandma Shen asks me to stay another week. Her sincerity and the warm afternoon sunshine draw me, but I have commitments to keep, so Hua arranges for a jeep to take me back across the mountains the next day. The services of a driver are not a problem, but I know how precious and costly is six hours' worth of gasoline.

"Please ask the driver how much the gas costs to get to Simao."

"Never mind. Never mind." I sense that this is not just Chinese politeness, that I'm in for a battle.

"Hua, you must tell me. I know it's very expensive."

"Never mind. We'll pay it. We have a large income and it's no problem."

"That you can afford it is not the point," I argue. "There is no reason in the world you should bear such an expense."

I sit on the edge of the four-poster bed while Hua moves around the room fidgeting with the wash basin, the thermos bottle, the mosquito netting. We are both upset now.

"Hua, let me tell you something truthfully. If you came to New York to visit me, I would happily house you and feed you and take you to all the sights and pay for local transportation—"

"You see, then—"

"But I would *not* pay your fare back to Washington or Chicago or wherever you had come from to visit me. I would consider that your affair."

She looks at me in silence for a while, then, recognizing that I am telling the truth, suggests that I leave her fifty yuan.

"I believe that's enough," she says. "If it's a little more, I'll pay it, O.K.?"

"O.K."

After a wild jaunt across the mountains and a good, long *xiuxi* at the little hotel, I awake to discover that my organs have resettled in their proper places in my anatomy, and that there's a woman sleeping in the other bed in my room. Over lunch I become acquainted with my new roommate, Wang Zheming, whose Chinese parents fled to Malaysia a few years before she was born in 1949, and then migrated to Australia. Wang is studying Chinese in Beijing, and I am most fortunate to have both her company and her translation skills during our adventures in Simao.

Wang and I wander aimlessly around the town that was wiped out before Liberation by a yellow fever epidemic and has only recently been rebuilt of brick and wood. We stop to admire a startling architectural feat: workers interlock wooden beams so that an entire house is built without a single nail.

Off the broad, clean main streets flanked by well-stocked food and wine shops are small communities of mud-soaked lanes where people are replacing worn bricks and door or window sections of their houses. Near a crowded doorway we encounter a bride's family moving brightly colored quilts, gleaming wood chests, and new furniture on horse-drawn carts to the room of the new couple. I ask if I may take pictures, but superstition forbids.

A shy teenaged girl is pushed forward by the crowd and urged to speak to me in English. I speak a little Chinese to encourage her. She's so nervous that she grasps both my hands and squeezes hard as she timidly but clearly articulates a few English book phrases. As we wander on through the winding lanes, she and her friends turn up again and again and repeat the scene until we finally wind our way out onto the main thoroughfare.

We pass a newly constructed complex housing a people's court, police station, fire department, lawyer's office, and PLA headquarters. On a wall near the airline office is a long list of all the families who have had only one child. On another near the hospital are superb cartoons that mock (and, one hopes, educate) those who throw garbage in the streets, spit and sneeze all over the place, chain smoke, or accidentally become pregnant.

We get hungry and walk from one restaurant to another looking at the fare. In one large, clean place we find a variety of foods artistically arranged (rather than heaped) on platters. This is clearly the place to eat, so we go in and ask the prices, only to be told the restaurant is closed. Closed? But there are still several dozen people enjoying all this delicious-looking food. We're discussing why we're being turned away when a man at a table near the kitchen tugs at our sleeves and urges us to join him and his friends.

"Oh, no, no, no. We couldn't possibly do that."

"Oh, come, come," he argues.

"No, no, no, no," we say several more times, and then sit down.

They pour red wine and a white rice wine that could double for dynamite and pile our plates high with vegetables, meats, fish, and poultry dishes. We laugh and talk and eat and drink and watch the men opposite us play a drinking game that works like this: Two people say something equivalent to "once, twice, thrice, shoot" and each raises one or more fingers, simultaneously shouting out his guess at the combined number of fingers extended by both players. The loser must *gan bei* or "bottoms up" (literally, "dry glass"); if both lose, both *gan bei*. As the fire water goes down, the game gets wilder and funnier.

It is, it turns out, a wedding feast. The man who invited us to eat is an old friend of the family who is responsible for organizing the wedding and dinner party. The others at the table are kitchen staff dining after the guests have all been served. The bride and groom come to greet us.

They are both workers and will live in a room at the local hospital where their parents are workers. How can two factory workers wine and dine two hundred people? It is customary, it appears, for each guest to give the newlyweds a wedding gift and a ten-yuan note.

They insist that we come to the wedding party, and gladly do we go, insisting on our part that we stop in a shop along the way to buy several *jin* of assorted cookies wrapped in shiny red wedding paper inscribed in our own hands in both English and Chinese. At the hospital we recognize the furniture and bedding we saw earlier in the day: a big, canopied double bed, a huge wardrobe, a desk, couch, and a couple of chairs. There are new pink curtains, elaborately embroidered bed and cushion covers, and a three-foot double happiness sign over the bed. The floor has been dusted with sweet-smelling pine needles. People ply us with candies, fruits, pumpkin seeds, peanuts, and tea.

In a large room down the hall, a couple of hundred men, women, and children chatter above the cassette recorder blasting out Hong Kong disco. Everyone is dressed up, some in velveteen jackets, most in corduroy or gaily patterned cotton. The little girls sport intricate hair combs with barettes and pretty ribbons, and one, I note, has bright red nail polish.

The master of ceremonies (our dinner table companion) offers some remarks on the young couple and on the nature of marriage, asks others to do likewise, and finally gets to me. I ask Wang to speak for me, which she does, but that isn't satisfactory, and they pull me to my feet and make me speak to all those people in Chinese. Wang insists my few sentences make sense, but in truth it doesn't much matter.

When Wang and I leave, we are each presented with a large red rose and a flowered plate and matching sugar bowl filled with double happiness candy. We are certain these had been gifts to the bride and groom, but protest as we may, we cannot refuse them. We walk off toward our hotel on this star-filled night feeling very happy with our treasures, and I am disturbed only by the realization that the "foreign guests"—and especially the non-Chinese foreign guest—received as much attention as the bride and groom.

"Don't worry about it," Wang assures me. "They'll brag about our presence at their wedding for years to come, and tell the story to their grandchildren."

The next morning Wang and I walk in the direction of a local commune. We photograph cabbages big as human heads. The peasants tell us they're happy here, make a good living, and have no intention of converting to the new family responsibility system. As we head back to the airline office for our tickets, a man strides toward us babbling and gesticulating wildly. He marches right up to us and announces that if I—

as I am clearly not Chinese and there must be some confusion about Wang—if I, the "foreign devil," wish to walk on this street, I must pay one fen for every step I take. He proceeds to punch me in the chest hard enough to momentarily take my breath away, then prances on down the road, no one taking the least notice of the whole matter. We see him again later, bellowing at some newly arrived foreigners.

Strange, wonderful little town. But oh, how many hours we pass holding up licked fingers trying to determine when our little airplane will be able to make its ascent up and over the mountains.

# 21
# Sun, Fun, and Frustration

They don't like it. It isn't what they have in mind for me. Perhaps they're even insulted, or at least hurt that I should wish to spend one of my few precious days in Kunming visiting strangers. And then we get lost. Of course I don't mind a bit. From my point of view the Yunnan Astronomical Observatory driver is taking me on a grand, sunny tour of the Kunming countryside.

At first it's pleasant riding with my students and hosts, Yang and Xiao Tu. Yang describes the countryside, and Xiao Tu fills me in on the details of his honeymoon after he and Mei Mei left Hangzhou. By 10 a.m., however, they suggest we abandon our search; we are wasting a great deal of expensive fuel on this jaunt to locate this Mr. Xing, a man whose company I had enjoyed on the long train ride from Hangzhou to Guilin. I had promised him I'd come and visit, and promised myself I'd find a way to keep my promise.

It's nearly 11 a.m. when an odd jumble of sounds guides us to our destination, for neighbors have told us the address we seek is a music school. We pull into a Fellini scene: beyond the row of lightly swaying palm trees lining the driveway lies a large field littered near and far with young men and women in shirtsleeves or jackets, seated or standing, with or without music stands, faced any and every which way, absorbed in violin, erhu, viola, trumpet, tuba, or cymbals, practicing scales, folk tunes, love songs, or arias from Chinese or Western operas, each oblivious to the others and all apparently oblivious to us.

A tiny, frail old woman comes out to greet us. She has been expecting me, she says, for her son-in-law told her I would certainly arrive sometime soon. As he is a policeman and his wife a music teacher, neither is around during the day. Now why didn't I think of that? I suppose when you aren't working it doesn't occur to you that other people are. But it seems perfectly reasonable to Mr. Xing's mother-in-law. She apologizes for being ill, and she does move and speak slowly and with difficulty as she leads us inside a one-story stucco building, and into a small, square room with grey, crumbling walls. An exquisite, handcarved canopy bed dominates the room. She bids Yang and me to take the chairs and seats Xiao Tu on the bed. In a room across the hall she loads a tray with tea and cups, peeled oranges and shelled peanuts, candies and sunflower seeds. She flutters about like a feeble bird, pouring tea and passing dishes. I'm relieved when she finally settles herself next to Xiao Tu on the bed. He seems bored and sneaks glimpses at his watch.

Ms. Tai is retired. Retired from what? She worked in the Yunnan Provincial Museum. She must have been a ticket-taker or janitor, I say to myself, looking at the tired, thin-haired, toothless woman in tidy, worn pants and jacket, but I notice that Yang sits forward on his seat as she answers.

"I was the vice-director of the museum," Yang translates. "I come from poor city people, but my father was educated and somehow managed to enable me to study. I became a Communist, and in the early forties moved to the Red base area in Yan'an where I studied painting and politics at the Lu Xun Arts and Literature College.

"In Yan'an I worked as a researcher for the *Jiefang ribao* (Liberation Daily). In 1946, shortly before my daughter was born, I quarreled with my husband, so when the paper moved to Xian, I went with it." Ms. Tai sighs deeply. "The man was impossible to live with," she says, "but he was brilliant. He was a political researcher and philosophy professor at Beijing Normal School. During the Cultural Revolution he jumped from a window and died." Yang and Tu sit quietly. I notice that even I have become inured to these matter-of-fact statements.

"In 1950 my father urged me to come up to the capital for a short archaeology training course. When I completed this course I was assigned to the Yunnan Museum, so I moved here with my daughter."

I guess she's lucky to end her days down here, for as she speaks the sun-speckled palm leaves outside the window sway gently, and the faint sounds of the instruments float up through the window. Three hundred days of sunshine every year—how bad can life be in a city with four seasons of spring?

"Since the fifties," Yang translates, "I have mostly been excavating minority relics." Out comes the "bible" and the two men struggle to translate the terminology. "I was involved in the excavation of a Western Han dynasty tomb while I was manager of the museum. I like to study books, but I like best to do the 'real things.'"

Tai's blue-grey eyes light up, and her voice grows younger and stronger as she describes the important bronzes they learned about from minority peasants living near a tomb site in Jin Yang county. "They still argue today," she says, "about whether some of the pieces are Dai or

Yi, but most say they are Yi relics and I think so too. The relics are wonderful. I found a golden chop in one tomb; it belonged to the head of Yunnan at that time and he was Yi nationality—"

She stops suddenly as Yang and Xiao Tu look at their watches and at each other. Oh, no. We absolutely cannot leave now. This woman is a national historical treasure. She lived at the Communist base in Yan'an with Mao and Zhou, studied at Lu Xun College where Jiang Qing (then Lan Ping) was an instructor and unsuccessful actress, worked on *Jiefang ribao*, was involved in major archaeological finds. She must have had staggering experiences during the Cultural Revolution. Was it then she became so ill? How can I walk away from her after twenty minutes' conversation?

I insist they go without me. We argue about how I will manage to get back. I could get back, but I realize that there's no way I can handle this without a translator. Perhaps, I suggest, we can pick up Tai tomorrow and visit the Yunnan Museum with her. Yang and Tu agree that that's a good idea, that "perhaps" we can do that, but I understand, and so does Tai, that it will not come to pass.

She will not allow us to take her picture; she is too ill, she says, looks so bad, and I must come another time when she's better. "Tomorrow," I say, "we'll pick you up tomorrow—." It is with great reluctance that I finally agree to leave. We sit in silence for some time as the car speeds along the winding mountain road, the driver leaning on the horn, irritating me and startling the donkeys and indigenous small horses that draw carts piled high with goods and people.

Yang and Tu are clearly annoyed with me but too polite to say so. I am not so polite: "Can I ask what the big hurry is?"

No one answers. Finally Yang turns to me and says very quietly, "Mei Mei will be at the railway station at noon. She is not supposed to be here. It isn't a good idea to leave her standing at the station waiting for us. Someone may recognize her."

"Oh. Well. Why in the world didn't you say so before?" I ask, forgetting, as always, the Chinese propensity for indirect communication.

Xiao Tu blushes deeply, which exaggerates his boyish features and crew cut. Mei Mei, who works for an import-export firm in Wuhan, is entitled to two trips a year, but the nature of her work allows her to sneak off now and then for extra visits to Kunming. We pick her up at the train station and whisk her off to a local hotel—it isn't safe to take her back with us—then drive back up the long hill that winds up to the observatory.

Perched high above the city, the new apartments at the Yunnan Astronomical Observatory take full advantage of Kunming's three hundred days of sunshine. Each apartment has two balconies, so you can shift your clothes as the sun arcs, and at night breathe in the clean, quiet air and wonder at the astonishment of stars.

The apartments are the nicest I've seen in China, with tiled kitchens and bathrooms, the latter combining Eastern habits and Western technology, i.e., a hole in the white-tiled floor and a flush system that also serves as shower (cold, of course) if you simply straddle the hole.

The hallway is separated from the living room by a half wall topped with a wood divider designed like a Chinese knick-knack shelf. This makes everything seem more spacious, and I find much warmth in the addition of wood to so many tons of cement. The apartments are also well lit, for unlike Zhe Da, where 15-watt bulbs are the norm because of the scarcity and high price of electricity, here electricty is plentiful and cheap. As it's never very cold in Kunming, there's no need for heating, and if the summer should get very hot—and I'm told that's rare—people hang out in the labs, which are air conditioned to protect the sensitive instruments.

An apartment like the one I've been given (living room, kitchen, two bedrooms, and two balconies) is three yuan a month. I have been placed next door to friends of Yang, a couple with a young child who attends the observatory's six-day child care center for a small fee and the cost of meals.

I am "practice" for a Ms. Li, who will be *wai ban* (handler) for "the old American lady" who will occupy this apartment next year. "How old is she?" I ask. "Oh, over sixty," Li answers with reverence. "We're concerned that she won't be able to walk the two flights of stairs." I laugh. "An 'American lady' who's coming out to live and teach in China for a year will keep you all hopping," I tell her, and then I have to get up to perform the act of hopping and explain the metaphor. Li is also seriously concerned about the lady's morning toast. There is no toaster or oven, and all the textbooks she's studied indicate that Americans eat bacon, eggs, and toast for breakfast. However will she manage? I point out to Li that *I'm* an American and I've managed very well—not to worry.

The next day Xiao Tu and I pick up Mei Mei early in the morning and drive for hours out to the Stone Forest. We have had a long discussion, Tu and I, about using the observatory car for so long a trip. I am perfectly willing to take a bus, but Xiao Tu won't hear of it, and it isn't difficult to understand why; without me as an excuse to use the car, they'd have little chance at so many private hours together. They chatter like lively teenagers all the way, and the Stone Forest offers lots of opportunity for hand holding as we all climb up and down the natural rock formations that create this phantasmagorical prehistoric forest with stone pterodactyls and brontosauruses amidst stone trees and bushes. (How I wish Nayim were here to hold *my* hand.) I will balk later at the sixty yuan I must pay for the gas, but then room and board and all other transportation are free, and they haven't even asked me to lecture for my supper.

I get a tour of the observatory. Like everywhere else in China, the grounds are littered with construction materials. Several major new buildings are going up next to the modern marvels already in use. We climb several staircases to the dome of one building. Yang pushes a button and the whole side of the dome slides back. When was this building built? 1972. And that laboratory? 1974. Most of the labs were finished between '72 and '75. The question leaps to mind: In the midst of the Cultural Revolution, when science came to a virtual standstill across the face of China, how is it that all these buildings were under construction?

"This was part of Jiang Qing's plot," is the answer. What? Can it be that something good is attributed to the ubiquitous enemy? "This was her showplace," says Yang, "the place she took guests and foreign visitors to demonstrate how the government was fostering science."

Kunming was a front-line battleground in the early days of the Cultural Revolution. Wanting nothing to do with it all, Yang and others took off for their homes in various corners of China. But in '72 they returned to find a flourishing, well-funded institute where they worked in peace while their colleagues in neighboring institutes suffered. "Did you know what was going on elsewhere?" I ask. "We heard," says Yang, "but what could we do?"

Several other buildings have just been completed, like the apartments and the attractive dining room with much better food than Zhe Da, though it is a bit more expensive, twenty-five instead of eighteen yuan a month for three meals a day. But the residents here are all wage earners, not students.

The following evening, Mei Mei is smuggled into my apartment for an elaborate hot-pot dinner. It's a lively party. Zao, Yang's wife, tells me that down here vegetables are plentiful, and I find platters heaped with lamb and beef as well. We drink warm beer and thimblesful of wine and laugh and feed the children, and they all make fun of me when I drop things in the soup.

Li and Zao and I move out on the balcony for a breath of air. Though we've had a few meals together, I've been unable to penetrate Tsao's reserve. She has spoken a bit about her husband and his work, about their nine-year-old and his schooling, about the numerous advantages of their new accommodations, but I have yet to learn anything about her.

"Where does Zao work?" I ask Li, for Zao speaks no English.

"At the factory way down there," she answers, pointing down the hill. I remember it. As our car swung around the foot of the hill on which the observatory is located, I noticed the gates of a large, grey factory flanked by brightly colored two-dimensional paintings of cars, trucks, and buses.

"Does she like it?" I ask, wishing that she would ask Zao rather than answer for her.

"Oh, yes," says Li, "very much."

This will not do, so I lean across Li and ask Zao in Chinese if she likes working at the factory.

She's startled by my question. Zao and Li hold a quick conversation in local dialect, then this quiet, reticent woman begins to speak in a strong, clear voice as Li translates.

"I am one of several thousand workers in the factory," she says. "Our factory makes parts for cars and trucks and buses. We make them so badly that no one wants to buy them."

The three of us burst out laughing. I have heard of other huge, state-owned factories where sloppy production results from bad management and bonus systems that encourage quantity rather than quality. Here's that old "red" versus "expert" contradiction again. Many of those still in charge of major industries are good, honest, well-meaning revolutionaries who know little or nothing about industrial production and management, and in some of the institutes I've visited, the scientists complain bitterly of waste and confusion created by uneducated cadres in charge of their work.

"The government will probably hire foreign quality-control experts to help reorganize the plant," Zao continues. "But in the meantime, since our wages are guaranteed and we have to do something, we study politics and manufacturing techniques. There is now a big battle going on at the plant, an ideological battle, of course," she adds quickly. "Some cadres at the plant argue that the way to save the factory is to retire women with children. Others say that since they would be forced by law to give us 75 percent of our wages, it doesn't pay to lay us off. 'Ah, but then we could close the infant and child care facilities,' says the first group, and they go back and forth like this."

"How do you feel about it?" I ask.

"It's an attack on women's right to work," Zao says firmly, her hand grasping the balcony railing so tightly her knuckles turn white.

The idea of "retiring" women has also cropped up in Shanghai and Beijing newspapers as a "solution" to China's severe youth unemployment problem. I've heard that the All-China Women's Federation is fighting it tooth and nail.

"Here, too," says Zao. "One thing is clear: if you don't work, you are nobody. We women don't want to be nobody anymore."

"What will you do?" I ask.

"We don't know yet," says Zao, "but we will not be driven out."

"Bravo!" I cry. I'm about to launch into a lecture on strategy and tactics in the American women's movement when we are called in by the menfolk for the second round of dinner.

I hate to leave Kunming. I hate to leave my friends, and I hate to leave the warm sun. As the plane takes off, I think of those deep male voices in the old black and white Movietone travelogues. Did I believe—did it even occur to me back then—that it would be *me* flying off into the sunset?

"Remember the Red River Valley," croons a tenor from behind a high grey wall as I walk the quiet morning streets of Chengdu in search of the house of one Tang Qubai, a friend of a friend whom I have never met. Once out of the quainter (i.e., poorer) areas, the walled compounds leave little to please the eye of the wandering tourist.

Or maybe it's me. I'm grumpy. Last night I had trouble at the airport getting someone to direct me to the free bus to town. "You will be most comfortable in a taxi," a China Travel hack assured me, "and it is only twelve or thirteen yuan to your hotel." I found the free bus, which left me at the hotel door, but then had a fight with the clerk who refused to give me a room at foreign expert prices, despite the law requiring him to do so. He finally agreed to give me a triple room for sixteen yuan a night on the agreement that if other travelers showed up, he would put them in with me and reduce my rate. I turned over my passport and travel permit and headed upstairs. Fortunately, no one showed—I was worried about all the cash stashed in my pockets.

Turning off the broad avenue (it has separate bike *roads*, not lanes, on both sides), I collect an entourage of children who escort me to Tang's house. Inside a wrought iron gate and down a narrow path through a garden of gaily colored flowers, I come upon a boy so absorbed in his book he doesn't notice me until I'm standing before him. He freezes, then leaps up and runs into the house shouting *wai guo ren, wai guo ren*, "foreigner, foreigner" (literally, "outside country person"). Out of an old wood and stone house with large windows topped by diamond-shaped panes comes a woman wiping flour smudges from her nose and chin with her apron. Tang and her husband are on vacation in Kunming, Tang's mother tells me, but she insists that I come back at six tonight to share their New Year's feast. She will try to find one of Tang's English-speaking friends to join us.

Wending my way back, I stumble on a holiday market gay with balloons, clothes, food, and multicolored crepe-paper dragons on sticks. The crowds following me are at last diverted by the street entertainer,

I return to the Tang house for dinner.

a bald-headed man in a karate outfit who breaks bricks, rides a unicycle, does magic tricks and clown routines. Tables of watches, clocks, medicines, china, bamboo, lacquerware, and even junky-looking 200-yuan washing machines line the streets. At an outdoor garment factory the men stand at large cutting tables, the women bend over sewing machines. I pass a motorized wheelchair with a side car big enough for two small children. It's easy to find the hotel; I just close my eyes and follow the sounds of civil war or the Fourth of July. (I'm a little frightened of the fireworks, for there seems to be little caution in their use.)

I return to the Tang house for dinner, and what a dinner! Colorful, aromatic, and simply delicious hot and sweet and sour and delicately pungent dishes, one after another, feed a dozen lively adults and children crowded around two tiny tables. (It occurs to me that one of the reasons the Chinese table settings are different from ours is that there's rarely space for large, individual dinner plates.) Everyone is jolly except sourpuss Zhu, who is sarcastic about everything except the food. In his early twenties, Tang's friend Zhu, who has been studying English by himself for more than two years, is doing remarkably well translating for me, but he is so serious and so cynical the rest of the family often laughs at him.

After dinner we gather around the TV to watch a children's program of puppets and robots playing music, and a Mr. I. Magination sort of thing where we get to travel the land via letters written to a PLA soldier by a young friend.

Zhu gets me back to my hotel by a series of sidestreets, for it's illegal to ride anyone, no less a foreigner, on the back rack of your bike.

The next day Zhu and I go to the People's Park, where I remain the center of attraction even in the playground with its elephant trunk slides, see-saws, swings, and merry-go-rounds. We have a good lunch in the park restaurant, owned and operated since the fall of the Gang of Four by the local commune. We share our table with three workers from a machine factory who earn about eighty yuan per month plus bonuses. "Now it's good," one man says as the others nod agreement, "because if you work hard, you earn more, so we enjoy working now and we live just fine."

The park is pleasant, but I do tire of parks and temples. "What would you like to see?" asks Zhu.

"I'd like to visit the commune," I answer.

"The commune?" he says with disdain. "Why?"

"Well, uh, I'm interested in learning as much as I can about the lives of the peasants," I answer, unsure why I suddenly feel so silly.

"These aren't real peasants," says Zhu. I look confused. "These are rich peasants," he explains.

"'The only good peasant is a poor peasant,' huh?" Zhu misses my point.

"Can you take me out to visit 'real' peasants?" I ask.

"No," he says.

"Then let's go visit the 'fake' ones," I suggest. Zhu manages a smile.

Carrying a one-year-old in a sling on his back, a young man is completing the third room of his new brick house. He stops to offer us coffee. Yes, instant coffee in little plastic packets, alas, very presweetened. The family now earns one to two yuan per day, plus thirty-two *jin* of rice per person per month provided by the government. Things are getting better and better, especially in the last four years since the fall of the Gang of Four. They get an extra four yuan a month for having only one child; if they have a second, they must give it back. (I think of the block-long billboard downtown featuring an exuberant family of three, floating symbols of modern science and industry, and that nasty Britishism, "You had better have only one child.")

"I used to want to be a worker," says our friend, "but now young people want to work the land as we can earn a good living here, especially because it's close to town so we have no transportation problems."

We walk on through rows of thriving vegetables and come to a whole clan gathered in front of a large new house, all of them dolled up in their holiday best. We must, of course, partake of tea, candy, cookies, peanuts, etc. Many years ago there were few people in this village, says Grandpa. "We were very poor. Sometimes we had breakfast, but never was there dinner. We only had hard work. There was much land, but only a few landlords. After Liberation some of the landlords ran away, others died of old age.

"After Liberation life got better, but now is the best time. Rice and vegetables—even pork—are plentiful, and if our family works hard, we can make over 1,000 yuan per year from vegetables and pigs, and from the restaurant and wine brewery in the park. We can now buy medicine, food, clothes, a bicycle, a sewing machine, a TV, a new home," he adds, displaying the latter with a flourish. "Soon our brigade will buy more tractors. The work is easier than before. There's less land and more people, 200 *mu* of land and 600 people. These little ones will never know how hard it was," he says, gathering in his arms his grandson all decked out in a sailor suit. "They should hang the Gang of Four," he adds. "Even hanging is too good for them."

"You see," says Zhu as we leave the family, "rich peasants." On the other side of the pig sties, however, we find a different story. We are served cups of hot water by a family in patched clothing seated on broken-down furniture before a crumbling house. They recite the same story about how bad it was before Liberation, how things got better, and, after '76, better still, how the family now earns several hundred dollars a year from their share in the brigade's enterprises.

If this is "better," I hate to think of what worse was. And why should one family be so much poorer than the others in the same brigade? They have three children, one of whom has a blood disease. He needs regular transfusions costing about fifty yuan each. "See," says the mother, pulling up her son's pants leg to exhibit his swollen ankles and calves. "The co-op covers standard medical treatment but will not pay the city hospital for regular transfusions." She is retired, and though they get rice and each earns about ten yuan per month, they never have any money because of the child's illness. "Last year his father had to sell matches for money for blood, and we often have to borrow as well. Because there are many people, the commune has no medical plan to help with amounts so large."

Commune family celebrates a wealthy new year.

There goes another of my utopian dreams. Surely, under socialism, that sort of individual expense could be shared by 600 commune members. But if it is suddenly glorious to be rich, then it's surely less glorious to help thy neighbor.

No sooner are we out of the commune and headed for the bus than we come upon a toothless old man with a full head of white hair, wispy white beard, and heavy black clothes sitting on the ground behind a sign that reads: "I am so-and-so. I come from such-and-such Mountain. My two children died of cancer and left me with my two young grandchildren. This year my house burned down. We have nowhere to live, there's almost nothing to eat in the mountains, and I'm too old to work, so we've come here to ask you city people to help support us." In his basket are coins, food coupons, candy, nuts, and fruit.

The Lantern Festival is fabulous. I'm already dazzled by lanterns shaped like fish and mermaids, elephants, and monkey kings when we reach the elaborate sets of revolving silk pictures: dynasties rise and fall, lovers woo and win and jump off cliffs together, gods and goddesses cavort with mere mortals. The crowd is happy and so am I, but I'm tired and eager to get to bed. Zhu, however, has another idea. His apartment is between here and my hotel; he would like to show me his apartment, and then he'll ride me home on the bike.

I'm reluctant to do this, and say so, but Zhu has been extremely nice to me and I feel I can't refuse. I'm not concerned for my safety, just uncomfortable.

Zhu's room is on the second floor of an old wooden tenement. It is one narrow room, cramped with furniture. Its only saving graces are a high ceiling, wood floor, and whitewashed brick walls. Zhu lives here with his wife and baby who are away for the holiday—this is the first I've heard of them. Zhu warned me the place was a mess, but I'd assumed this was ordinary politeness. It wasn't. Clothes and books are intermingled on the unmade bed, the desk, the floor, the chairs with canvases, messy paint tubes, and half-cleaned brushes.

Zhu is an artist, or "was" as artist, as he says bitterly. Now he's a factory worker who paints. His paintings are mainly of nature and of faces: an arbor in winter where the dark tree limbs, black against a bleached sky, stretch upward like Martha Graham figures, or a face of an old Yi woman, peaceful, pleasant. He submits his paintings to institutes and art contests, but nothing has ever been accepted, a result, he is certain, of "politics," though he will not be any more explicit than that. I have no way to judge.

Zhu spent three years in the countryside with the "real" peasants. He liked it and learned a lot but can't say what he learned. It occurs to me that I may have found someone who supports the Gang of Four (or at least the Cultural Revolution). But I'm eager to leave, for I'm uncomfortable, cramped in amidst the rubble of his room, my elbow endangering the three white porcelain nudes on the table next to me.

Perched precariously on the back of Zhu's speeding bike, I wonder: Is Zhu just a bitter personality, or is he a child of the Cultural Revolution, one of the throng that wandered the streets without parents or schooling during their formative years? He will likely live in a state of permanant bitterness, blaming his failure on "the system." Were he in the West, he would no doubt work as a waiter or taxi driver, and blame his failure alternately on himself and on *our* system.

As Zhu leaves me a block from my hotel, he gives me a small painting and seems genuinely sad to let me go. Suddenly I feel that I have judged him harshly, that I ought to stay another day and hear his story—how many stories have I left behind? But I've determined to take the boat down the Yangzi, and I've already made arrangements to meet friends on the boat dock in Wuhan some days hence. I will never find out what makes Zhu tick.

At the hotel desk I ask if there's a bus to the train station. No, but a taxi is a mere twelve yuan, and there just happens to be a taxi office in the hotel. I walk right out the front door and stop a passerby. Why, yes, the bus to the train station stops across the street and costs ten fen. I go back to pay my bill. Again we haggle. I hand him the thirty-two yuan we agreed upon, storm out of the hotel, catch the ten-fen bus, and settle myself, still fuming, on the train to Chongqing. In the middle of the night I realize I have left behind my passport and all my travel documents.

With a bit of ingenuity, a lot of help from my friends, and a major fleecing by China Travel Service, I manage to get a hotel room for the night in Chongqing, the boat to Yi Chang where you change for the bus around the Qutang Gorge where river passage is blocked by dam construction, and another boat on to Wuhan where some of my students await me on the dock.

Despite my dearth of documents, someone manages to get me a plane ticket to Shanghai. But in the big metropolis signatures and seals are serious business; no one will take responsibility for selling me a train ticket to Hangzhou. I show the old train master my only remaining official document—my little red work permit that proves I belong to a unit. I assume the train master will call someone—the Shanghai police, the Hangzhou police, my unit, someone—but after a couple of hours my rumbling stomach tells me otherwise.

"I hope you're a good cook," I offer pleasantly.

"Cook?" he says, assuming he has misunderstood my Chinese.

"Why, yes," I answer. "If I'm going to sit here in the Shanghai train station indefinitely, well, then, you're going to have to feed me. You wouldn't want the poor American teacher to starve to death, would you?"

The man is now seriously perplexed. He picks up the phone and has a long conversation with someone in Shanghai dialect, then pushes paper, pen, and ink toward me. He says that if I write out an explanation of where and how I lost my documents, he will allow me to return to Hangzhou.

Lucifer whispers in my ear that the man doesn't know a word of English, and I could write a devilishly comical letter. But I restrain myself, scratch out my story, and telegram Lao Fan to come and pick me up in Hangzhou.

Forty-four days after my departure, Hangzhou is still grey and gloomy. But everyone is there to greet me at the station. I'm glad to be home.

# 22
# Mayday, Mayday

Letters bound above the line. Others sag below it. Some hang upside down. Some have fainted flat on their faces. Numerals stand in for some. Others are missing altogether. This will not do. We came to no arrangement about money, but the Shanghai Foreign Language Education Press promised to produce an attractive textbook, one we could all be proud of. These galley proofs are outrageous.

So much seems outrageous nowadays. I have actually fired my *aiyi*, Miss Mei You. I, who so admired the iron rice bowl, could not go on paying her twenty yuan a month for work that I do myself. It isn't as though I'm starving her or sending her to the streets to beg; she still works half a day for Jenny, and the university will have to fill in the other half of her pay. But think of China's dilemma: some people, like my former *aiyi*, Xiao Zhou, work very hard for their wages while others, like Miss Mei You, do as little as they can manage. If people cannot be fired, how do you get the lackadaisical to work? And if you multiply Miss Mei You on a Chinese scale in agriculture and industry, consider the implications for productivity. On the other hand, won't the freedom to hire and fire lead China right back to exploitation, sexual harassment, all the things socialism is supposed to eliminate?

Well, that's China's problem. As for me, I'm exhausted. I'm trying to teach my classes, finish the text, and do all the shopping, cleaning, and laundry. No wonder the teachers bitch so much about housework. And for the first time in two years I have actually said no to Li Xumei, who asked me to record some books. I think she's annoyed because the textbook is a project neither created nor agreed to by my unit. *I* decided where to put my time and energy. *I* decided this book is needed in China. Individuals simply don't make those kinds of decisions.

I'm tired, crabby, confused about what's worth arguing about and what isn't. Maybe the textbook *was* a mistake. In this, my last half year in China, at a time when I have finally learned enough to begin asking the right questions, I remain cloistered in my bedroom hacking away at the typewriter. I regularly get letters from America: "What about democracy?" everyone asks. Well, what about democracy? I don't know. I have pages and pages of interviews with everyone from top cadres to ordinary people on this question, but we don't seem to be talking the same language. We can't even agree on definitions of "democracy," "freedom," "human rights."

Worst of all, Lao Fan and I have begun to quarrel. We're working on a chapter about filling out forms for visas, grants, graduate school, etc. "Forms, forms, and more forms," I begin. "If you think there's a lot of bureaucracy in China, wait until you start filling out the multitude of forms required by Western institutions." Lao Fan says we cannot come right out and say that China is bureaucracy-laden. I say that every eight-year-old child in China knows it is, so why not say so? Suddenly there seem to be so many points to niggle over. And these horrendous proofs are the last straw.

Lao Fan and I take a trip to Shanghai—at our own expense—to meet with our publishers. I'm hopeless at this sort of negotiation; they want to chat about the price of tea in China, and I want to get to the point about the book. Lao Fan does his best to bridle me, but I cannot hobble about the point for long.

Their story is this: they've been waiting almost a year for people from London to come and repair their broken printing presses (probably smashed during the Cultural Revolution). They want to get the book out before I leave China, so their non-English-reading printers have been handsetting from remnants of pre-Liberation fonts as best they can.

"If you want to market it widely," I argue, "you need a properly printed, well-illustrated book." Chinese textbooks are uniformly dull—page after page of uninterrupted text.

"Illustrated?" they gasp. "That costs money. And we've already spent 1,000 yuan on this first printing."

I argue that it's in their own interest as well as ours to produce an attractive book. "Besides," I add, trying to best them at their own culture, "you promised." After much discussion and guilt-tripping on both sides, they agree to wait until their presses are repaired.

And the cover? Certainly the American flag, they insist, or the Capitol building. Good grief, no. No one will be able to distinguish the book from the propaganda distributed by the American Embassy in Beijing. How about embossed gold lettering? Too much like all other Chinese texts. We agree to leave the matter to the imagination of their art director.

The title? After much serious debate, our students have named the book *Modern American English: Living and Learning in the West.* Good. Settled.

Deadlines? I agree to get the book done before I leave China and to supply them with illustrations. They agree to air mail ten copies of the book to me in America as soon as it is published. And payment? That depends. As we're escorted out of the wonderful old Victorian house that serves as the Press offices, I still don't know what payment depends *on.*

Last time we were in Shanghai the Press took us to dinner. This time, Lao Fan says, I must wine and dine them. I comply, always trusting his guidance on Chinese protocol, but I feel ripped off. It isn't that thirty-five or forty yuan is going to break me, but I'm me and they're a company. However, *mei you ban fa*—there's nothing for it. We arrange to meet them for dinner that evening at the Peace Hotel.

Over lunch, Lao Fan gingerly raises another issue: the university wants me to agree in principle to pay some unspecified sum to their typists out of whatever I make on the book. I'm confused. The typists have been typing my classroom lessons, which they would have had to do book or no, and no one said anything about money all these months they've been doing the work. Furthermore, the Press has yet to give me a figure, no less a contract, and I've already signed over half of that mysterious amount to Lao Fan—a small way of paying him not only for his time and energy on the book, but all that he has given me over the last two years. I flatly refuse to pay the typists, though I'm troubled to know that Zhe Da will continue to pester him to pester me.

The more I think of it, the easier it is to guess what happened. Zhe Da feels cheated. There have probably been meetings to discuss the matter. Aren't they paying huge sums for my services twenty-four hours a day? Didn't I make the decision all by myself without their permission to work on this book on *their* time? Can't they devise some means of compensation for the hours I'm stealing from them? Yes, it's the *jinjinjijiao* mentality fine tuned—square accounts to the last fen.

After lunch we go shopping. Shopping in Shanghai is always fun. There are so many things I'd like to buy (like a bolt of cashmere to make a suit for Nayim), but after fighting with Lao Fan over the typists' fees, I can't bring myself to do it, so I buy practical wool instead. This has been going on for two years; I earn so much more than people here that I'm reluctant to spend large sums on what are certainly luxuries.

There are no parades, no speeches, no demonstrations in Shanghai this Mayday. It is a celebration of families who at long last have enough money to buy the goods that have at long last begun to appear in the stores. No, not enough goods, but infinitely more than there were five years ago or even two years ago. Is this, too, a form of freedom—or does it muddle matters to link economic and political freedoms? Can a definition of freedom exclude the rights to food, clothing, housing, education, medical care, child care, jobs?

It seems as though all of Shanghai's eleven million people are here today: The accordian buses are so packed we cannot pass our fares to the conductor; the department stores are so stuffed we have to do as the natives—shove people out of the way and shout for the attention of a clerk. The streets are so jammed with holiday-clad families we are sometimes swept along toward other people's destinations. By the time we get to the Peace Hotel, I'm exhausted.

Seated around a large table in the opulent restaurant overlooking the Bund, the gentlemen seem quite at home. On my left is Mr. Pu, a sophisticated, multilingual intellectual who, not many years ago, was paraded through the streets of Shanghai with a dunce cap on his head. On my right is Editor Li, son of a Shanghai industrialist who, not many years ago, was grinding stones for the foundation beneath my room at the Jing Jiang Hotel. Editor Li was jailed in 1957 during the anti-Rightist movement and was under arrest or "supervision" until 1978. Now he has a good job and a new wife; soon he'll have a good apartment and a new baby. Next to him is Lao Fan, my intellectual peasant friend who surely suffered as much in his early years as these gentlemen suffered more recently. Across from me is Pu and Li's driver. I know nothing of his history. His presence seems like a token acknowledgment of socialism, unable as he is to participate in the conversation.

Mr. Pu says how pleased they are to add my excellent book to their small list. I'm curious to know on what basis they select books, and how much freedom they have in choosing. They are seriously restricted by the amount of paper available, he says, but are now free to publish whatever they choose without interference from the government.

"You mean no one in the government oversees your publications?" I ask in surprise.

"Well, of course, we're under the Ministry of Education," Pu answers, "and we discuss our work with them. But they do not interfere. We are free to publish what we like. Of course, we're also responsible now for our own profits and losses," he adds.

"And what sort of books have you chosen?" I ask.

"Our latest project," Li announces enthusiastically, "involves the translation of children's books. We have just put out the first edition since Liberation of *Cinderella*."

I groan. They stare at me. "You have limited paper, the hard-won freedom to publish whatever you wish, and you choose the most sexist literature to feed to Chinese children?"

"Sexist?" asks Mr. Pu.

"What does *Cinderella* teach children? That ugly is bad and beautiful is good, that girls should be patient and passive even in the face of vicious abuse, that their only salvation lies in the love of some man attracted to their beauty—and in China, of all places, that beauty lies in lily feet!"

No one says anything. Lao Fan changes the subject. I look out the window. From up here, the crowds on the Bund, the boats of many eras on the muddy Huang Po River, and the old British buildings across the street seem unreal, like a blue-filtered shot of old Shanghai in a 3-D movie. Somewhere down there, in 1975, I sat across a rickety table from a wrinkled old dockworker. His eyes gleaming with tears, he spoke of his life as a coolie, a half-clothed, half-starved bearer of burdens. In 1949, for the first time in his life, he had been addressed as "brother," as "comrade," and provided with food, clothing, housing, medical care, and the guarantee of a decent burial.

I didn't think then—I don't think now—that the old dockworker was exaggerating. How many accounts have I read of old Shanghai, always exciting and teeming with life—but what life! I remember Helen Foster Snow's description of debarking in Shanghai exactly half a century ago, setting foot upon the Bund for the first time: "We thought we were being attacked by a mob—they turned out to be competing rickshaw men—and then had to thread our way through filthy, ragged beggars in all stages of disease."

I turn back to our table. We toast the success of our book, the success of the Press, the happiness and health of Mr. Li's forthcoming child. But I am moved to propose another toast on this Mayday, this international workers' holiday. Fumbling for phrases from my tiny, toneless vocabulary, I toast our driver, saying as best I can how wonderful it is to be today in the busy Shanghai streets and find ordinary men, women, and children on a Mayday shopping spree. Whatever suffering there has been over these last thirty years, hoorah for New China, no longer the Sick Man of Asia. Hoorah for the People's Republic of China. "*Gan bei*," I conclude, lifting my glass.

Glasses of lead are lugged up to the lips. "*Gan bei*," they repeat politely. What have I done now! You were perfectly fine, I say to myself, a foreigner giving a fevered lecture on Chinese history—on Mayday, no less—to a group of Chinese intellectuals repeatedly beaten, jailed, and humiliated over the last ten, twenty, thirty years. It occurs to me that the driver probably speaks Shanghai dialect and understands not a word of my abysmal Mandarin. It's doubtful that anyone but Lao Fan could interpret my Chinese, and he's so embarrassed he can't even look at me. Henceforth, I promise myself, I will stick to "Long Live the

Friendship Between the Chinese and American People."

They drop me off at the Jing Jiang Hotel, but I can't sleep. The disco music from The Club below pounds on the walls, the floor, the furniture. I'm going back to America in a few months. What will I say to the friends who ask "Well, what do you think about China now? Can China modernize? What about the 'fifth modernization'—democracy? Will more freedom bring more Cinderellas? Is China going capitalist? Is it totalitarian? Could the winds shift? Could there be another Cultural Revolution or some other leftist movement? What will happen when Deng Xiaoping dies? Will all the rehabilitated get unrehabilitated, and all the Gang of Four followers be exonerated? What about— What about—"

I throw on some clothes and go down to The Club, where half a dozen Chinese waiters in starched white uniforms serve Johnny Walker Red and Black while half a dozen others idly drum their fingers on the polished wood bar and watch the Westerners wiggle around the room. "If the standard of living in China improves," Americans will ask, "won't the Chinese become just like us?"

"Well, you see, it's a transition period and it's hard to tell," I say to myself, testing out responses to all the questions that are to come. "You see, one always divides into two—" How about, "You see, the Chinese are always Chinese—" That's a big help!

The train back to Hangzhou is so crowded that several people must rearrange themselves before a man can put his hand in his pocket for a cigarette. The chatter and laughter are exhilarating, but the heat, the smoke, the press of bodies, the poking packages (including ours) will not be fun for three hours. Lao Fan convinces the conductor that the foreigner must have the snap-down seat in her own two-by-two cabin. However squashed the two of us are in here, it's lots better than being out there. We chat with some brewery workers sitting knees to chest on the aisle floor. Once out of the fray, I enjoy the liveliness of the crowd, the pleasure of conversation with strangers. It occurs to me that as much as I resent the endless restrictions on my independence, so much do I enjoy the security of being perpetually cared for by Lao Fan and virtually everyone else. "It's like having a billion mothers," I often tell Li Xumei, certain that she gets but half the double entendre.

Do I want to leave China? Despite all the recent tensions, I have been happier, more alive, more productive here than I have ever been before. Why don't I just take a year to study Chinese and stay here another year or two? Maybe then I could begin to answer some of the questions. I am giddy with heat and fatigue, mesmerized by the rhythms of the train: "Why not stay here?

Why not stay here? Why not stay here?"

Two reasons. A letter from the Borough of Manhattan Community College, City University of New York, the first and only letter from my erstwhile employer, says: "You have been away two years. If you do not return in September, you will lose your job and your tenure. Inform us immediately of your decision." Nice. Very nice. Not even a "hope your leave was productive." Really makes me want to rush back. But am I ready to give up my tenured job, my own iron rice bowl? A letter from Nayim says he's working closely with his adviser on his dissertation and simply cannot arrange to come to China. But he misses me. When, he wants to know, am I coming home?

So I am going home and, willy-nilly, I'm going to be the "China expert." It's one thing to describe the life I've seen, but how am I going to answer all those people who write to ask about the big issues like democracy?

A telegram comes from a friend who's whizzing through Hangzhou with a tourist group. I'm eager to talk with her, so I join her group for the day. In a deluxe, air conditioned sightseeing bus we head out to a commune on the outskirts of town, and visit with Grandfather Wang, who has just built a spacious home for his family. The peasant proudly explains in detail what building materials he selected and why, how many years it took to amass 5,600 yuan, how the neighbors pitched in to help at each stage, and how many generations of Wangs will enjoy its comforts.

An American asks: "But do you have the right to sell your house and move to another area?" The interpreter does not understand the question. The American elaborates. The interpreter asks Grandfather Wang. He doesn't understand the question. Of course he owns his house and *could* sell it, but— We go back and forth for some time, the American pushing his point, the purple-faced interpreter apologizing because the difficulty must surely lie in his translation skills.

In the commune office we find Grandfather Wang's new daughter-in-law. "How many children do you want?" asks an American woman. "One," she answers dutifully, lowering her eyes. "If you later decided you wanted more than one child," the woman asks, "would you be free to make that decision?" "Oh, no," answers daughter-in-law. "It would depend on the number of children and the number of pregnancies in the brigade as a whole." She turns to a wall chart listing every married woman in the brigade, number of children, method of contraception, and when or if she might be permitted to become pregnant. "In some cases," she adds, "it is possible to have two children if there are not already too many." "But you do not have the right to make that decision for yourself," the American reiterates. "Oh, no," says daughter-in-law.

Over lunch in the Tianwaitian (Heaven Beyond Heaven) Restaurant, the tourists discuss the stupidity of Grandfather Wang, who doesn't even recognize that he isn't free. Someone suggests that perhaps the interpeter is a party hack unwilling to translate the question because it might awaken the peasant to the totalitarian nature of the state. No, no, says another, certainly the daughter-in-law understands and resents the restrictions on her civil rights but is saying what she's supposed to say to the tourists—what else can you do in a police state?

I ride off home thinking: Americans. Bah! We are obsessed with some abstract notion of democracy. Everyone must be free to do everything and anything he or she pleases regardless of the consequences to anyone or everyone else. Let them procreate at will and starve like their neighbors in India—as long as they're free. Let them flock to the cities and spur poverty, crime, disease, prostitution, hunger, homelessness, unemployment—as long as they're free.

The very next afternoon as I'm out biking, I bump into an American woman studying at the Hangzhou Institute of Art. "Remember Lei Feng," she asks, "the guy who did good deeds in the dead of night?" I certainly do—Xiao Liang had given me a pretty strong dose of the young hero. Well, a large gold bust of Lei Feng has been planted in the entranceway to the institute. A student wryly suggested to a companion that he kow tow to the new Buddha. He was overheard, hauled in by the administration, and is rumored to have been either suspended or dismissed from school—or worse, who knows? It's all arbitrary, depending on the whims of the cadres.

Bah! These Chinese, I say to myself. They really do need democracy. If a bunch of petty bureaucracts can wield so much arbitrary power over individual lives, how will people ever feel free to take enough initiative to bring China into the twenty-first century? It may be idiotic to suggest that Grandfather Wang needs the freedom to move, and idealistic to think his daughter-in-law should be free to have as many children as she pleases, but it's perfectly clear that this student must have the right to criticize party policy—surely no crime against the state.

So there's democracy and there's democracy. And what will I say to my American interrogators?

I will say that I have met Chinese leaders (some Western-educated) who understand the urgent need for democratic reforms but admit they have little notion how to go about it. They have no experience with democracy, and no socialist country has done well enough in this regard to emulate. Nor do they wish to copy Western-style democracy; they fear the loss of control, the possibility of two seats of leadership which, as they see it, can only result in another Cultural Revolution-type situation. "Who do you want to vote for, Jiang Qing or Lin Biao?" one cadre joked. There is genuine fear even among the most liberal of cadres that freedom may lead to disunity, fragmentation, to individualism, to anomie—that lack of purpose, identity, ethical values, rootlessness that characterizes much of our society. Since the Cultural Revolution, these very problems have arisen among Chinese youth, and China's leaders haven't yet figured out how to cope with those problems, no less open the doors for more.

Every time I asked about democracy, Li Xumei described to me the ideal Marxist-Leninist concept of democratic centralism embodied in the phrase "from the masses, to the masses." The idea is this: There are party members at every level of society—every school, office, factory, farm, neighborhood. They pay close attention to what the "masses" (i.e., ordinary people) like and don't like, do and don't complain about, and they pass on that information to the next level of party organization, which sends it up another level, and so on all the way to the top. At the top, based on all this information from all these masses all over the country, it is possible for the leadership to make decisions that reflect both the needs and the most advanced inclinations of the people. A bit cumbersome, perhaps, but not a bad idea.

But there's a catch: for democratic centralism to function, every person must feel free to say what he or she believes, however "backward" it may appear to his or her superiors. Superiors, however, are prone to assume that any hint of dissatisfaction reflects on their own ability to carrry out party policy (i.e., they fear reprobation—or worse—from those above them). So they punish the free-speaker in any number of concrete ways. Thus the party can never carry out the mass line because almost no one feels free to say what isn't in vogue.

The result is what Lu Xun described in 1925 in "Expressing an Opinion":

> I dreamed I was in a primary school classroom preparing to write an essay, and I asked the teacher how to express an opinion:
>
> "That's hard!" Glancing sideways at me over his glasses he said: "Let me tell you a story—
>
> "When a son is born to a family, the whole household is delighted. When he is one month old, they carry him out to display him to the guests—usually expecting some compliments, of course.
>
> "One says, 'This child will be rich.' He is heartily thanked.
>
> "One says, 'This child will be an official.' Compliments are paid him in return.
>
> "One says, 'This child will die.' He is given a thorough beating by the whole family.
>
> "That the child will die is inevitable, while to say that he will be rich or a

high official may be a lie. Yet the lie is rewarded, whereas a statement of the inevitable earns a beating. You—"

"I don't want to tell lies, sir, neither do I want to be beaten. So what should I say?"

"In that case, say: 'Ah ha! Just look at this child! My word . . . did you ever! Oho! Hehe! He, hehehehe!'"

The Chinese want Western science and technology, but they need more. They need to learn from us how to free the strengths and creative energies of the individual, how to frame a social environment wherein the individual is free to experiment, to err, to try again, and to fail again—without losing face, no less being expelled from school or jailed or worse. And things must be clear: it is not enough to put platitudes about freedom in the constitution; there must be written laws that guarantee specific freedoms.

I am not convinced (as some American journalists seem to be) that Chinese democracy must or even could take the same forms as our own. Whether we like it or not, the Chinese have a different starting point— the needs of society as a whole, rather than those of the individual. But I do believe that China urgently needs democratization—indeed, that the current system cannot survive if it remains unable to create forms of democracy appropriate to its level of economic development, its own culture, and its own needs.

But I will say that we, too, have much to learn. If the Chinese must learn to free the individual without creating excessive individualism, we must learn how to provide our independent children with a sense of security, roots, something equivalent to the Chinese network of family, community, and nation so fundamental to the structure of Chinese society.

My friends will say to me: O.K., wise guy. You who always tout the concrete over the abstract, how would you go about creating democracy in China without our excesses? And how would you solve our problems without restricting our much-cherished and hard-won freedoms?

I will say: Are you kidding? I don't know!

As May slithers into June, the mercury oozes up from mark to mark, the humidity oppresses, addles the brain. The night song of the cicadas is driving me to distraction. I am ill. Lao Fan has dragged me from one hospital to another until we determined that I have an intestinal infection. But there are no oral antibiotics, and I will not go three times a day to the clinic for shots because there are no disposable needles—I'm frightened of hepatitis.

I am sick and I am tired. I'm dragging myself through the final stages of the textbook and hardly doing justice to my classes. People come every day to put dibs on my belongings: my refrigerator, my bicycle, my radio, even pots and pans and glass jars. I'm trying to sell my electric typewriter to the university; they suggest that as I am American (read "rich"), I should simply give it to them. I'm trying to make travel arrangements, and trying to get a visa for Terry to come and travel with me. If she were my mother or my husband, it would be easy; for my niece there are reams of red tape that even Lao Fan cannot wade through.

And then the fateful tea. This is the last of many dozens of formal teas I've suffered through over the last two years. The administration has gathered sundry deans and vice-presidents, all of my students and all of Jenny's to wish us a formal farewell. Jenny gets up and gives a brief speech. It's my turn. I begin to cry. I simply cannot control myself. Unable to mumble even a few proper words, I give up, completely humiliated. The officials are shocked, the students dumbfounded. I feel utterly idiotic. If ever I had to write a freshman composition on "my most embarrassing moment," this one would win hands down.

# 23

# Tourists and Teachers and Other Strange Creatures

After the rains comes the heat, the heat that weighs upon the limbs, upon the lungs. Thin bamboo matting has replaced my mattress, but it sticks to my skin and a sheet on top negates its advantages. I rise after a few hours of fitful sleep to get in some time before sunrise, but even now the sweat drips into my blurry eyes, into my cottony mouth, into my soggy brain.

I think I speak aloud, but the words seem muffled in the palpable air: *Oh, Nayim: I am so hurt, so disappointed. After a hundred letters of yes and no and maybe, you say you cannot come to China after all. This simple fact seems more painful than all our battles of the previous year, a sort of physical pain that makes me laugh: "Well, my dear, you're experiencing 'heartache.'"*

But I will have good company on my travels. My niece Terry arrives tomorrow, and as soon as I finish the textbook we can take off for points north, away from this sweltering heat.

Lao Fan and I went to some municipal office to try to get a visa for Terry. Some Person of Consequence behind a large desk in a large office told us Terry could get a visa from China Travel Service in Hong Kong. All she had to do was pay for a full tour around China, then leave the tour group when it arrived in Hangzhou and pay all over again for her trip with me. Lao Fan ushered me out of his office. I insisted he go back in there and tell that man I won't take no for an answer. He refused. As the heat intensifies and the time to leave China approaches, I have less and less patience with Chinese bureaucracy and what I have come to call the "new greed," and Lao Fan—as always—bears the brunt of my foul humor. But Terry is very resourceful; after her own set-to with China Travel, she got an independent visa and an inexpensive train ticket to Hangzhou through the Hong Kong YMCA.

During the week it takes me to finish the book, Terry and I have many dinners with friends, who are delighted with her Mandarin and her knowledge of things Chinese. I inform her about my "husband" (lest she goof when someone refers to him in conversation), so she gleefully chats about her *gu fu*—"husband of the father's sister." Worse, she's now taken to calling me *gu gu*—"father's sister."

One night Yao and Wu take us to a basketball game (China vs. Mexico) at the new sports stadium. We're chatting about rules and munching Quaker Oats Man popcorn when in march some forty Americans in painfully tight jeans and T-shirts with messages about Mickey Mouse and what is and is not invited to be done to this person's person.

The game begins, and with it the whooping and hollering. The Chinese team makes a basket. The Chinese quietly applaud. "Boo, boo" shout the Americans, waving ten-gallon hats, which Wu recognizes from photos of Deng Xiaoping's visit to Texas. The Mexicans make a basket. The Chinese applaud quietly. Amid whistles and cheers of "Mejico! Mejico!" paper bags with large bottles of Tsingdao beer emerge out of pocketbooks and bowling bags. "Mejico, Mejico. Kill 'em. Tromp the yellow dogs," they shout.

Terry and I slump down in our seats, but our companions miss the slur. They're delighted by the uninhibited fun, the unbounded enthusiasm of the fans, but they're mystified: Why, they want to know, do these Americans feel so strongly about the Mexican team?

George has finished his two years at Hangzhou University, so the next morning Terry and I stop at the hotel to bid him farewell (and to use his bathtub). At breakfast George points out his replacement sitting alone at a distant table. When he refers to Mary Elizabeth as a "fruitcake," I insist he's being subjective; as responsible people we might at least offer her some orientation. "Be my guest," says George.

I approach Mary Elizabeth and tell her who I am. Her face lights up. You see, I tell myself, she's just lonely. Can I give her some books about teaching English? I've given my books away, but I toss off some reassurance about experience spiced with imagination.

"But I've never taught English," she says.

"Then what in the world are you doing here?" I ask.

"It was the only way I could get in," she says. I stare. "To spread The Word," she adds, as though this were a perfectly reasonable explanation, and proceeds to tell me about the tasks God has set for her. Of course she's sorry to have fooled the Chinese with a false dossier, but isn't all fair in God's work?

"I worked in Africa for several years," she says. "but here it's very difficult to figure out what to do." I stare again.

"Well, people here are so Christian," she says. "I don't understand it. How can they be so Christian without Christ?"

"Got me," I answer, and rise to leave.

"Wait," she urges, grasping my arm. "Wait. People say you're a Jew. Is it *really* true? I've never actually met a Jew." This time we stare at each other.

"I'm sure you've met many Jews before," I assure her. "You just didn't know it—we hide our horns."

Not a hint of a smile. "Do Jews have tails?" she asks. I can't believe this is happening. And in China! I don't know how to take her. I decide not to take her at all.

"Wait, wait," she says frantically. "Is it true that the Jews and the Arabs are related through Ishmael?"

"Honey, the only Ishmael I know was a whale-chaser," I answer. *She* stares. One point for George. This one *is* a fruitcake.

Lao Fan escorts Terry and me to the police station where we offer our itinerary: Shanghai, Beijing, Beidaihe, Huhehaote, Lanzhou, Xian, and down around again. Terry adds a dozen places she'll visit when I come back to Hangzhou in a month to pack. No hassle. The police sign our travel permits without question.

On a summer evening, at the end of a long, hot day capped by a crowded, stuffy, smokey train ride to Shanghai, the weary travelers, pushing their way out into the streets, are confronted with the full force of Chinese life. Take Atlantic City holiday crowds, dress them in Chinese underwear, take them out of their tiny, stifling rooms, sit them on stools or stretch them out on lawn chairs that cover the sidewalk so a pedestrian cannot begin making his way through, move them out into the street so bikers and drivers must crawl around them honking and cursing, light the whole scene with flashing Times Square art deco neon signs like a steaming teacup perhaps twenty feet high, and you have some sense of a summer evening in metropolitan Shanghai. The travelers, of course, take a taxi to their air-conditioned hotel.

I have but one task in Shanghai. While Terry goes sightseeing, I go to see the good gentlemen of the Shanghai Foreign Language Education Press, who eagerly await the manuscript. The time has come. I want to get paid.

"Oh, no," they intone, "our policy is to pay the author when the book is *published*."

"Then you had best change your policy because I won't give you the book if I don't get paid for it."

"We will send money to you in America."

I am not so impolite as to say aloud that the renminbi is only good for Monopoly money in America, but I'm beginning to lose my temper. There are hints about "rich American," about how much more they need the money than I do. I grow evil. "My understanding is that China exists at present under socialism, not communism. Under socialism, the slogan is: 'From each according to his ability, to each according to his *work*.' Later, under communism, the slogan will be 'From each according to his ability, to each according to his *need*.' Is that not correct, comrades?" Oh, lord, I have overstepped the bounds again. But what *am* I supposed to do?

At long last they agree to give me 1,000 yuan (about 650 dollars), and I agree to take it—having not the least idea how fair this is. They hand me a wad of money to count. I count it.

"But this is 920 yuan and we just agreed on 1,000. What happened to the other 80?" I ask quietly.

"There is a new law," they explain. "Twenty percent of all earnings over 800 yuan goes directly to the government."

"O.K. That's 40 yuan. What happened to the other 40?"

"That's for the typists at Zhejiang University," they respond. "The university has written to ask us to subtract the sum from your payment." I hit the ceiling. They bring me the other 40 yuan and with no further formality escort me to the door.

Does that explain why I never learned from them that the book was published eighteen months later? Does it explain why they never sent me one, much less the ten copies agreed upon? Does it explain why I have never heard from them that the book went into one reprint after another? If I had somehow learned to conduct business Chinese style, would it all have come out differently? And is it possible that I am still *so* angry!

On the nineteen-hour train ride from Shanghai to Beijing, I tell Terry at length about my see-saw relationship with Nayim. We talk family feuds and personalities—great fun because we've hardly known one another all these years. We rattle on and on, comparing our memories of childhood incidents as I unconsciously begin preparing myself to go home. I rattle on and on about my two years in China, beginning the awesome task of digesting this stupendous experience.

In Beijing we call several hotels but end up, as usual, at the Youyi, the Friendship Hotel some eight miles from Tiananmen Square. How appropriate—this is where it all began two years ago, in this seedy, unkempt, 1,500-room and apartment complex built in the fifties for Russian experts. There are several dining rooms, bars, food stores, and tennis courts, and I remember on my first afternoon in China watching Chinese, European, and African children frolicking in the swimming pool, calling to one another in Mandarin. The grounds are now littered with the tall wooden packing crates of foreign experts headed home, and the trunks and bags of those arriving to replace them—*us*.

Perhaps I need to be here. While my Beijing students escort Terry to the Great Wall, the Ming Tombs, the Summer Palace, I spend much of my time with foreigners. Foreigners! Funny how I've come to regard all non-Chinese as "foreigners."

Everyone eventually turns up in the experts' dining room here. (The new arrivals listen intently to the old-timers—now I, too, am a voice of experience, tossing around Chinese phrases and code words.) Some can't wait to get out of here. Some are genuinely sad to leave. Some have chosen to stay for at least another year—after that, they'll see. Some of the scholars are bitterly frustrated by a year or more of bureaucratic interference with their research, while others describe remarkable freedom of travel, inquiry, and access to libraries and documents. Some people feel they've been continually spied upon, while others resent being regularly lied to in the guise of "saving face." The teachers agree this has been the best teaching experience (and, for many, the best experience) of our lives, though some point out that the younger students enrolled directly out of middle school are generally not so conscientious as the older ones. Everyone has contract stories: some bureaucrats bind experts to each contractual duty and obligation while sidestepping their own, while others are fair and flexible. Everyone has China Travel Service horror stories. It's so bad that *China Daily*—yes, there's actually an English-language daily now—reminded CTS that its mission is friendship first, avarice second. (Ah, for the old "red" CTS of 1975, so eager to show you China they couldn't let you waste precious hours on shopping!)

I'm surprised to hear people who have lived in Beijing a year or more say they've never been to the home of a friend or colleague. (How lucky I am—*was*—to live in Hangzhou.) They, on the other hand, are savvy about political developments, documents, policies, factional fighting in the party's Central Committee. Some argue that China is marching boldly down the capitalist road, abandoning all socialist principles: private enterprise grows apace and with it exploitation; communes have been disbanded, women's issues are at best neglected. But perhaps the party had little choice if it were to survive—people get very tired of being so poor, and all of us recognize the significant improvement in the standard of living everywhere any of us has lived or traveled.

But did the party have to go so far? Couldn't they have given more control and policy-making power to lower bodies without abolishing nearly all socialist forms? China is being Westernized; with the miracles of modern technology come the worst of Western ways—materialism, the get-rich-quick mentality that has already led to a greater gap between rich and poor, to uncontrolled corruption at every level of the party and government. And all this concern for artists and intellectuals, such a tiny fraction of China's population. Sure, they're entitled to a good deal after the absurdities of the Cultural Revolution, but who will speak now for the vast majority, for the workers and peasants? Was Mao right after all? Will China soon have a new elite class like the Soviet Union?

Nonsense. This is a transition period. The party understands that opening to the West has inherent dangers—corrective measures will be taken when needed. In fact rumors are flying about a new antipollution campaign, for the party is deeply concerned about Western cultural influence, about eroding traditional and socialist values. What values? It isn't clear. Maybe it's lectures and discussions about freedom and democracy that worry the authorities, or maybe it's our fierce individualism and moral (or immoral) outlook they fear. Maybe both. (This campaign may explain why my Beijing students always arrange to meet us in public places, maintaining that their apartments are too small and wretched for company.)

We agree it is neither me nor thee at whom this campaign is aimed, but admit we've all bumped into a lot of odd-balls. So much for politics— now for gossip. (How I would love to have a Fulbright grant to study foreigners in China. What a collection we are!) First we run through all the juicy sex stories, then I relate my encounter with Mary Elizabeth. Across the room we spot Bunny's bright red hair and freckles. Bunny's still "doing grass," but there's debate about whether she actually offers it to her students.

Does anyone know what happened to David Wordsworth? I met him in this very room on my first day in China. "The name's Wordsworth, David Wordsworth-as-in-William. Ha ha ha." Months later George and I were having dinner at the Hangzhou Hotel when we heard an odd wailing outside. A funeral, perhaps? "Remember David Wordsworth-as-in-William?" said George. "He's parading around the streets with his bagpipes." Sure enough, bagpipes and all, David bounded into the room, his rotund body and jutting appendages tipping waiters' trays and disturbing tourists' equanimity. Later we heard about David's grandiose Shanghai church wedding—imported a bride from England, you know. And here's the latest: In the Shanghai foreign experts' building one night, David drinks all the beer in the communal refrigerator, flings the refrigerator down several flights of stairs, waves, Mao-fashion, at the masses gathered below, then unzips his fly and pisses over the railing. The authorities take him into custody for a couple of weeks, then politely escort him and his weeping bride to the airport.

God, the stories! One follows another. Even my friend Arthur turns up at the Youyi. He's going home to Roger after all. It's his birthday, so Terry and I take him out to dinner and give him *Menggu yifu*—a full-length, wide-sleeved, turquoise and black Mongolian costume bought second-hand in Shanghai.

To mitigate the heavy dose of bitching and gossiping they're subjected to every day in the Youyi, I introduce some of the newcomers to my Chinese students. Dell Bisdorf has come for a year to polish translations at *China Reconstructs*; Marcia Marx, who has come to teach, intends to live in China forever. She offers to run a weekly discussion group with my Beijing-based students so they won't forget their English. They'll love it; she'll love them. I feel, as the students see Terry and me off to Beidaihe after a touching parting banquet, that I've managed at last to proffer a valuable gift.

On the beach at the old seaside resort of Beidaihe, frequented mainly by high cadres (on one beach) and foreigners (on another), I watch a solitary figure, pants rolled above knees, bending near the shoreline, selecting shells and putting them in a little plastic bag—no doubt the makings of the shell sculptures on sale all along the route to town. The sky is magnificent, the air fresh and clean and cool. The only sound is the sea. I think Terry is bored, but I'm relieved to be here, to relax, to clear my head.

Lots of luck. Arthur turns up again, and he's very agitated. He has invited a teenager, a high school art student from Beijing, to visit him here, but the hotel clerk is adamant: it is not lawful to give the boy a room without a travel permit from his unit.

The boy arrives carrying two ugly, modernish paintings. He's clearly under the impression that Arthur is going to wing him off to America where he will live happily ever after, earning fame and fortune in the gold-paved streets of the free world. He spends the night in the pouring rain in a latrine outside the hotel gates. Terry and I are slightly hysterical. Does Arthur understand this little episode could destroy the boy's life? Does he think the authorities will slap the boy's wrist if they catch him traveling without permission, much less engaging in homosexual activity? And, by the way, if Arthur's having an affair with this wild child, why didn't he share his room with him instead of leaving him out in the toilet to catch pneumonia?

The truth pours out through the tears. Arthur never touched the boy. In fact, Arthur has never touched *anyone* in China. All those descriptions of secret codes, of midnight trysts, of body types, of the sexual behavior of this or that waiter or teacher—all fantasy. All those stories he'd told me were fantasy. He'd wanted so badly to have something more than the male-male contact or handholding normal in China, and he'd thought maybe at last with this boy—but the boy didn't even understand what he was getting at.

Lecture time. You go right this instant, take that child directly to the train station, give him roundtrip fare, explain that you never had any intentions of taking him to America and that he had best keep his mouth shut about this little adventure.

He does it. I'll give him that.

How thrilled we are to be going to Inner Mongolia. And what a pain it seems to be. Apparently CTS hasn't gotten the word up here about friendship superseding greed. We want to go to the grasslands. The grasslands! We've seen the fine animated film *Little Sisters of the Grasslands*, about two heroic children braving ice and snow to save a single commune sheep.

Ah, yes, the American friends can be taken on an overnight excursion by jeep for only 350 yuan. Taken is right. I go through my two-years-in-China-on-Chinese-salary routine, and we get down to 60 yuan. In a tiny local restaurant we find a group of Hong Kong college kids who are going out tomorrow in a bus for 8 yuan apiece. Yes, we'd *love* to go with them.

We set out early next morning in a junk heap that reminds me of the school buses we used to rent for demonstrations. We take an unpaved road for two hours and then at one point—God knows how they know what point—we make a left and then a right and then there's no more road, and we go on and on, hour after hour, stopping now and then to pet some sheep, to open pop bottles—the driver does it with his teeth—to look north, south, east, and west at flat, scraggly grassland, to crank up the bus and set off again—in circles, I'd swear to it.

We don't dare complain about discomfort or even ask questions because the CTS guide—Terry calls him "Cookie"—will have nothing to do with cheap Americans. (Surely if the 350 yuan were going into the CTS pot, Cookie wouldn't be so burned up about it.)

Cookie is not Mongolian, but Han. As far as we can tell, he knows little and cares less about the land and its people. (Is his assignment here some form of punishment?) He assures us we'll learn all about Mongolian life from the people themselves at lunchtime. We alight some hours later at the only house—the only thing—visible in any direction, a pleasant, utilitarian home. A Mongolian woman serves us wonderful bread and cheese and goat's milk, then disappears. Cookie starts to lecture the assembly on the poverty and misery of Hong Kong life as compared with the glorious motherland. The Hong Kong students are mortified. A few try to argue. Most walk out.

In the bus I tell Terry about Yao's experience teaching in the Minor-

Terry with Mongolian guides in the grasslands—the only way to dress
for camel riding.

ities Institute in Xian. She found the Tibetan students dull, slow, unable
to master grammar, unwilling to interact with their teachers. Yao concluded they weren't too bright, these Tibetans, so she taught her
classes and read novels at night. On the last day of the course the
students stood dumbly before their teachers, heads hung. Suddenly Yao
realized they were crying at the departure of their teachers. It shocked
her. She began to think about what had happened, to realize she really
knew nothing about these people, their family lives, their educational
background, their culture. How can you know how to teach people
about whom you know nothing? I told Yao of our comparable experience
with open admissions in New York City—white teachers, black and
Hispanic students—and we talked long into the night about the roots
and consequences of racism.

The grass grows thicker and greener as we near a town with a
temple, a store, a restaurant, and a dozen yurts. It's clearly a little
tourist town, but who cares? After dressing up in an exotic rent-a-robe
to sit astride a double-humped rent-a-camel, it's a fabulous Mongolian
hot-pot dinner with a whole lamb, a good night's sleep in a cold yurt
under several warm quilts, and a lovely Mongolian sunrise in the company of our yurtmates.

# 24
## Slow Train

It's called the the *man che* or slow train. We take the slow train because we can't get tickets on the "fast" train for several days, and we're expected in Xian.

Thus we're destined to see but a flicker of Lanzhou, this 2,200-year-old Silk Road city. At the train station, a tall, leathery-faced young beggar spots us. Her mouth falls open. She rushes to us and with a wrestler's grip grasps one of my hands and one of Terry's. There is nothing threatening in her face or gestures; she's simply as fascinated by our strangeness as we are by hers and wants to touch us, to make us real. We try to communicate but find no common language.

As the train pulls out, we're tantalized by the diversity of face and dress seen only in minority areas, by the number of beggars, by an old Hui man in a white yarmulka selling sheepskins, by a barber shaving patrons on the street. We must come back here some day.

The slow train *is* slow. It takes eight hours longer than the usual sixteen from Lanzhou to Xian because it runs slowly and stops at scores of tiny stations along the 350-mile route.

Three things strike us at once: the price is half that of the ordinary train; the only hard sleeper car is, unlike any Chinese train I've ever been on, sparsely populated; and the snowy white sheets of the regular runs have been replaced by sets of uniformly grey bedding—"Gucci Grey," Terry calls it. They're all clean, the sheets and blankets, no doubt scrubbed by industrious hands, but cold water and coarse soap cannot contend with the hazards of the northeastern environment or the coal-burning engine.

It is dry. So dry. The Yellow River ("China's Sorrow") winds into sight from time to time. It's desert terrain. Are we in the Gobi? We check our maps but it isn't clear; there are two rail lines and no one knows which goes where. But it is certainly desert terrain. Unlike the

Scratching a living out of bone-dry soil.

South, where peasants normally work in long rows, here a solitary
figure leans into a walking tractor, though it seems a hopeless attempt
to scratch a grain of millet much less a living from this brittle, crusted,
sunbaked earth.

Station scenes confirm the notion. Children sell a few eggs or apples
to passengers. They are ill-clad and dirty-faced. I heard tell when I was
down in Xishuangbanna that up north where it rarely rains there are
people who have but three baths in their lives: at birth, at marriage, and
at death. I look out at our young vendors, who are well past their
initiation rites but have a long way to go before enjoying their nuptial
ablutions.

Terry and I are wonders to them all. Most stops are just long enough
for local passengers and traveling peddlars to toss their bundles on the
ground and jump down behind them, but at one station we have time to

From the window of the slow train—our friends find it funny we should pretend
to be Americans instead of overseas Chinese.

bargain with children for some awful confection. The children are delighted with us, hopping and chirping and chattering among themselves. No, we are not really foreigners! Certainly we are teasing them
when we say we are Americans. Americans cannot speak Chinese, and
they most certainly would not be on the *man che* that stops in *their*
villages. What are we then? Why, of course—overseas Chinese. Terry
and I turn to one another and remark in unison: "Funny, you don't look
Chinese," and then, to the amazement of the urchins, we burst into
peals of laughter. It strikes us that the children understand and speak
Mandarin (their elders do not); however they may look to us, they must
attend school.

Oddly enough, the meals are excellent. Our cook's specialty is our
favorite Sichuan-style noodles, which are *la la la*—very hot. He is not a
Northerner, none too happy to be stuck up here in the boonies, and
delighted with passengers who want his southern specialties. We con-
jecture that, like Cookie, he's been banished from his hometown for
some Cultural Revolution evil-doing.

Yet each meal is an agony. Three times a day the conductor comes to
escort the two foreign ladies to and from the dining car. Each time we
pass through three hard-seat cars, rectangular boxes containing rows of
small, wooden benches—no such amenities as tea tables, doilies, or even

hot water thermoses. Each bench, designed for two tiny rumps, supports the supine figure of one peasant, towel-wrapped head pillowed by a sack of millet or wheat, surrounded by mounds of sale goods, living and dead.

As he whisks us through each car, the conductor shoves dangling legs out of our path. There's grumbling and growling—entirely justified—and, to make matters worse, Terry tries to apologize to the peasants who, nonspeakers of Mandarin, surely imagine she is excoriating them in some devil tongue.

We rebel: we will not eat if he does not stop this nonsense. He agrees to walk a car's distance before us to assure our safety—which by now might be necessary—and to refrain from shoving the peasants out of our royal path. But the damage has been done; the peasants stare at us with a mixture of scorn and confusion as we tromp six times a day back and forth through their sleeping quarters.

On the PA system, waltz follows fox trot follows tango—"Strange Sensations" indeed! The hours roll by. The scenery becomes monotonous. We get bored and goofy. We sit on the beds, Terry on the top bunk and me below her, telling idiotic ethnic jokes and singing "I wanna getcha on a slow train in China." We make a great sideshow for the other passengers, who are by now as giddy as we are, and they laugh at our laughter and encourage us to tell more stories and enjoy ourselves. We are far better entertainment in the flesh—two foreign women on the *man che* rolling about on their beds—than the cross-talks on the loud speakers.

It's difficult to sleep. The heat is stifling and the air thick with dust and sand tossed up by the train wheels into the windows—open because one must have something resembling air, no matter how gritty. (By the time we arrive in Xian, Terry and I resemble the sheets and the local children.) So it's with great trepidation that I rouse Terry to look out at the night sky flooded with moonlight filtered through dust and sand. Aside from the rhythmic clacking of the wheels, all is quiet and eerie and utterly beautiful.

In the morning, an astonishing sight: cave houses carved in loess mixed with straw, hundreds of miles of rounded clay dunes with small black eyes staring out at us. Imagine living in a cave! But people tell us the caves are spacious and comfortable, cool in summer and warm in winter, and that the local soil encourages wheat, corn, and cotton.

Joyous mob scene at the Xian station. In sundry branches of the Academia Sinica in Xian and nearby Lintong, I have five students (four of whom are here) who have four spouses (none of whom are here) and eight children (six of whom are here).

We all pile into the *mian bao che*, the "bread loaf car," a squarish blue Japanese van provided by one of the institutes. I catch up on all the news: Da Liang is back from Hungary but may soon leave for Paris; Xiao Liang has been accepted into the Communist Party; Young Wang has a fiancée in Beijing; Serious Wei (as all the other scientists call him) is packing for two years in the States.

But where is my friend Liu, the man who gave me my Chinese name, the one man who said—and meant it—that he would stand up for himself and his colleagues regardless of consequences? Liu's four-year-old daughter has been in the hospital for several weeks now. Liu and his wife take turns feeding Ye Ye three times a day, and because she's so young, so ill, and so frightened, Liu curls up with her in her crib every night and sleeps there. But we will see him soon. They promise. The wide, poplar-lined avenues are well designed to accommodate the plentiful traffic, but peasants have spread their wheat and hay across the road so the traffic will flatten it for them. Our driver tries to maneuver around it.

As we approach the Xian city limits where new six- and seven-story brick buildings gradually replace crumbling hovels, we discover we're following the Silk Road. Over a thousand years ago this was Chang'an, the capital of China through eleven feudal dynasties, the largest city in the world, the cradle of Chinese culture, the hub of international commerce and art. Yet Terry and I end up in a pointless discussion with our driver, who wants to live the easy life in New York City where he could own his own cab and make scads of money.

In response to my request, and in exchange for a lecture on "How to Study English" (their idea, not mine) and my ever-popular slide shows on New York City and Chinatown, the students have booked a room for us at the Xian branch of the Academy of Sciences. Of course they must apologize for the accommodations.

The guesthouse is a two-story cement building with a few dozen large, immaculate rooms. Ours has a twin bed, a double bed, a large desk, a huge dresser, two big stuffed chairs, lamps, tea things, and the standard enamel wash basins.

Xiao Liang escorts us across the hall where we take in two rows of sinks on the left wall and a row of toilet stalls along the right. Built into the center of the room is a square, knee-high basin with faucets. It's fun to lather up, lean over the big sink, and pour pitchers of cold water over ourselves, though we note that it wouldn't be a whole lot of fun in winter.

In the thick morning mist behind our quarters, trudging through a muddy courtyard of graceful old buildings on our way to a hearty breakfast, we stop to listen to the wind and make out an old man sitting on a doorstep among his chickens. He is playing the *san hu*, a three-stringed instrument that sounds like a flute or recorder. Delicate and beautiful, it seems a whisper from Chang'an (Everlasting Peace) to Xian (Western Peace), a whisper more haunting than all the museums and tombs and walls and towers we will visit this week.

Terry, who knows a good deal about Chinese history, bubbles about Qinshihuang, the first emperor to rule a China united under a centralized imperial system (221–207 B.C.). I, however, who have had enough of glassed-in relics, I who remember only stories (never names, dates, chronologies), I am none too eager to go to tombs and vaults—even less so as we approach some exhibition hall that looks like a hangar for a small fleet of Boeing 747s in the middle of a hundred acres of nothingness.

How could I ever have imagined—how can I describe—the sensation of walking into this room. Amidst the hundreds and hundreds of larger-than-life terra cotta soldiers standing, kneeling, leaning, following their chariots, leading their horses, lying prone upon the rough earth—amidst them are living men and women in blue pants and white shirts, some towel-headed, some white-aproned. These mostly young peasants are trained by the Provincial Committee for the Preservation of Historical Relics. As they gently touch at these figures with hair-thin brushes, working at a mustache, an ear, a button, a hairline, a smile, I share the thrill and pride I'm certain they must feel.

The next morning Young Wang takes us by bus out to Qianling, the joint tomb of Gaozong, the third emperor of the Tang dynasty, and his consort, the infamous Empress Wu (often compared with Jiang Qing nowadays). As I casually rest my camera on a seventh-century headstone, I look up at a field of large statues—all decapitated. The statues, says Wang, represent guests from fifty foreign states and regions invited to the Emperor's inauguration festivities. Later there was a drought in the area and the starving peasants, convinced by the local shaman their ruin was due to the presence of foreign spirits, came up and hacked off their heads.

"Did it rain?" asks Terry, holding her neck with both hands.

"Don't know," Wang laughs.

On the outskirts of the town below the tombs, we stop to look over the edge of an enormous pit and find ourselves peering into the family courtyard of a cave dwelling. Grandpa looks up and invites us down. In the sides of this hole, perhaps twenty by twenty-five feet, large rooms are carved out of the loess: three bedrooms with *kang* (beds with built-in coal stoves), a sitting room, a kitchen, and a goat stall, complete with goat. The cool rooms are whitewashed, each has a bare bulb hanging from the ceiling, a decorative calendar, a picture of Zhou Enlai, and as much furniture as the best peasant houses in Hangzhou.

Wang feels right at home. When he graduated from middle school in the early seventies, he was sent to Yan'an to farm. He lived in a cave there for four years and twice a week gave lessons to the peasants, mainly about what was in the newspapers and party documents. He feels strongly that intellectuals must spend *some* time—perhaps a year—in the countryside, that they are better people for it, but four years seriously interferes with scientific education and production. I'll say!

Now he's thirty and a physicist. He has a girlfriend in Beijing whom he plans to marry this year. Since the policy is to move people out of, not into, the biggest cities, he says, she's more likely to be transferred to Xian than he to Beijing. But he is about to take the national physics exam; if he passes he'll go to the States for three to five years. Aiya! Terry and I later comment to one another that he'll be an ideal husband, sweet and smart, patient and helpful, but who'd want to spend the first five years of marriage 3,000 miles apart!

Next morning, another astonishing experience—the stone library, a scholar's dream, an artist's heaven. "In the beginning was the word . . ." Here are hundreds of thousands of characters carved for all eternity by the best calligraphers century after century on row after row of stone stelae. With the invention of paper sometime around the birth of Christ, the emperor decided that in repeated transcriptions of the classics on paper mistakes might be made, so an accurate, permanent record should exist. Each emperor thereafter preserved on stone the most important works and the best calligraphy of his period.

We amble through the *Analects* of Confucius, records of Han and Song and Qing dynasty peasant uprisings, interlinear calligraphy illustrating the evolution of characters from one period to another, rows of poetry of the Spring and Autumn Period. And we actually come upon the famous seventh-century Nestorian stele in Syriac with a cross on top.

At lunch, Terry has a fight with Serious Wei. She wants to spend the afternoon wandering about Xian by herself. Wei is certain she will get lost. Wang points out that Terry speaks Chinese, but Wei is adamant. I'm amused at the personality differences between Wang and Wei, annoyed with Wei's silly concerns for Terry's safety, and irked by Terry's unguestlike behavior. I realize that I'm embarrassed because it's like watching my own contradictory behavior here in China over the last two years.

They all appeal to me. I remind Wei that Terry has traveled much of the world without getting "lost," that after we reach Shanghai I will go on to Hangzhou and Terry will travel alone for several weeks, and that

Terry and Naomi with scientists and their families at Huaqing Hot Springs.

even I, with my mere mouthful of Mandarin, have maneuvered all over the face of China. Wei pouts all afternoon, but when Da Liang and Xiao Liang arrive from Lintong at the same time Terry shows up for dinner, he, too, is caught up in the lively chatter of children and grown-ups.

Next morning we all pile into the bread loaf van along with three scientists who need a ride up to Lintong. Terry calls them Groucho, Harpo, and Chico because they giggle all the way. We head out to the 6,000-year-old village of Panpo, thought to be a matrilineal society, then stop at the Huaqing Hot Springs, a resort with a mere 3,000-year history of emperors, concubines, court intrigues. Day after day I find myself awed by the sophistication, the humor, the beauty of ancient Chinese science and art, but I remain unable to absorb the meaning of "ancient," the concept of thousands upon thousands of years.

But never mind cold history; this is July and Terry and I luxuriate for an hour in the hot springs' warm mineral baths of sodium, sulfur, and magnesium. Neither of us suffers from rheumatism or skin diseases, but we sure are hot and dirty.

We drop the Marx Brothers at the institute and drop our bags at the Lintong guesthouse. Lintong is wonderful, a place to take a peaceful stroll down country roads and admire the tall-as-people sunflowers, a great relief after our tour of big cities. What do they do here? Da Liang's field is astrometry.

"Ast . . . what?" I ask.

"Astrometry," she says. "It's a very narrow field. We draw longitudinal and latitudinal lines on the earth by sighting off the stars, and we set the nuclear clock used for PLA movements and bomb detonations."

"Does it make you very punctual?" Terry asks. This is translated for the children, who find it *very* funny.

Back in Xian, I am happy at last to see Mr. Liu, though I feel awful that he and his wife have gone to so much trouble and expense to make dinner for us. Their daughter's illness has been a terrible drain on family time, energy, and money. As Meng is a part-time librarian at Liu's institute (which she doesn't much like because she was always a peasant and has many years' experience as a barefoot doctor), she gets no pay when she takes time off to care for Ye Ye. The institute gives them fifty yuan toward medical costs, but the hospital bill is one hundred yuan a month.

Would Ye Ye be pleased if we came to visit? Liu's eyes light up, then dim. "I would have to make arrangements with the hospital . . . they might refuse and . . ." Liu and I look at each other. "Never mind," he says, "let's just go. What can they do?"

The following morning Terry and I buy a set of wind-up toys—turtles, butterflies, rabbits. In the children's ward we sit on miniature chairs circling a low, round table and set the dozen noisy creatures scurrying about to the great delight of the children, who range in age from two to nine.

Ye Ye has a liver disease requiring cortisone treatment. She is not a child, but a big ball of misery—puffed up cheeks and lips and eyes, ballooned abdomen and arms and legs. It's heart-rending. She cries bitterly at our arrival and weeps softly during our entire stay. Liu assures us over and over this has nothing to do with our strange appearance. We're unconvinced but relieved to find that the other children respond to us as visitors, not foreigners. These children are ambulatory; there's another ward for more serious cases, and a third for children with pneumonia.

Every few minutes another member of the hospital staff asks us to come to his or her office for tea and a briefing. We refuse as politely as we can, explaining that we have only come to see the children and do not wish to bother them one little bit—though it's clear they are bothered a great deal by our spontaneous visit.

The room is crowded, but immaculate. Three walls are lined with eight small beds and two cribs—imagine Liu curled up in this tiny box with his baby every night, getting up to go to work in the lab, then feeling he must (and wants to, I know) spend time with me.

Terry signals me to look in a corner near the door where two squatting figures converse quietly in a language I cannot recognize. Nor can I identify the woman's flat, black toreador hat or the magnificent silver clips in her jet black hair, which trails behind her on the floor. With a dancer's grace, she has assumed a position that brings her precisely eye level with the child.

She is Tibetan, Liu says. This is a provincial hospital, so people bring children from great distances for problems that cannot be treated locally. They're given beds so they can stay with the children. She is one of the clean ones, he tells us. Many Tibetans are very poor and dirty, so the doctors and nurses often have bad attitudes toward minority and peasant children, don't treat them nicely, and don't give them such good care. You have to have a little *guanxi*, he says, so he tries to use his status as a scientist to help people.

Ye Ye bawls hysterically at our (really her father's) departure, but the hospital staff is relieved to see us go. I worry about what may happen as a result of our visit, but Liu believes that because he lives nearby, comes regularly, and is a scientist, there will be no repercussions. We've clearly had little conciliatory effect on Ye Ye, though the wind-up toys—which didn't survive the length of the visit—were at least a lively diversion for the other children.

But I regret having no time to sit and talk with Liu. There are so many things I'd like to discuss with him before I leave China.

"Next time," he says warmly. "Next time."

Everyone sees us off at the train station and loads us down with goodies.

"Do you know anyone down South?" Serious Wei asks Terry.

"No," she replies.

"Oh, you will get lost!" he gasps, and then, with a big grin, hands her a large, tissue-paper-wrapped package. "This will help you find your way," he says.

"What grand adventures you will have," says Wang, handing me another neatly wrapped package. The instant the train pulls out Terry and I tear the paper off a spectacular reproduction of the famous Xian horse from Wei, and a dark green hard-cover Chinese-English dictionary from Wang inscribed "To Dear Teacher Nan Hua Mei."

# 25
# Leaving Home, Going Home

Terry heads to scenic sites south and I to Hangzhou to pack and, somehow, to say good-bye.

I pack only to unpack so I can make a list of every item packed so customs can come and unpack to check the items against the list so I can pack again before their eyes so they can themselves seal the boxes so nothing, not a single traitor Lin Biao button, can be slipped in after they leave.

Despite the heat, the university hosts a formal banquet and presents me with a delicate wine decanter and glasses. Even the Foreign Affairs Office celebrates my departure with a marvelous meal in my favorite vegetarian restaurant. Seated next to the Dragon Lady, I take this final opportunity to ask her about her early days in the revolutionary underground, but she doesn't respond.

Tormented by the heat and stress of leave-taking, I'm soaked in sweat and misery and those eternal Russian tears.

Lao Fan comes with gifts. "A snake," Suzy Fast had called this man whom I have come to love like a brother, this man who did indeed work me hard—but not a bit harder than he himself worked.

From Ming, for Nayim, a flowered tea service that was her mother's. From Lao Fan, for me, a set of six flower paintings in round wooden frames that had been *his* mother's.

And this: On my final evening with Lao Fan, Ming, Li Xumei, Yao, and Wu, someone suddenly says, "But you can't leave. You're one of us now."

# Afterword

The new chairman of the new foreign languages department at Zhejiang University does something most uncharacteristic: Lao Fan gives me a big bear hug right here in the train station in Hangzhou.

It has been more than five years. I'm eager for news. Two couples whose marriages I attended are divorced; people whose divorces I witnessed are remarried; Xiao Zhou, my *xiao meimei* who didn't know where babies come from, gives me photos of her toddler; Madam Lo is in the hospital with heart trouble; Dean Miao is vice-chairman of the Provincial Bureau of Higher Education; Liu Dan has at last relinquished university leadership to a "youngster"; Zhe Da students consistently take the honors in national English exams; some of the recycled Russian teachers are again teaching Russian. (Rumor has it they spend their leisure hours doing comparative analyses of Chinese, English, and Russian grammar.)

And my Chinese family? In their five-room garden apartment, Lao Fan proudly complains about the work associated with his promotion, Ming is delighted to be teaching in a local school (gone the three-hour commute), and Fan Ming has graduated with honors from Zhe Da (which he chose because of its proximity to home).

And how is Nayim, they want to know. He has long since finished his doctorate and is doing well, I answer, but neglect to add that we have separated. For years we struggled over the same issues that plagued us in our long-distance correspondence, then finally agreed that enough was enough.

And how, I ask Lao Fan, shall I dispose of my pocketful of renminbi? In Shanghai I was ceremoniously received by our publishers, presented with a dozen books and sets of tapes (to schlep all over China), and given 1,375 yuan (now worth 346 dollars), which, of course, a foreigner cannot legally spend. *Modern American English: Living and Learning in the West*, now in its eighth printing, has sold

537,000 copies to date. They'd like to do a sequel.

I bring Lao Fan greetings from our many students in Beijing. We had a grand reunion in my room at the Friendship Hotel (where Chinese as well as foreign guests are now welcome). Liang Tai took me to visit my old students in their new appliance-laden apartments. We looked through lots of family photo albums: here we are on vacation at Mount Tai or Beidaihe; here I am with my colleagues in Berlin, Budapest, Boston; here's my daughter at Michigan, my son at the Sorbonne. They spoke exuberantly about scientific breakthroughs in China, but all conversation stopped abruptly at 6 p.m. daily as Huey, Louey, and Dewey (in living color) quacked Mandarin at Peking Scrooge.

The scientists still meet weekly for English practice with Marcia Marx. She learned Chinese, married a Chinese widower, and works for Panda Books. She's the first foreigner to win a Model Worker award. Dell Bisdorf. too, is still in Beijing and has been honored with a promotion to managing editor of *China Reconstructs*. At Zhe Da (in Building 30, Room 207—my old apartment), I find Hillary Wilson, a thirty-five-year-old British woman who arrived soon after I left. She's as happy here as I was. "Why have you chosen to stay?" I ask, echoing my own internal question, why did I choose to leave?

Hillary represents the third generation of expatriates. The first, like the hero of John Hersey's latest novel, felt "the call" at the end of the last century. In the fifties, a number of Americans hounded out of the country by McCarthyism came to work and live out their lives in China. But the newcomers of the late seventies and early eighties have no single identity; they've come and stayed for innumerable personal, vocational, and, less frequently, political reasons. Hillary has been made an associate professor at Zhe Da "and everyone is so thrilled about it for me," she says. She speaks fervently of what I have called "gifts," the significance of your work, the sense of community, the mutual affection, respect, and trust, the depth and permanence of bonds.

Of course Hillary and I have mutual friends. Sally's husband John is back from UCLA, and Sally and her daughter are at Ohio State. Li Xumei looks not one minute older. No longer party branch secretary, she clearly remains the community confidante and problem solver. Her enthusiasm is now directed toward teaching and compiling English texts, and the family will "really soon" move to a larger apartment.

Yao and Wu have each, in turn, spent a year in America. In my apartment in New York they shared their experiences "living and learning in the West." Now they insist on hearing my impressions on returning to China. I've been struck by odd bits and pieces on my one-month journey. On the trains, for example, covered styrofoam containers and disposable chopsticks have replaced unsanitary tin boxes and unsterilized utensils. A meal is more expensive, but people earn more now. (I don't know if the food is any better.)

There are the obvious signs of modernization. Every cityscape is dominated by construction cranes—"the national bird of China," people quip—and major cities are building elaborate highway systems to deal with horrendous traffic jams. World-class tourist hotels (many, sad to say, so un-Chinese in design they could be anywhere in the world) contrast sharply with Chinese hotels and housing, which remain without hot water and, in the South, without heat. The comparison is a sore point for many.

But development is uneven. In a phone conversation with Lao Liu (whose child, by the way, is healthy and happy), he asked if I remember the little mountain village he'd once described for me in an essay. Of course I do. He recently returned to the Qiling Mountains to find no signs of new roads or the electrification he so ardently hoped for.

True, say Yao and Wu, but you have to start somewhere. Beside the "Three Olds and Three News" stand "Three Newer News": Before 1976 when a girl married, she wanted a watch, a sewing machine, and a bicycle. After 1976 she looked for a sofa, an electric fan, and a tape recorder. Today a couple expects to start with a washing machine, a refrigerator, and a TV set—preferably color.

But they insist that the barrage of reports on Chinese capitalism they encountered in America are seriously misleading. They fear that if Americans see China as a sort of semicapitalist country, they may be deeply disappointed when they learn it isn't, and the backlash could be unproductive for both peoples. There are aspects of the Chinese economy that are capitalistic, but they amount to a fraction of the whole and exist in the context of a planned, controlled economy. For better and for worse, Chinese society is absorbing elements of Western ideas and ideals, but the emphasis is on elements. In too many ways China remains unacceptably undemocratic and repressive, but beware of shibboleths: China is neither "totalitarian" nor "a bitter sea." China is Chinese. It was. It is. It will be.

Everyone knows the Chinese consider themselves superior to everyone else in the world. But everyone knows that Americans are really superior, and that everyone really wants to be like us.

And so it goes, but with a difference. Chinese superiority is, in the words of Francis Hsu, "passive," while ours is "aggressive." The Chinese smile benevolently at the foibles of others and go about their business, while we feel we must convert all the peoples of the world to our ways, whatever they may be at any historical moment.

Certainly we have much to offer. What I said in 1981 is still true: the

Zhe Da students voted to leave Mao where he was, but erect a bronze statue of
Zhou Kouzen, president of the university in its formative years.

Chinese need more than Western science and technology. They need to learn from us how to free the strengths and creative energies of the individual, how to frame an environment wherein the individual is free to experiment, to err, to try again, and to fail again without losing face, no less being expelled from school or jailed or worse.

But what about us? While I'm down here in Hangzhou, Secretary of State Shultz is up in Beijing asking the Chinese not to sell arms to Iran. ("The nerve of some people's children," my mother would say.) Shultz also chastised Deng Xiaoping for his handling of the recent student demonstrations. Ah, yes, Deng responded, you have your *xiao mafan* and we have ours. Ah, yes, we all have our "little troubles."

Deng was referring to the Iran-Contra affair, but he might have added any number of domestic ills. As usual, John King Fairbank is right: Despite "some convergence of Chinese and foreign elements in a new cultural synthesis," we must not "jump to the conclusion that *they* are becoming more like *us*. It can also be argued that under the pressure of numbers and uncontrolled social evils, *we* are obliged to become more like *them*."

Though somewhat abashed by the experience, American business and financial interests have recently been forced to admit they have much to learn from Japanese economic successes. Can we be humble enough to recognize we have something to learn from the social structure of a poor and underdeveloped Third World country like China? Can we learn to provide our independent children with a sense of security, roots, something equivalent to the network of family, community, and nation so fundamental to Chinese society?

Yao and I tour the Zhe Da campus. Outside the majestic new gates the free market displays a wide variety of fresh vegetables, fruits, fish, and fowl—all day every day, no lines, no coupons. There are new classrooms, dining rooms, and dorms, but Chairman Mao retains center stage. In response to my questions about democratic reforms, I'm told of open and heated debates about doing away with the immense figure. The students voted to keep it, but in front of the new million-volume library, workers are polishing a lovely bronze statue of Zhou Kouzen, the famous geologist who was president of the university in its formative years. The statue must be finished quickly; in two weeks begin the festivities for Zhe Da's ninetieth anniversary. How I wish I could stay!

"When are you coming back?" I'm asked again and again. I don't know. The temptation is enormous. But even in America the gift continues. Chinese friends and their friends regularly turn up in New York, and I still thrive on letters like this one from Wu Jianguo:

I am studying at the Department of Chemistry at the University of Pennsylvania in Philadelphia. Even in America I have been receiving a lot of benefits from your English lessons. The written material and tapes are very helpful to me to use the American society. Just like a coach, it often guides me how to act in the States.

I have never forgotten you were so kind to teach us in Zhejiang University. You see, my English level is very poor compared with my classmates, but you encouraged me to keep practicing and gave me a lot of help. Step by step, I made big progress. Whenever I recall, I have very warm feelings with confidence you gave me to overcome difficulties. So, there is nothing more happiness than I could meet you again . . . .